RALPH RICHARDSON
AN ACTOR'S LIFE

As a man and as an actor Sir Ralph Richardson is
a phenomenon, famed for his eccentricities
offstage and his subtle, poetic acting onstage. In
this first full-length biography Garry O'Connor
reveals an enigma: an elusive, complex and
mysterious man whose power to enchant an
audience remains unrivalled in the history of the
theatre.

"This is the most exciting theatrical biography I
have ever read. It is an astounding book, original
in form and fascinating in content"

Sir Harold Hobson

RALPH RICHARDSON
AN ACTOR'S LIFE

"Exceptional . . . a sensitive, searching and exact account of a supremely elusive man"
The Times

"Exemplary: carefully researched, sensitively attuned to the subject, agreeably written and well documented . . . it reads effortlessly"
Washington Post

"O'Connor has succeeded not only in bringing the man alive but he has also preserved his aura of mystery. This is a most remarkable biography as well as a most readable book"
Canberra Times

"Richardson's presence, oblique, subtle, absurd, eccentric, above all truly felt, makes this book a worthwhile monument to that astounding genius"
The Guardian

"A very notable biography indeed, as finely written as it is deep in understanding and sympathy"
Books and Bookmen

RALPH RICHARDSON
AN ACTOR'S LIFE

"It is a work of literature . . . on every page one
sees and hears the man and the actor"

Punch

"It must have been a daunting task, trying to
capture the essence of a man so expert at hiding
himself, but O'Connor draws a portrait that
finally convinces"

The Observer

"As a profile of a master craftsman it is
absorbingly perceptive"

New Zealand Herald

"An enlightening insight into the social history of
the theatre"

Plays and Players

"Researched with great care and particularly well
written . . . well worth reading"

Los Angeles Times

"Indispensable in any theatre collection"

Library Journal

GARRY O'CONNOR directed in the theatre for six years before he became a full-time writer. He has published four books, a survey of English Theatre written in French and had six plays performed, among them *Semmelweis* and *The Musicians*. He formerly reviewed for the *Financial Times*, and he was awarded an Arts Council Writer's Grant in 1978. He lives in Oxford, is married, and has four children.

Ralph Richardson

An Actor's Life

Garry O'Connor

CORONET BOOKS
Hodder and Stoughton

Copyright © 1982 by Garry O'Connor

First published in Great Britain 1982 by Hodder and
Stoughton Ltd

Coronet edition 1983

British Library C.I.P

O'Connor, Garry
   Ralph Richardson
   1. Richardson, *Sir* Ralph
   2. Actors—Great Britain—Biography
   I. Title
   792'.02'0924   PN2598.R/

ISBN 0-340-33968-3

Printed and bound in Great Britain for
Hodder and Stoughton Paperbacks, a
division of Hodder and Stoughton Ltd.,
Mill Road, Dunton Green, Sevenoaks,
Kent (Editorial Office: 47 Bedford
Square, London, WC1 3DP) by

Photoset by Rowland Phototypesetting Ltd.,
Bury St Edmunds, Suffolk.
Printed in Great Britain by
Richard Clay (The Chaucer Press) Ltd,
Bungay, Suffolk

As to the poetic character itself, it is not itself: it has no self—it is everything and nothing.

JOHN KEATS

For B. A. Young

CONTENTS

Part Two: *Middle Layers* 1942–1949

Part Three: *Close to the Heart* 1949–1982

The Career of Ralph Richardson

ONE

The Skin of the Onion

1902–1942

Regent's Park, London. The end of an elegant winged attachment connected by a paper-thin triumphal arch to John Nash's longest unbroken terrace composition. The house is tall, five storeys including a basement, with white-stuccoed walls and numerous decorated pilasters. There are seven steps curving up to the front door, which has a window in it, with wrought-iron spirals behind. Ralph Richardson has lived here ten years, having returned to the neo-Corinthian and Ionic shapes of Cheltenham, where he was born: the names of some near-by streets where he takes his morning walk are interchangeable with those in Cheltenham's Regency quarter.

5.30 p.m. I park outside the front door. The road is private and virtually deserted. Beyond the arch, before a foreign embassy, stands a policeman, lone deterrent to some invisible bomber or hostage-seeker. Dark clouds lower overhead, and thunder intermittently sounds—rather meek thunder. I press the button and after a suitable length of time Richardson descends from the first floor; he is clearly visible behind the front-door glass. His manner is warm and affectionate, though it is our first meeting.

"Ah, dear boy, come along in," he says. "Quite a storm, did you get caught? 'Blow, winds, and crack your cheeks! You hurricanoes, spout, till you have drenched our steeples!' Follow me."

I follow him in. He begins a slow ascent of the narrow, elegant and deeply carpeted staircase, holding on to the polished wooden rail. On the stairs he turns and asks, "What will you drink?"

Our meeting is the result of a very tentative approach I had made some weeks earlier by letter, wondering "if there was any hope at all of approaching you as a possible subject for a book". The reply, which came some weeks later, was handwritten and carefully printed down the centre of a sheet of notepaper. Sir Ralph thanked me for copies I had sent of my previous books, and continued: "I am quite astonished that you say you would like to write about me; you cannot; there is nothing to write about. I am a PRINTER that is all—I make copy after copy of a performance and only I know the difference between the bad and the not so bad that it is my job to do—there is nothing to say to anyone about such an occupation."

On a second sheet he had added a postscript ("and add a P.S. to the matter") in handwriting half the size, but still down the centre of the page, giving even more the compact effect of a poem:

> I am reading the three long volumes of Vincent Van Gogh's letters to his brother Theo, these letters are rather boring, they go on and on about his difficultys, one has to keep patience to read them but it is really very interesting because one knows all the time the great sun of his gift will eventually break through. Any memoirs of me might be a little less depressing because my life has not for so many years been so stricken with poverty—but the theme had I kept a diary, as these letters of Vincent to Theo are such a writing would be rather the same —perhaps like this vanguard specimen:
>
> > THIS WEEK I WAS A LITTLE BETTER, PERHAPS I HAVE FOUND A NEW WAY TO OVERCOME THE NERVOUSNESS THAT HAS BEEN HOLDING ME BACK SO FAR.
>
> Could be interesting to read if one could tell that after all this digging in a waste land—a streak was just within the digger's find. Were I to find it you might have an excellent book to write. You will have to wait a bit I think and I do not think Ladbroke would give you a very good bet on the chance.

On receiving this I wrote back and reaffirmed my interest. He telephoned one Sunday night and we arranged to meet.

We are now in the first-floor drawing room: the rooms

are less spacious than appears from outside. Behind its imposing façade, the house is comfortable and elegant.

"Come straight from Oxford?"

"Yes," I answer.

"Down the new motorway?"

I nod.

"How long did it take you?" This clearly interests him.

He pours drinks; he takes a gin and tonic and does not stint himself. "Gin is a good glass before dinner; a very smooth take-off," he has said, "leaving no fume behind." I settle down with an uncomfortably large whisky.

"About an hour and a half," I answer. For some minutes talk flows easily. On plays. Politics. Novels. Some of his favourite novelists: Elizabeth Taylor, Henry James. He has said he has read all of Henry James, that he likes the "twists, turns, puzzles and mazes in his mind". Nervous, I begin to feel the effects of the whisky. At this point he becomes more purposeful.

"Finish your drink, and I'll give you another. I'm going to make a little speech. It will be over soon."

I do as I am told. He rises from his chair and helps himself to more gin, at the same time generously replenishing my own glass.

"Take your glass—and this bottle here, we'll go up to my study. It's better there for talking. You go first."

I again do as I am told, preceding him up two further flights of stairs to the top floor. I wait; he is taking each step with measured grandeur. He ushers me into a pale-green-walled, carpeted room with magnificent views west over the Park. He sits down in a battered black chair in front of a desk. He motions to me to draw up another chair right next to his. In the corner the Windsor chair which, as I find out later, used to belong to his father remains empty. I place the bottle and my glass on a pink-marble-topped table whose balance seems unsteady. Perception is becoming somewhat too heightened; I eye my drink uneasily. He opens the sloping desk-top before him and with a sudden acceleration of activity noisily turns over the dozen or so pipes inside. Selecting first one and then another, deciding each is not right, he finally, with the choice made, closes the lid.

Having filled and lit the pipe, he sits back and allows smoke to envelop him in a comforting cloud. He grips the pipe hard in his teeth—the teeth look ferocious and strong, like those of a landowner. The presence is very Russian. His face suddenly seems very near, as in one of the close-ups of Karenin in *Anna Karenina*: intensely strange, broad and sober, the nose irregular and prominent, never quite letting the face settle down to give a consistent picture, the eyes sometimes cold, grey-green—for a moment I convince myself they are blue—sometimes warm in the voltage with which they flash out humour. Then a shock of recognition: Russian, why not? He is after all appearing just now in Tolstoy's *The Fruits of Enlightenment* at the National Theatre. An actor's face: his canvas.

1   *Family landscape*

> God is very economical, don't you think? Wastes nothing. Yet also the opposite.   RICHARDSON, *The Observer*, 1975

The Richardsons came from Northumberland. "Puritans from the North. When I go to Newcastle . . . they come round to see me in my dressing room after the play. They're all farmers. They all talk about their pigs. 'I had swine fever last month, Ernest,' one says to the other. 'How's it going, George?' asks Ernest. 'Better Ernest now' says George. And, never once does any of them mention my performance in the play. They down their drinks and say good night until the next time and go out into the streets, still talking about swine fever among themselves. But as they drive home through the hills, I like to think they turn to one another in their car and say, 'Young Ralph looked bad when we first saw him. Worried, weren't you, about him? But when he got all that stuff off his face after, he looked a lot better!' "

Caution. This, like much of what Richardson (talking here to William Douglas Home) may say about himself, is a simplification, the striking of an attitude at once humorous and paradoxical. It is part of the problem, as Cedric Hardwicke—Richardson's mentor and oldest friend, predating both Laurence Olivier and John Gielgud—notes in his memoirs, "of anyone who has been an actor for any length of time: he does not know whether he has any true emotions or not." Richardson himself has gone further: "We don't know exactly who we are, do we? We hardly know anyone else, really completely. We none of us know when we're going to die. . . . We're a mystery to ourselves, and to other people."

We do know that his father, Arthur Richardson, was a painter and an art master. He is listed, along with nine other Richardsons, in Marshall Hall's *Artists of Northumbria* (1973); they were all landscape painters, and related directly or indirectly to Thomas Miles Richardson, Senior, the most celebrated Northumbrian artist of the nineteenth century.

Arthur Richardson, born in Newcastle upon Tyne in 1865, was the son of a successful leather manufacturer, David Richardson, whose wife, Catherine, belonged to the Fry cocoa- and chocolate-manufacturing family. In the 1880s Arthur's father sent him to Paris to study art. There he became a pupil of Adolphe Bouguereau (1825–1905), a salon painter of meticulous technique, averse to Impressionism, recently prized by collectors.

Ralph Richardson has claimed that his grandfather David, who was a devout Quaker, a keen naturalist and a gifted linguist, showing the same breadth of practical in-

terests his grandson was to exhibit later, disliked his son's
being a painter and would have preferred him to work in
the family business. Arthur Richardson's drawings, said his
son Ralph, were not as good as those of his grandfather,
who drew as a hobby. But then, in Ralph's early years at
any rate, his father did not behave towards him in a way
that gave him the security and confidence he found in his
grandfather.

In Paris Arthur Richardson met his future wife, Lydia
Susie Russell, who was also studying painting. A Roman
Catholic convert, she was the daughter of John Russell—
related to his Whig namesake Lord John—a merchant sea
captain who sailed the first steamship up the Thames.
Though Arthur remained a Quaker like his father, they
married and by 1890 were living in Newcastle at The
Gables, Elswick Road, built by David near to his own
Ashfield House, and near the family's Elswick leather
works. Arthur and Lydia's first son, Christopher, was born
there in 1890. In 1893 they moved to Tivoli Road, Cheltenham where Arthur Richardson, aged twenty-eight, was
to take up an appointment as senior art master on the staff
of Cheltenham Ladies' College, the well-known boarding
school for girls. In her report for that year the Lady
Principal records that she has engaged "Mr Richardson,
who is highly recommended". Arthur Richardson had
made the classic compromise of the middle-class artist by
becoming a teacher. He was to remain at the Ladies'
College for the next eighteen years.

At the end of the nineteenth century Cheltenham was a
comfortable and favoured town. Unlike even near-by
Gloucester, it had virtually no typhus or smallpox. The
streets were broadly laid out, the buildings designed with
style and imagination: a credit to the speculators who in the
earlier part of the century had transformed a small market
town into a fashionable spa, with a splendid Pantheonic
Rotunda dominating a network of tree-lined avenues and
drives. The domestic architecture had a neo-classical unity
and taste which today remains largely unspoilt. Far from
being shut-in or airless, the atmosphere was one of optim-

ism and evangelism. "There are great spiritual advantages
to be had in the town," says Bulstrode in *Middlemarch*. On
one side the Malvern Hills could be seen—although over
twenty miles away—while from the town's highest point,
on a fine day, sixty or eighty miles of England, which
included the Cotswolds, the Severn Valley, even the distant
Welsh hills, could also be scanned. The situation was, for a
landscape painter such as Arthur Richardson, ideal.

The Principal of Cheltenham Ladies' College, which had
been founded barely forty years before Arthur Richardson
joined the staff, also quoted George Eliot one year in her
annual address to the school: "No man can be great, he can
hardly keep himself from wickedness, unless he gives up
thinking much about pleasures and rewards and gets
strength to endure what is hard and painful." The College
day began at 6.30 a.m., when the girls in white blouses and
resplendent house ties made their way to Assembly, with
the pinnacles of the College buildings silhouetted against
the pale sky, like a miniature city. The principle of good
conduct was thought more important than ambition, which
was held to be narrowing and productive of envy and
malice. Even so, standards of learning were high, while all
kinds of extramural activities flourished, among them the
Department of Art which yearly expanded its numbers.

Arthur Richardson, a "shortish man with a beard and
cold blue eyes", who wore, according to his son, a multi-
coloured waistcoat, would take a cab with yellow wheels to
College. (The cab was somewhat of a mystery, for Tivoli
Road is only a few minutes' walk from the College.) He
worked hard at his job: almost every year in the College
magazine some reference was made to the progress of his
pupils. In 1897, we find them showing a "decided advantage on former years, both in power of drawing, in appreciation of tone value and colour". Later, their life paintings
are described as "vigorous", or "bold", or, at yet another
time, "direct and effective."

He didn't neglect his own career as an artist either,
exhibiting not only at the Laing Art Gallery, Newcastle,
thus maintaining his connections with his family, but for a

number of consecutive years at the Cheltenham and County Fine Arts Society Exhibition. In 1889, before moving to Cheltenham, he had achieved what represented the summit of his attainable ambition: his water-colour, *A Groyne at Leigh, Essex*, was selected for the Royal Academy Annual Exhibition, and he repeated this success in the following year with *Ryton Church*, and in 1897 with *O River, flowing to the sea!* His paintings also found their way into the Walker Art Gallery, Liverpool, and the Manchester City Art Gallery. Giving an idea of the character of his work, the *Cheltenham Examiner* wrote, of the Cheltenham Exhibition of 1907, that "Arthur Richardson, RBA, is represented by two charming water-colour drawings—*Evening on the Wye* and *A North Country Ferry*. The first is a particularly beautiful work. . . . Mr Richardson is a poet painter, selective and interpretive, but also true to nature." The same was to be true of his son's work, very much later, as an actor.

Langsyne, the house in Tivoli Road to which the Richardsons moved in October 1900, having lived previously at two other addresses in the same road, was a substantial villa in pale gold stone, with Ionic pilasters on either side of the front door. Detached, it stood—and still stands—set well back in a very private road of tall hedges and stately trees. Though he did not own the house, only rented it, Arthur Richardson liked to live in style.

It was at Langsyne, on 19 December 1902, that the Richardsons' third child (and third son, a second boy, Ambrose, having been born in 1892) was born. For some reason the birth was not announced in the *Examiner* until 4 February 1903. A week before that the Registrar signed the birth certificate of Ralph David Richardson.

CHESTER TERRACE, *21 May 1979:*

"Are you Catholic? I assume with a name like that . . ."
Without waiting for an answer Richardson goes on: "Someone told me this silly story—I don't suppose you've heard it."

He takes his time, puffing at his pipe every half-sentence:

"A good man is met by God at the entrance to Heaven, and God says, Let's go and have a look at the other place. When they reach it they find somewhere to sit down in a corner and have something to eat. Over in the distance are millions of people all roasting on fires. God says—in the meantime they're tucking into cold food, tuna fish sandwiches and the like—'I'm not cooking—as there's only the two of us.'"

I laugh, uneasy as to the point of his story. "Are you still a practising Catholic?" I ask. You never quite know if he will answer or not.

"My mother was Catholic. As a boy I used to be one. Then I had a whole revulsion against it. But sometimes I find it a great comfort."

His eyes seem on mine even while he is doing the talking, as if seeking something out. They take on a mysterious baffled power, and an eyebrow cocks balefully as he says:

"On occasions I've been a bit evil, but on the whole I've tried to be good. Haven't done anything really bad."

"Do you go to confession?"

He laughs, amused by the question. "If I went to confession it would be like Voltaire on his death-bed. To confess all my sins would take me seven hours." He looks uncertainly at me, wondering if the levity of his reply might have upset me.

"Do you really think when you die, there will be anyone there?" He stops for a long time, his great eyes staring somewhere over the top of my head. "I don't think there's going to be anyone there at all."

At this point, without warning, he suddenly breaks into coughing and spluttering and grows extremely red in the face, while his eyes, quickly turning bloodshot, begin to pop out in a sinister way. For a moment or two I think he is going to choke. He regains control. Still breathes heavily: "Too much damn smoking!"

He slams the pipe down. He sneezes quickly four or five times, and having at last calmed his breathing, turns to me with an amused look on his face.

"Much better if I died while you were working on your book," he says. "You know—I might go off at any moment. Might be next minute."

Silence, as I watch the great uneven waves of rain sweeping across the Park. In spite of his teasing tone a slight suspicion flickers in my mind that he might well be right.

"Best from your point of view if I did. Like the waiter, totting up the bill." He does a quick little sketch, deftly executed, of a French waiter scribbling his *addition*; swiftly drawing a line under the total. "That will be— . . . Or a spectacular death would be just what you want; like Eleanora Duse."

I hardly know whether to treat this as a joke or to reply seriously. He stares off towards his built-in bookcase, and in a far-away voice adds: "I'll see what I can do."

2   Peer the dreamer

Until the age of eighteen Richardson was, by his own admission, a mother's boy. He might have liked it to be otherwise, but one night in 1906 or 1907 his mother left his father, taking Ralph with her: "She eloped with me, then aged four."

The departure was dramatic. The Church was Lydia
Richardson's accomplice. A black cab was drawn up round
the corner of Tivoli Road: a tall nun in black was standing
by. "Hush boy," she said to Ralph, as a box filled with their
belongings was fixed on the roof. Ralph and his mother got
inside, the window of the cab was let down, and the "nun
with her starched white veil put her head in. 'Now goodbye
dear,' she said to my mother, 'and be a good boy,' she said
to me. 'But why have you got a moustache?' I said to her.
'Drive on, cabby, please,' called my mother." His mother
reproved him: "Always remember, Ralphie, never to say
things like that."

In a memoir of his early days published in the *Sunday
Times* in 1960, Richardson disclaimed knowledge of what
caused the rift between his parents, saying it was over
something trivial. In an article in *Vogue* some 19 years
later, he partly attributed it ("I've never discovered the real
cause") to his mother, for having had his father's studio
painted out of her own pocket money while he was away for
a day or two. On his return, "domestic fury struck the
household with the suddenness of an avalanche." Some
time later, he said, he was told—presumably by his mother
—that his father was a wicked man. However, on meeting
his father fourteen years later, when he was eighteen, he
had doubts about his wickedness.

Again Richardson turned what was probably quite ordinary into something mysterious and paradoxical—for why
should he have believed when told his father was "wicked",
that it was over something trivial? It seems more likely that
his father had begun an affair with another woman and his
mother, incensed and hurt, ran off taking Ralph with her.
The records show that, like a future king of England,
Arthur Richardson became attached to a Mrs Simpson
—though in his case there was no remarriage. In 1911 he
was no longer living in Tivoli Road, but had moved to, and
was sharing premises at 10 Suffolk Square, Cheltenham,
with a Mrs Alexander Simpson. It may be that in his youth
or even later Richardson did not know of this lady's existence—or even if he was told, wasn't inclined to believe it.

The event of his leaving Cheltenham was important: from then on he became the sole object of his mother's care and attention, his two brothers having remained with their father in Cheltenham. His father's presence had been a benevolent one. His background in Cheltenham was secure and ordered. Now he was to suffer a degree of deprivation that created in him not only the need for secrecy which his life so curiously illustrates, both at a conscious and an unconscious level, but also that need for self-expression in a creative form to which his long and unusually rich career stands as a monument. At his departure from the Ionic porch of his Cheltenham home, with its Victorian certainties, and from his gifted father, nurturing his pupils in the highest ideals of selfless service, the terrain of Richardson's life becomes one of bohemian irregularities, of muddle and confusion. He became isolated from his social peers, ceasing to feel sufficiently respected by his neighbours. But he was to be given a more expansive and uncertain canvas on which to form dreams. And he had all to himself someone who shared and stimulated his private life.

Arthur Richardson provided his wife with £2.10s. a week. She and her son, with an old nanny called Joey who had been in service with the Bird family, makers of the famous brand of custard ("She fed me on Bird's custard almost every day")—thus preserving in poverty a flavour of middle-class gentility—moved to Shoreham-by-Sea, on the coast. There Lydia's sister Maud Russell, once a musical-comedy actress of some note, had a house. The best the Richardson ménage could afford was a makeshift bungalow of discarded rolling stock, consisting, as Richardson wrote, of

two complete railway carriages with all their original doors and windows. The carriages were joined by a tin roof. The space between the carriages made a large room. There was a front porch and verandah and a kitchen added at the back. So, we had a front door and a back door as well as about twenty side doors, these with brass handles and leather strapped windows. We had

lamps and candles for illumination and we caught the
rain water off the tin roof into a butt, and we boiled it for
drinking.

But they were happy here. His memories—of the rain
rattling on the carriage roof, the smell and savour of a
particular soap or, more succulent, of seafood caught in a
huge shrimping net, of climbing breakwaters or groynes
and falling down and rolling in the soft shingle of the beach,
practising deaths, pierced by an assegai or shot by an
arrow—all showed how he coped with an isolation he felt
deeply, but also how he developed at an early age a capacity
for catching imaginative reverberations.

For a time he was befriended by the world-famous
wrestler George Hackenschmidt. When Hackenschmidt, a
short, thickset man, went shrimping he used to take Ralph
on his shoulders—giving him the feeling of being carried by
the strongest man in the world.

Unlike most other boys, Ralph grew up in this seaside
place with an almost complete absence of trees and shrub-
bery. And already he was in costume. His aunt Maud
brought him back from Turkey a wonderful scarlet jacket
with brass buttons all the way down the front and with
epaulettes on the shoulders. He wore this a great deal, and,
alone on the beach, his dressing-up period was much
prolonged.

An incident was to heighten this isolation. He knew one
of the daughters of the suffragette leader Mrs Pankhurst,
who was a neighbour. One day when they were playing, an
iron hoop he was twirling round on the end of a stick came
off and struck the Pankhurst girl on the head, causing a
copious flow of blood, though it proved to be nothing
serious.

"You brute! You have killed my daughter," shouted Mrs
Pankhurst in a rash display of unegalitarian feeling. Ralph
was never allowed to play with the girl again.

One day his aunt Maud led him to the window of her
house on the front at Shoreham, pointing at three or four
smartly dressed gentlemen striding along the beach. She

called out to them, "with an effortless ring," "God save the King!" One of the gentlemen stopped, looked at the house, raised his top hat and made a little bow. "That," his aunt told him, "was King Edward VII. You might remember that."

Lydia Richardson's ties with the Church remained strong, not always to her son's benefit. Once he was sent to be chastised by a priest, Father Christie, for taking without permission an orange from a bowl, eating it and then lying to Joey about it. Lydia was deeply distressed but refused to punish the child herself, instead writing a note for Joey to take to the priest. Ralph was determined he would never be punished by Father Christie, "the person I first hated . . . my hatred was a sin." On the way to the sacristy, by the Norfolk Bridge, he slipped away from Joey and hid successfully in the oozy mud by the river Adur. When at last he returned Lydia forgave him, her soft heart melting with joy to have him back: clearly an indulgent mother.

Ralph's most vivid memory of childhood remained of a bath given him in a convent, where he was kept for a day or two when his mother had gone away somewhere:

I remember the bathroom. It was spacious, warm, steamy. We only had a tin bath in the bungalow. "Now Ralph," said two charming nuns, "you put on this nightgown and then into the bath and we'll be back. . . ." The nightgown was not my own, which was, I think, oatmeal-coloured flannel and was friendly and smelt like my teddy-bear. This nightgown was white and it was too long for me but I put it on. "Now Ralph," one said, "get in the bath." I sat in the bath, the white nightgown billowing around me, refusing to sink. I was like a poached egg, surrounded by white. The nuns did not move. Neither did I. This is all I remember of bath night in the convent.

The background of Richardson's early years has strong similarities to that of Henrik Ibsen, who at the age of seven was moved into a smaller house outside town because of his father's debts and drunkenness (his plays are frequently about the attachment of mother and son). At the end of

Peer Gynt, a play about a poet's development in which Richardson was later to have one of his greatest successes, Peer asks Solveig, who has remained faithful to him all through his life, "Where is the real Peer?" She answers, "In my faith, in my hope, in my love." It was the devotion of his mother, Äase, that first brought Peer the courage to be a poet, just as it was Solveig's emotional support that sustained him in his life without an identity of his own.

Peer was luckier than Richardson's father seems to have been. As an artist Arthur Richardson's subsequent progress was less than fortunate. If our assumption is correct, he had acquired a mistress as an object for his inspiration, but this was probably not the same thing as having a woman like Lydia behind him, and may have proved more of a limitation than a fulfilment. In any event, he did not exhibit again at the Royal Academy. At the end of the summer term of 1911, aged forty-six, Arthur left his post at the Ladies' College. An advertisement in the Cheltenham *Looker On* of 30 December 1911 stated that he had left off teaching but was taking private pupils at the Montpellier Rotunda Studio. Members of the College staff presented him with a book, appropriately titled *Turner's Golden Visions*, together with silver tobacco and match boxes, which were "suitably engraved, as a mark of their regard and esteem".

3 Bold outlines

Like Peer the dreamer Ralph found every subject at school boring. From the age of five he attended several Roman Catholic institutions, one of which, the Xavierian College,

Brighton, was a seminary for intendant priests from which he ran away. These schools were chosen in preference to a "common" school because they had a certain tone, but also because their fees were remarkably low. One day, he did make an impact on his class, by standing up and reading from one of Macaulay's *Lays of Ancient Rome*, giving it "the works". The class was spell-bound, horrified. And he, too, frightened himself with his own power. "That's enough," they said—and never asked him to read again.

Like Olivier, who attended an Anglo-Catholic school and enjoyed its flamboyance ("We had six blazoned candlesticks, a crucifix and the Host with a lamp in front") and Gielgud, who loved the smell of incense and felt exaltation watching the ceremony of Brompton Oratory, Richardson found in the rituals of the Church an early love of ceremony. He got his first moments of formalized drama swinging the censer as an altar boy at St John's Church, Brighton.

He also read much: all of Shakespeare by the age of fourteen, and later H. G. Wells, an author with whom he was to identify as a young man and who made him question his religious beliefs. And he formed other, shorter-lived attachments. When he was about twelve he met a girl named Francesca. He said he never kissed her, never even touched her. He saw her no more than a couple of times. "But," he said, "as long as I live I shan't forget her."

His love of fireworks began with Halley's comet ("Look up, look up at the sky, Ralphie," his mother told him). Later they moved to the London suburb of Norwood, near the Crystal Palace, and fireworks became commonplace. But he always preserved a childlike wonder at these marvels. (There was to be a famous incident in 1937, when his friend Olivier had set up house with Vivien Leigh in Chelsea and Richardson arrived on Guy Fawkes night with a large rocket, which instead of going up into the air ravaged the drawing room. In commemoration of this deed, every time a new production opens at London's National Theatre, a rocket is let off from the roof. It is known as "Ralph's rocket".)

Although his mother never again saw his father, friendly relations were kept up with the Newcastle side of the family. When he was six Ralph had been summoned to Newcastle to see his grandmother, Catherine Richardson. He took with him a pet mouse called Kim, precursor of numerous unlikely pets. The servant sent to meet him off the train shook her head and told him, "You'll never be allowed to take that creature up to Ashfield House." "Why not?" asked Ralph. "I've been invited to see my grandmother, and I never travel without my Kim." "She won't let it in the house," said the servant. "In that case," said Ralph, "When's the next train back to Brighton?" The matriarch of the family was forced to capitulate, and gained a strong impression of her grandson's character: it was to stand him in good stead later on.

One day when Ralph and his mother were living in Norwood his grandfather David, then nearly eighty, came to give his grandson a special outing. "I took him," wrote Richardson, "to the Crystal Palace and we spent hours on the switchbacks: he never turned a whisker. I was told afterwards I might have killed him. To me, he behaved as if he were the same age as myself."

Outwardly the boy who was growing up was vague, somewhat clumsy, with the hefty frame of a Northumberland farmer, but friendly and affectionate. Inwardly he was a muddle. H. G. Wells, who had a similar background and described his autobiographical hero Kipps as "By the nature of his training . . . indistinct in his speech, confused in his mind, and retreating in his manner", might well have been describing Richardson. He rarely attended school for more than a couple of days a week. With all the moves mother and son made in those years, from one flat, boarding house or small hotel to another, and with the loss of a father still an ever-present shock, he turned on himself the aggression he must have felt towards his father and towards the outside world. To this day he does not know if he was really ill or not, or ill because he didn't want to go to school, but he seemed to catch everything that was going— diphtheria, scarlet fever, measles, mumps, chicken-pox

—and spent a great deal of his life in hospital. The diphtheria he had caught was supposed to have left him with a
weak heart, so he was forbidden games. As well as cosset-
ting him, making him go to bed at twenty minutes to
nine—"I can remember looking out of my window and
seeing the boys playing on Norwood Common while I was
undressing for bed. I envied their freedom"—his mother
made, as he himself said, a "bit of a hobby" of her own
health, "which wasn't really so bad." She was impractical
but loving, spoiling him and overprotecting him.

By the end of his school days he claimed he had learned
nothing: more important, he had no discipline of mind and
absolutely no ability to concentrate. In fact he was so
backward that for a time he had a private tutor called
Ernest de la Grave, but this was no great help to him,
and he ended up giving de la Grave lessons in bookbind-
ing.

Temporary salvation came when he left school and found
a job as office boy with the Liverpool and Victoria Insurance Company in Brighton, to which mother and son
returned in 1917. Richardson was very conscious of small
sums of money, and each wage day he deposited in the Post
Office 7s. 6d. out of his 10s. salary. With this job, not only
did he feel, for the first time in his life, better off, but it was
the end of his social isolation; at once, as if by a miracle, his
health improved.

At the insurance company he first showed signs of having
the imagination to invent the character "Ralph Richardson" who was to grow in time into such a rich and many-
sided creation. He tells how he constructed for his boss, Mr
Barry, "a character of an office boy of immense solemnity
and a marvel of neatness that seemed to rebuke his easi-
ness. It came off very effectively with him. I suspect that I
have a talent as a butler. If I half subconsciously pulled his
leg in my pantomime, I sincerely admired him."

For the first time was seen the other side of the Richardson personality: on the one hand the imagination and
formlessness of a poet, but on the other the finished and
eccentrically detailed "character", rich in type, with always

a dominating trait clearer than other features which are an integral part of the picture. At seventeen, half of his being remained unformed, searching without direction, but the other was already presenting defined and typical attitudes, the bold outlines essential for humour and the inspiring of affection in others, which he achieved early.

He liked to see himself in the office at the corner of North Street and New Road, as half buffoon, half daredevil, the butt of fortune, also the tempter of fate. One day he went climbing round the ledge outside the building, high above the crowd in the street below, just to amuse himself. His boss returned unexpectedly early from lunch. Richardson smiled to him from outside, waved and put his head in through the top of the window. "Mr Barry, sir," he said affably, "a pigeon."

He opened the mail, changed the nibs on the pens, and later edited the office magazine. He sent off cheques and claims to the wrong people, so that people who should have got demands for premiums received cheques and those who were due to have their claims settled got the demands.

On 20 October 1913, in Newcastle, his grandfather David died peacefully in his sleep. Six years later his grandmother also passed away, and though she had a large family she remembered the distant and estranged existence of her grandson Ralph, and particularly his stubborn will; she left him £500, in his eyes a princely sum, to be spent on furthering his education. Kim, the mouse he'd taken with him to meet his grandmother, had cost him sixpence.

He and his mother decided how they should spend the money, and the uncle who was executor agreed. Richardson went along the following Monday morning to tell Mr Barry the news.

"May I speak to you, sir."

"Yes."

"I have bad news for you, I'm afraid, Mr Barry."

"What is it, Richardson?"

Richardson could see Mr Barry knew of his posting of valuable cheques to the wrong clients.

"I have to give you two weeks' notice. I am leaving your

employment and I am going to the Brighton School of Art."

"Oh thank God," said Mr Barry. "I was going to give you the sack at the end of the week, but I was putting it off as long as possible."

CHESTER TERRACE, *21 May 1979:*

"Didn't you once want to be a painter, Sir Ralph?" I ask, thinking a change of subject might do us both good.

"Oh yes." The question is the right one: it seems to awaken him out of some inner slumber as if he has temporarily switched off his presence in our world. He snaps out of his trance, changing gear again. I too have been spellbound with his notions of death, of dying, and catch up more slowly.

"I was too lazy to be a painter, which I should like to have been. It was like riding a bicycle—I hadn't got the persistency—but then I hadn't got very much talent—"

I expostulate. He turns again, this time clearly bored, as if he wants to get rid of me. "Are you going back to Cambridge—"

"Oxford—."

"Oxford," he corrects himself, "—tonight?"

Time not to withdraw, I reflect: we have hardly broached the subject. I ask quickly.

"What about this new play—by David Home?"

"Storey." He seems to regain energy and the awkward moment passes: talking more quickly now.

"Very good job—I like it. Don't know if I shall do it. We'll have to see. Lindsay Anderson and I went round with some comments, to ask him to rewrite. Instead of disagreeing, Storey said 'You're absolutely right.' We both thought, Fine, but when we next met Storey said 'I don't want it done.' Splendid writer. No horrible 'that's' and 'which's' . . . sets a rhythm and sticks to it . . . Look here,'—he turned to face me—'why do you want to do a book about me, I've no great talent—felt standing on a stage, saying 'Dinner is served my lord'—I could make something of it. Theatre—it's the demands of others—I'm basically lazy by nature, but it's set up and you can't get out of it, and it's the fear that drives you on: I might be found not to know my part—oh God." He puts his hand to his head in mock consternation. "But I'm jealous of painters. Picasso—wonderful tricks. Everything very clever but couldn't in the final reckoning deliver. But the way of seeing things—suddenly he showed us a woman, a delicate wonderful creature with her arms folded in a certain way." He folds his arms across his chest—he seems to be enjoying himself again. "And suddenly we see women in a new way—that was his skill. But nothing like Pissarro, the way the eye sees and carries it through. And the loneliness, the courage of being a painter, just going on day after day by yourself, the heroism of it."

Later, visiting the Pissarro exhibition at the Hayward Gallery, I notice two pictures directly evocative of Richardson's own childhood, the painting of a railway siding and embankment at Norwood, and a scene near the Crystal Palace: in such a road Ralph might have lived as a child. Another painter of whose work Richardson is an ardent admirer is the English artist William Nicholson, who taught Winston Churchill to paint: Richardson has called Nicholson "one of our greatest painters", and used to see him frequently in the 1930s and 1940s at the Savile, a neat figure in olive green who played a stylish game of snooker. He was something of a character in his later days, and would sometimes go about sporting ostler's braces in bright orange.

Of Nicholson once giving him sound advice, Richardson spoke in a BBC interview in 1969:

> In Harriet Walk, in Lowndes Square, where I kept a mews house, was the most beautiful Regency arch which used to tower above my little house; and I was painting in my upstairs room this arch one day, and I went downstairs to my little dining room and the arch of course looked quite different from down below, so I took my painting down and I painted it from down there and then I didn't know whether to paint it from upstairs or down, and so, when I went to the club that day I met Nicholson. "I've got a problem—I'm painting it from upstairs and I ran down and painted it from downstairs and I wasn't quite sure . . . another bit from upstairs . . . a bit from below . . . is this all right? Shouldn't I make a decision?" "Perfectly all right," he said, "perfectly all right, Ralph. But why run?"

Richardson owns five of Nicholson's paintings, three painted before the First World War: *Rottingdean, Winter* (1908), *Seascape* (1908) and *Shingle and Sea* (1910): painted in oil on board, they are again scenes intensely evocative of Ralph's childhood.

4 First thoughts of the stage

At Brighton College of Art Richardson discovered he had no great talent for painting, or at least no commitment to go on seeking the talent. One deduces something holding him back from following in his father's footsteps. "Vitality" and "originality" were the qualities he found lacking in the drawings and water-colours he kept from those days; though he painted later as a hobby, his capacity for execution in no way satisfied his sense of possibility. It was fortunate he had the opportunity to explore the limits of his talent for art at such a crucial moment. He buried the landscape painter once and for all, but the buried painter remained alive inside him, as did other possibilities awakened later—the engineer, the aviator. As an actor he was able to call on this submerged potentiality.

In 1920, after a few months, he left art school. He still had half of the £500, and wondered quickly what to try next. He thought for a time he might be a pharmacist. He felt that being dressed in white and mixing things in bottles, and saying "Take this three times a day" was rather a good idea. So he went along to a pharmacist and there they told him how long it took to qualify, and he had second thoughts.

He went along to the *Brighton Herald*, thinking he might try his hand at journalism. Again, and very nicely, they asked him what examinations he had passed and he was forced, reluctantly, to admit he had never passed a single examination. So they next said, what about shorthand and typing? "It's quite simple," they told him. "Buy a book." He went away and bought the *Easy Guide to Pitman's Shorthand* but got nowhere, finding it appallingly painful and difficult: still the old problem of being unable to concentrate. He abandoned this idea.

As a child he had often visited Brighton's theatres: the Theatre Royal, the Grand, the Hippodrome, the West Pier, and the Palace Pier. He never had much success in getting his mother to accompany him or share his love. As he described what he had seen—Grand Guignol or Sybil Thorndike as St Joan perhaps—"a particularly glazed expression" would come over his mother's face. He is quoted in Elizabeth Sprigge's biography, *Sybil Thorndike Casson* (1971): "Since then I have often observed this expression and learnt that I must avoid expressing too much enthusiasm to someone who cannot appreciate it. I'm afraid I bored my mother to death, but I don't regret it, because this was something I could not keep in—and motherhood has its penalties."

He had also seen, in the weekly changes of bill, all the great music-hall performers, among them Little Tich, Harry Tate, George Robey and Marie Lloyd. But it was at the Theatre Royal, during a performance by Frank Benson as Hamlet, that he first pin-pointed for himself a specific excitement in and ambition for straight acting. Strangely enough, what attracted him was not the actor's magnetic appeal, or the emotion aroused by some passage, but an almost mundane piece of stage business which for him took on a magical significance.

It was even stranger in that Benson was much past his prime, and his memory had begun to founder, although his athletic prowess had remained constant, as had his zeal to promote Shakespeare. He had gained a blue at Oxford and would trot through each town he toured, corks gripped in his hands, while his manager in starched collar and dark suit panted alongside gasping out the business of the day. Fifty years after beginning he was still playing Hamlet and Richard II; it was said that when he began to fumble for lines he would take Horatio aside and exclaim, "Crouch we awhile and mark," and dart into the wings to refresh his memory.

His Hamlet embodied rugged individualism and old-fashioned staging. The Ghost appeared in white, while in the scene with the players, Benson, raking up Ophelia's dropped fan, would cover himself with it as he lithely stalked across the stage, ending with a "blaze of triumph at the King's rise". In the final act he wielded a fisherman's net—to remind everyone he had been to sea, and with which, like a Roman gladiator, he finally enmeshed Claudius.

It wasn't so much the explosive, hysterical quality of Benson's performance that impressed Richardson. But when, after the Ghost says to Hamlet: "Revenge his foul and most unnatural murder," he answered with his drawn

sword, by scraping it across the floor of the stage, making a
weird and wonderful noise, to Richardson this sounded like
Hell, where the Ghost came from, and it absolutely mesmerized him. My God, he thought, if I could do that; and
he found his heart was beating quite wildly. Oh, oh, he
thought, if only I could be an actor, if only I could have a
sword and scratch it on the floor, I wouldn't want to do
anything else.

In December 1920 he began to make enquiries. Near
where he and his mother lived in Brighton, not far from the
railway station, a small company—half amateur and half
professional—was performing in a disused bacon factory
known as St Nicholas Hall. Being unlicensed, it was not
allowed to charge for tickets, and made a precarious living
by taking collections. The director was one F. R., or Frank,
Growcott, who had acted with Benson, and modelled his
company along the same missionary lines. Benson was
often referred to as the "bishop"; the much less eminent
Growcott was sometimes teased, in his former bacon factory, for re-starting the production of "ham".

Early one Sunday morning Richardson cycled to Growcott's house in the Port Hall Road and knocked on the
door. Growcott himself answered. He was the first actor
Richardson had ever seen off stage: he wore a dark brown
woolly tweed suit, a shirt and tie, and was cleanshaven. He
had somewhat hawkish features which reminded Ralph of
Benson, though Growcott was smaller. His eyes were
friendly and blue. He stood in the doorway and looked
Richardson over.

"What do you want," he said.

"Well, my name's Richardson and I'd very much like to
be an actor, if I could. I mean, you've got an acting
company, could I join it?"

"Well," he said, "what acting have you done?"

"Well," said Richardson, "I haven't done any acting at
all. Never."

Growcott was playing with the door handle, impatient to
get on with his breakfast. Richardson was so eager he didn't
even seem to be aware of the time of day.

"What's all this about?" said Growcott. "I mean you say you want to be an actor, you've never done any acting. I mean, look here. What did you say your name was?"

"Richardson."

"Look here, Richardson, why fiddle about with this?"

Richardson was very disappointed. "I couldn't possibly be with you then?"

"Well," Growcott said, "I don't know about that."

Richardson was thinking hard: he had formed a plan.

"Look, Mr Growcott, a short while ago I came into some money, and I've still got a little of it left. I mean if I could come to you in any way as an apprentice I could pay a little premium, you know, Mr Growcott."

"Well," Growcott said, "what was the name?" He straightened up in the doorway.

"Richardson."

"Come inside, Richardson."

This was Ralph's entrance into the theatre world. He went upstairs with Growcott and over the remains of breakfast talked it over more. Richardson who, in spite of his bungling way in the insurance office, had gleaned some small insight into financial matters, said, "Well, I think it would be fair if I paid you ten bob a week for twelve weeks, and if you kept me on after that, you paid me ten bob a week until we've sort of equalled the thing out, then we can think again, eh?" Being no businessman at all Growcott was nonplussed: Richardson was decidedly the sharper of the two.

After reflection Growcott said, "Well, that's all right. Come and recite something to me tomorrow, at the theatre. Learn it and let me listen to your voice. Let me get some idea if I could employ you as an actor at all."

Next morning at 11.30 Richardson was at the theatre. An hour passed. No Growcott. An hour and a quarter and still no sign of the man. At nearly one o'clock Growcott strolled in as if nothing had happened.

"Mr Growcott, you have kept me a long time waiting," said Richardson crossly.

"Young man," said Growcott, "if you are going to get on

in the theatre you'll have to learn to wait."

He motioned him on to the empty stage. "Very well, come along now. Let's see what you can do."

He watched Richardson go forward. He wasn't much taken. Richardson tripped on the steps and made the whole forestage shake: Growcott had built it with his own hands. A lumbering kind of chap—six feet tall—who walked with loose limbs, head well set forward, marking energy, perhaps, all right for a farmer or builder. But an actor?

The features were equally unpromising. One might call his face attractively plain—the nose, the "funny round nose" as the influential critic James Agate was to dub it later, sizeable and slightly flattened at its tip, might on occasions and with the right expression in the eyes, be humorous. But not the face of a tragedian, by any stretch of the imagination: no stern classic mobility, no eagle glance of command. Nothing of the reverse either—no inkling of suffering or of pale intellectual gloom. At first sight Richardson was hardly inspiring.

"What are you going to do?" said Growcott.

"Falstaff's description of being thrown into the Thames, from *The Merry Wives of Windsor*."

"Well, then, take your time. Don't rush now."

Richardson began: "Nay, you shall hear, Master Brook, what I have suffered to bring this woman to evil for your good." He went on with the elaboration of Falstaff's absurd plight in the laundry basket of foul clothes as he is doused first in the stinking hot water of Datchet Lane and then, hissing hot and half stewed in grease, slid into the Thames. He took comfort from Growcott's expression, which remained throughout tolerant and good-humoured.

"Well," he said, when he was through.

Growcott rose from where he'd been sitting.

"Oh," he said, "it's absolutely awful."

Richardson's expression fell. His high hopes were dashed. "It's the first acting I've ever done," he said plaintively.

"It's frightful, Richardson. I mean you don't even know the goddam thing. Shapeless, senseless, badly spoken, and

I can't think why you chose the piece—you could never, never be any good as Falstaff."

Richardson made no reply. He took up his copy of Shakespeare into which he had folded the £2 premium his mother had lent him to advance to Growcott for the first four weeks. It now caught Growcott's eye.

"But don't let's despair, Richardson. Don't let's despair. No doubt we can do something with you. I mean you're handy with the brush, aren't you? I mean, you could fix up the lights, eh? Sweep the floor, and that sort of thing. Of course, you'll have to start at the bottom."

He did. That same night he had to provide noises of a Zeppelin raid for a wartime comedy Growcott had written. He was supplied with two empty petrol cans tied to the end of a leather strap and shown to a small space underneath the stage where he was to conceal himself, where there was a little spill of light between the boards to see by. The signal was to be Growcott tapping with his toe above. But Growcott, who was short and very sensitive about his height, wore lifts, and Richardson, lying beneath the stage, was confused by the tapping sound of the actor embarking on his first entrance; he went into action prematurely with his tins, drowning the leading man's opening lines. "Thus," he said, "I burst on the English stage as a bombshell."

After this he made himself more useful by learning to fix the lights and even to wire them up. He learnt how to build crude scenery, which was the best they could manage. By day they would rehearse and then he and Growcott would sit up half the night painting the set. One of his first jobs was "mixing the black" for the tabs—getting powdered black paint to dissolve in water. It floated, and nothing on earth would get it to mix. He spent many weary hours.

Growcott chose to play a heroic character both on stage and off. Adventurous and undisciplinable, he did things with style. He was abstemious, never swore, and pronounced the word arrogant as "AG-ARR-ANT". His wife, Blanche, fascinated Richardson even more; sardonic in humour, older than her husband, she looked as if life hadn't been all roses, and she excelled on stage as Nancy in *Oliver*

Twist or Madame Defarge in *A Tale of Two Cities*.

In time they tested Richardson above board. His first, non-speaking part was the Gendarme in Balzac's *The Bishop's Candlesticks*, adapted and directed by F. R. Growcott, with F. R. Growcott in the leading role. They found him a scarlet coat to wear and as it reminded him of the coat he had worn on the beach when he practised death falls, he felt comfortable. Another Gendarme followed, this time in *Les Misérables*. Soon he was cast in small speaking parts, until he was playing everything short of the leads: Cuthbert in *The Farmer's Romance* by F. R. Growcott, the Father in *The Moon-Children* (by Constance M. Foot). By this time the company had moved to another theatre, in Queen's Road, fancifully called by Growcott the Shakespearian Playhouse. Here Richardson doubled Banquo and Macduff, who appeared in the same scene.

On Midsummer Day, 1921, he opened as Malvolio in *Twelfth Night*. The local critic applauded his make-up and wrote that he "gave a thoughtful impression of the conceited steward". This was in contrast to an Orsino who was "self-conscious" and an Olivia who was "colourless". The notice didn't encourage Growcott to honour his side of the bargain struck with Ralph, who hardly ever saw the ten shillings they'd agreed he should receive after twelve weeks; almost every Saturday night they had an argument which sometimes led to blows. "My first manager is the only one so far that I have actually struck," said Richardson later.

The funds left him by his grandmother were running low. Richardson reflected on this on a happier occasion, drinking cocoa with the Growcotts one evening in Port Hall Road, as he eyed the printed label on the tin: FRY'S COCOA.

5 *The good companion*

In 1921 live theatre was flourishing in England. Most cities
had at least four playhouses; Manchester had sixteen.
Charting the intricate mechanism of the living theatre, the
theatrical journal *The Stage* never showed less than 150
touring companies moving about the country at any given
weekend in the autumn. Railway junctions such as Crewe,
York and Birmingham were scenes of endless shunting and
coupling, "choked on the Sabbath with the entertainment
world in transit."

Richardson wrote to the leaders of four companies that
regularly visited Brighton: Benson, John Martin-Harvey,
Ben Greet (with whom Sybil Thorndike had acted) and
Charles Doran. From the last two only, replies came back.
Ben Greet saw him at the Palace Pier but had nothing to
offer. Doran asked him over to Eastbourne one Wednesday after a matinée of *The Merchant of Venice*. Oh my
goodness, thought Ralph, what a wonderful thing. He got
out his bicycle and gave it an extra clean. (His bicycle was in
fact so clean already that if there was a spot of rain in the air
he never dared take it out, but would walk.) He put on his
cycle clips and set off over the Downs, arriving in time to
see part of the performance. The theatre, in Devonshire
Park, was the pride of Eastbourne, with a domed roof and
two identical towers. The stage had a famous "metyza-
nium" floor, with machinery which enabled part of the
scene to rise while the other part was sinking—helpful for
the transporting of spirits and devils.

Making his way backstage after the play, Richardson was
nervous as a cat: aged eighteen and a half, he had still never
been behind the scenes of a professional theatre. He was
struck by the cathedral-like atmosphere that presided in
Doran's theatre: everyone was highly drilled and made to
walk on tiptoe.

Doran's dresser said to Richardson. "Come in, the
Guv'nor will see you." When Richardson went in Doran
was taking off his make-up as Shylock, and hardly looked at
him. He wore a vest and stage tights and wielded a towel

with red edges. He observed Ralph in his mirror.

"Oh yes, Richardson," he said. "Let's hear you spout something to get an idea what kind of voice you've got."

Ralph knew this was coming and had learnt, this time carefully, Mark Antony's funeral oration from *Julius Caesar*.

"Yes," said Doran in his pleasant voice with its slight Cork accent. "Stand over there, will you, just over there so I can get a look at you."

He stood over at the back where Doran's street clothes were hanging next to his Shylock costume. Doran was watching him in the mirror.

"Go on, start away."

Ralph began: "Friends, Romans, countrymen, lend me your ears; I come to bury Caesar, not to praise him," and went on with the speech:

You all did see that on the Lupercal
I thrice presented him a kingly crown,

becoming quite dramatic. Doran suddenly roared

"Stop it, man stop it! Pack it up."

Ralph was shattered.

"Isn't it any good, Mr Doran? Isn't it any good? Don't you like it?"

"It's fine," he said, "it's fine. But you're standing on my trousers!"

His trousers had been hanging on a peg behind Ralph and in his excitement down went the trousers and Ralph was plunging on them, feeling they might serve as Caesar's rent and blood-stained toga.

He needn't have worried. "I liked that, I liked that, Richardson, that's fine. Would you like to join my company?"

"Of course, it's been the ambition of my life."

"We might fix that up," Doran said. "How much do you want?"

Richardson's business acumen again came to the fore. He looked challengingly at him and said, "Mr Doran, I'm getting thirty shillings a week at the moment."

He might have said that Growcott owed him 30 shillings a week.

"Are you, are you? I'll give you three pounds. That's the Equity minimum." And he added, "But you'll have to give me a pound a week back."

In August 1921, Richardson took a room in a boarding house over Waterloo Road, where the Festival Hall now stands, to begin rehearsals with Doran's company. He was away from his mother for the first time in his life, with what seemed uncommonly like the wicker basket in which Falstaff had hidden himself. The difference was that inside the lid was oilcloth to keep out water. Each member of the company had a basket and these were travelled by the company and delivered to each theatre they played. Across the lid of his in bold letters was painted

RALPH RICHARDSON

The company was the school Richardson had dreamt of as a child, and missed. He had to provide

2 wigs—1 juvenile, 1 scratch character
2 court shoes—1 russet, 1 black
2 tights
2 ballet shirts

The reality was much harsher: rehearsals were long and arduous (Doran's company took ten plays on tour), and although Richardson had little to do at first, they were preparing six or seven plays and had only three weeks. Lorenzo in *The Merchant of Venice* was the most important of his first set of parts; others were Guildenstern in *Hamlet*, Scroop and Gower in *Henry V*, and Oliver, Orlando's elder brother, in *As You Like It*. The younger you were, the older the parts you played. Doran himself was in his early forties and like Growcott had acted with Benson. He had also appeared at Stratford-upon-Avon. The parts for which he was noted were Shylock and Petruchio.

The settings the company carried with them were fairly simple: black tabs, arches and a blue backcloth. Doran was one of the few producers who bothered about lighting and in *Julius Caesar* and *Macbeth* it was relatively complicated. Richardson, as usual with a novice, was Assistant Stage Manager and had to pack away props after the show.

Doran was a genius at picking promising newcomers, and in his company were Barbara Everest, Edith Sharpe, Neil Porter, Norman Shelley, Reginald Jarman, Abraham Sofaer, Arthur Young, Cecil Parker, Hilton Edwards and Don Woolfitt (Donald Wolfit), all of whom made their names later on. Richardson was wide-eyed with wonder, for up to then he had acted in total isolation; now he found himself part of an orchestra—designed to create the maximum of sound, bustle and vitality, to leave quiet, calm passages for Doran's virtuoso displays.

But he became confused again, as he had been at school: back in the world of muddle and disaster. He was painfully conscious of his lack of technical training, and Doran was highly critical of him. His concentration let him down and while he had a strong voice, he had no idea how to use it. He compensated for this by doing far too much: "Bewildered I shouted, I screamed, I rushed about the stage as if it had been on fire. I banged Solanio and Salerio on the back as if they were choking. I spoke so fast I felt my tongue must gabble out of my head. I laughed like a tipsy hyena, but 'Oh Richardson, do keep it up' was all the response I got from Doran." The final night of *The Merchant of Venice* in Lowestoft, after the performance, he stood packing his props into their basket and found himself meditating on his misfortunes: "My pattern of bright stars on the floor of heaven did not seem to be shaping well; I looked at the floor at my feet, saw the thick hard boards of the stage dyed with the left-overs of plays, musicals and variety shows, and patterned into them a constellation of bright screws, tacks and nails. Here was my floor of heaven and I was treading it."

In the long summer holidays, with the certitude of being re-engaged in the autumn, such torments could be forgotten. Ralph was now in contact with his father, who had, on his mother's death, retired from private teaching—presumably no longer needing the income—and in 1920

left Cheltenham for Dawlish, Devon. Lydia Richardson
had moved to London again, to Fulham, and Ralph's older
brothers Christopher and Ambrose, who were engineers,
would come to stay with her.* Ralph had not seen much of
them since he was very small, when one or the other of
them used to put him on the handlebars of his bike and
speed him down to the railway engine sheds in Cheltenham. Arthur Richardson punished them severely for
this, and Ralph felt ashamed that they should have taken
the rap.

Ralph's friend Norman Shelly remembered these
brothers:

> We went for rowing or cycling holidays together, would
> mess about in boats, or play boisterous games around the
> home. I was there one day when his brothers, as big and
> burly as Ralph himself, thundered on the front door and
> demanded to be let in. Soon I found myself involved in
> great rollicking games with them: of hide and seek and
> bears and ratmen, rolling about on the floor and being
> tossed—for I was small and by far the lightest of the
> four—as easily from one to another as a shuttlecock.

Richardson's nickname in the Doran company was
"Bonzo", after the famous and savage Staffordshire bull
terrier drawn by the cartoonist who signed himself "G.L."
"You never knew what he was going to do next," said
Norman Shelley, testifying to the uncertainties of the
apprentice—but also to his seriousness. "Bonzo didn't
think he was the least bit funny," Shelley went on, making
it clear Richardson had early turned the financial tables on
his second employer; "anything he wanted he just had." He
swopped his immaculately kept push bike for a motor bike,
his first, a Rudge, a powerful machine without clutch or

---

*During the First World War, in a bar in France, one of these brothers had
murdered a man. He hadn't liked some things the other man was saying so
had pulled out his gun and shot him dead. He was court-martialled and,
according to Richardson, some years later, "they were going to string him
up but it was getting towards the end of the war and they were beginning

gearbox but with an expanding pulley and a rubber driving belt. To start it had to be given a running push until it went off "like a rocket" and "if you were lucky you had landed in the saddle."

Shelley, later well known as a radio actor, had become Richardson's closest companion. It was he who introduced him to an even more dangerous hobby. During a visit to Wales, when they were playing in Swansea, Shelley suggested they should go out for a spin on his Rudge to a great stretch of sand known as The Mumbles. While they were there a couple of joy-riding Avro biplanes turned up, one piloted by a friend of Shelley's who was chief instructor at the London Aeroplane Club. They were taken up in the three-seater. When they returned to land Richardson went totally barmy, as if he'd suddenly drunk two bottles of whisky. He crowed like a cock, and did a couple of somersaults.

"This is bloody marvellous," he said. "We must do it again. Can we go up straight away?"

He was determined to become a pilot.

Meanwhile his parts improved: Cassio, in *Othello*, Horatio in *Hamlet*, Lysander in *A Midsummer Night's Dream*. By the end of his engagement with Doran Richardson was receiving £5.15s. a week. The work was hard but they had a lot of fun; practical jokes were even played which upset the holy atmosphere backstage while the play was in progress.

During one performance of the *Hamlet* in which Richardson was Horatio, the actor playing Claudius was told to make his red beard thicker and more bristly. The next time *Hamlet* came round the Claudius took his revenge. Before the performance he went out and bought a pound of prawns from the fishmonger, and instead of crêpe

---

this offensive at Zeebrugge and they needed chaps who knew about blowing up bridges and they remembered Richardson. He knew about explosives and there weren't many left who did. So they looked him up and said, get him out of prison, we need him. Bit hard on the other chap, though."

hair glued their legs and whiskers to his face. When Act I, Scene ii opened with

> Though yet of Hamlet our dear brother's death
> The memory be green . . .

a strong smell of fish smote the court, and they could barely contain themselves at the sight of the prawns' legs and whiskers. Fortunately Doran, as Hamlet, was downwind, with his back to Claudius, which delayed the fishy impact until his first lines, whereupon he nearly choked, and gave new and hitherto undiscovered emphasis to the line,

> A little more than kin, and less than kind!

Richardson toured Ireland with the company in 1921, and returned there in 1923, playing Cork, Dublin and Belfast, both times during the so-called amnesty between the newly formed Irish Free State, the Irish Republican Army and the newly independent Ulster. The Irishman Doran changed his politics to fit the venue: in his native Cork he was rebellious and republican; in Dublin sophisticated and Anglo-Irish; in Belfast Carsonite and Protestant.

Julius Caesar was one of the plays they took on tour. At the Opera House in Cork they played to General Mulcahy, Chief of Staff of the Irish Free State Army, who with his staff occupied two boxes. Doran was Brutus, Shelley played Caesar and Wolfit was Casca. Richardson, who was Mark Antony, had just delivered the funeral oration when he heard a great clattering of boots off-stage as troopers from the Irish Free State Army, all of them soaking wet—it was traditional Irish weather outside—sealed off the backstage, and mounted a guard. That night not only were Cassius and Brutus defeated at Philippi but 43 members of the audience were arrested, including the Countess Con Markiewicz, a leading Republican.

On their way from Cork to Dublin the company found the bridge at Mallow had been blown up and they had to get off the train and proceed by charabanc until they met up later with an unbroken bit of the track. In Dublin shootings were still frequent. One member of the company had the unpleasant experience of walking to digs behind his landlady, who was shot dead at his feet. Outside the Gaiety where they played two schoolgirls were arrested, the satchels they were carrying crammed with .303 bullets. Richardson told a newspaper reporter his costume for *Othello* was lost, and for one performance he had to borrow Doran's trousers while the latter sat and shivered in the dressing room. The Gaiety was in a road off St Stephen's Green, looking across on the other side to the Jacob's biscuit factory. In the course of a matinée some members of the company saw a man's head and shoulders appear by the factory chimney; next moment a rattle of machine-gun bullets, and everyone had to duck.

Richardson received his first really enthusiastic notice while playing at the Gaiety: "one of the finest performances of the night," wrote the Irish reviewer. "The oration over the body of the dead Caesar . . . was delivered with quite remarkable elocutionary effect . . . the actor seemed not to be giving utterance to a set speech, but rather to the spontaneous expression of his feelings."

They proceeded to Belfast. With them in the coach they had to take the bodies of two northerners who had been shot near the theatre. Yet in Belfast all was quiet. Norman Shelley had a striking memory of walking at 11.30 at night back to the Falls Road, where their digs were and where for a time he had to share a double bed with Sir Arthur Sullivan's nephew, and seeing "row upon row of what looked like waggling bottoms": Protestant housewives scrubbing their front doorsteps. Shelley and Richardson, unable to satisfy their love of aviation, amused themselves by making paper aeroplanes and launching them from dressing room windows into the square where they did circuits round a policeman.

Richardson recorded in a notebook, in which he made terse comments on his acting progress, or imagined lack of it, that "Doran hardly rages at me at all." Still, he never felt entirely comfortable with the company, and by the time he came to leave it, in November 1923, he had not resolved that inner sense of muddle and confusion, nor had he developed significantly his ability to concentrate.

But he'd enjoyed himself. Touring was fascinating,

though the "wicked stage" broke him of the habit of going to Mass, as Sundays were spent on training. "We had our own carriages with vans behind for the scenery. We were coupled up with whatever else that was going our way; coming out from Hull or Grimsby there would be chalked up on the board, 'Fish and Actors'."

6   *Types and prototypes*

In between tours Richardson was able to broaden his knowledge of other actors. Experience had tempered his enthusiasm for the graphic method of illuminating a text which he had found in Benson's Hamlet, and made him turn to modern actors and playwrights. There was danger in doing nothing but Shakespeare: the very richness of the speech and action meant that the actor invented little of his own. If one played him for too long one might become unfit for other dramatists.

At the opposite end of the scale from Frank Benson, Gerald du Maurier also became a prototype for the young Richardson. Du Maurier had played in Barrie's *The Admirable Crichton*, was the first Mr Darling and Captain Hook in *Peter Pan*, and Raffles, the thief, whom he had made into a gentleman and a hero; his later performances as Will Dearth in *Dear Brutus*, in *Alias Jimmy Valentine*, as Bulldog Drummond and in *The Last of Mrs Cheyney*, showed to perfection his light, throw-away manner, an art not only that lay in concealing art but mocking and elusive, and hard to define. "I have never had a happy day in the theatre," du

Maurier confessed, and his younger contemporary Cedric Hardwicke commented of him, that he "despised the playwrights who supplied him with such dross which with his alchemist's touch he persistently made to look like gold".

Du Maurier was undisputed leader of the English stage, and had acted at Wyndham's Theatre for some fifteen years, with the reputation of being always the same in every part he played. It was as a master of underplaying that Richardson saw him first. "Must you kiss her as though you were having steak and onions for lunch," he would ask an actor. "Can't you say, 'I love you,' and yawn, light a cigarette and walk away?"

Richardson never found du Maurier monotonous. "Inimitable," he calls him, and "un-inimitable too". Everyone would give imitations of Henry Irving, he said, but du Maurier began a whole new school of acting in which when actors came on to the stage they did what they would do in ordinary life. "Don't force it. Don't be self-conscious," were his watchwords.

Charles Hawtrey became another hero of Richardson's; he excelled at—significantly, where Ralph was concerned —parts where he had to lie and keep a secret. "Hawtrey was such a strange little man; there was really nothing to him; you couldn't believe how he fascinated you, riveted you, and charmed you and held you; he never seemed to be doing anything at all but sitting in an armchair but my goodness me, he was a magnet if ever there was one."

If Hawtrey and du Maurier delighted him with their charm and awoke curiosity and technical aspiration, Mrs Patrick Campbell as Hedda Gabler was to strike at the centre of Richardson's being with sheer awe and an admiration he never to forget. When he first saw her, in Plymouth, it seemed the greatest performance—in fact the only truly great performance—he ever witnessed, and so it was to remain. He recalled for Alan Dent, her biographer:

There was a marvellous kind of horror about her. I have never seen anything so terrifying. She turned the character—whether she was being true to Ibsen or not—into a kind of Clytemnestra. She did, in fact, take considerable liberties with her author. With her large black eye, huge mane of black hair, she began by practising pistol shots alone in the darkened room, without actual firing. She would take aim at some object and count—one, two, three, four, five, six, *seven*! She had all the terror and movement of a puma.* I was glad she was behind the bars.

When Aunt Juliana's ring was heard at the outer door she vanished from the scene. With a baleful glance, a sinewy step—I have never seen such incredible cruelty. She forced you to think Ibsen must have approved of it. She was a kind of Malignancy personified. The usual Hedda one sees is a small, spiteful, more or less enigmatic and inscrutable creature. But Mrs Campbell's was a big and majestic creature. . . . It was only for a fraction of a second at the very start before she uttered a word that the audience might be imagined as noticing how stout and old the enchantress was beginning to look.

In her burning of the manuscripts, the "child", she flings open the studio stove with a poker; the lid falls back with a clang. "My child I'll singe your baby's locks" —and she throws it into the flames. You look straight into hell itself in a fantasy whose painter was Goya.

At another time, in Portsmouth, her manager told Richardson Mrs Pat varied extraordinarily in her performances, and he got the impression that she was undoubtedly a tremendous social snob:

> would ask each evening who was in front—would tend to act pathetically if there was "nobody" and blazingly well if there was somebody. . . . Her delicate fastidious hand-movements reminded me of Chaplin licking the nails of the boots he was obliged to eat, in *The Gold Rush*, as daintily as if they were the bones of a roast pheasant. If she picked up any object or garment on the stage, she seemed to imbue it with a life of its own.

*She moved across the stage "with the awful symmetry of Blake's own tiger", he said at another time.

Beyond the impact of the playing of Mrs Patrick Campbell, although Richardson was less aware of it, was the crucial impression made by the part of Hedda and by Ibsen's technical mastery in showing it with such clarity. Max Beerbohm pointed out in his initial review of Mrs Pat's performance in 1907, how the audience comes to know Hedda as naturally as if she were a woman it had known for years in real life. Everything in the play is a clue and at no point is any speech superfluous. Continuing his catalogue of Ibsen's meticulousness, Beerbohm wrote:

> She has no instinct at all towards liberty. Life jars on her. She is too fastidious for any direct personal contact with life. She is inquisitive about life. She likes to know all about it at second hand, and she likes to build romances on this information. She wants, above all, to create something—to have a tug at the wires by which the puppets are dancing. She approaches life from the standpoint of an artist.

Part, at least, of the fascination of the play for Richardson was that in some more or less distorted form—and just as Ibsen had in *Hedda Gabler* provided yet another self-portrait, a feminine version of the artist hero—he must have seen something of himself.

CHESTER TERRACE, *21 May 1979:*

Later afternoon sunlight over Regent's Park. The trees, washed in the intermittent showers, have settled into a

muted damp calm before nightfall. On the third floor of
Richardson's house I await his proposition. The setting is
remote, like an eyrie. That of a man who likes detachment.

The latter days of Richardson's early mentors were
passed in very different circumstances. Hawtrey perished
unnecessarily at the height of his fame, from inadequate
medical care. For Mrs Patrick Campbell the glory had all
evaporated. Not long before she died she was to write a
begging letter from Paris to Shaw, just after the success of
the film of *Pygmalion*, reminding him "how loyal I was to
you when Tree came to me just before the curtain went up
and begged me to 'cut' the 'bloody' . . . of course you have
forgotten everything or you would send a Christmas Box."
Later she was to appeal to Shaw to bring her to London: "I
had as soon bring the devil over," replied Shaw. As for Sir
Frank Benson, he spent his last five years in a bed-sitting
room on the first floor of 18 Holland Road, where, as J. C.
Trewin noted, "he would never complain even when the
curry powder strayed into the coffee." He had no financial
resources, but had been granted a Civil List pension of £100
a year.

Since then a change has come about in the status and
earning power of the actor. He can no longer be thought
beyond the pale. Henry Irving, the first actor to be
knighted, said: "It is a recognition of the stage . . . we
are now as other citizens." As other citizens? So great has
been the recent change that now the actor's life-style is a
condition to which society apparently aspires.

"Now", Richardson says, addressing me by my correct
name, "I'm going to make that little speech I promised."

He has an old friend who is a well-known publisher, and
he thinks we should go to this publisher and see about doing
a book together. Richardson asks me what I think I should
do first and I say, Perhaps I should prepare a synopsis. I ask
about sources of material: letters, for instance. He says he
has none, only books of press cuttings. As a start he lends
me some material he has sorted out: Kenneth Tynan's 1977
New Yorker profile of him; the autobiographical piece he
himself wrote, called "On Looking Back", which appeared

in instalments in the *Sunday Times* in 1960; a monograph by Harold Hobson published in 1958, the copy inscribed to "Ralph Richardson who has given me more joy and exaltation than any actor I have known".

I rise unsteadily and we begin our long, slow and sedate descent of the Nash staircase. On the first stage, before we reach the second landing, Richardson pauses balefully over the gap down the stairs.

"I'll throw myself off the Eiffel tower—how about that as an ending for the book?"

We are on the stairs between landing two and one: "I suppose you know," I say, "about Tynan having to stop writing his biography of Olivier." Olivier had objected to the biography, it was said, because it contained intimate details disclosed to Tynan when he was Literary Manager of the National Theatre.

He nods and stops. "Tynan put all these things in his book about Laurence, about his weaknesses, but it's unnecessary—there's good and bad in all and you can't pretend there's only weakness. Naughty boy, he made me say some things about other people which I didn't say."

Clutching the Tynan article under my arm, I start forward once more. We have almost reached the *entresol*; the doorbell rings; above us a door off the landing opens, apparently noticed only by me; behind it a swift and hushed feminine presence can momentarily be detected, undecided as to whether to come out or remain behind. Flute music plays in the background. The door almost closes. I realize, with a *frisson* of ghostliness, that someone else has been in the house all the time—his wife "Mu." Richardson has noticed nothing, apparently.

A small pug dog pushes its way through the gap left in the door and bounds down the stairs, overtaking us. Through the glass of the front door a blurred image can be detected. I point this out and Richardson, suddenly galvanized, shoots towards the door and opens up. By now I expect two middle-aged detectives in severe dark suits: "Inspector Goole, can I come in, sir . . ." But it is a middle-aged woman of comfortable appearance—she holds a magnificent, larger-than-life-size bunch of red roses.

"For Lady Richardson," she says, in a broad Irish accent. "From Sir John Gielgud." Richardson takes the flowers carefully on his arm, a cavalier gesture. "Oh thank you so much." He places them inside, and comes down into the street.

He pushes down on the suspension of my Citroën, parked by the curb: "Jolly extraordinary cars—the way they bounce!" Turns to me swiftly: "Goodbye, dear chap, see you again soon." The pug dog has by this time escaped from the house and is prancing about cockily at the end of the Terrace where it joins Chester Gate.

Ralph motions towards it. "And you can kill that dog —he's my wife's!"

7   First wife

In 1923 a girl student of fifteen joined the Doran company. Doran always had a scattering of students among his ranks, and as theatrical unions were only just beginning to exercise their muscle, a two-way process was in operation between student actors and managements—the one supplying virtually free labour, the other experience which no amount of formal teaching could replace.

The student's name was Muriel Hewitt. She was small, slight and extremely pretty, with something oriental about her looks, with dark eyes that slanted at the corners. Her father, Alfred James Hewitt, was a clerk in the Telegraph & Cable Company, and she had been brought up abroad:

her middle name, Bathia, suggested a colonial birth. She moved beautifully, instinctively, like a dancer; she had, according to Richardson, the courage of a lion. Returning one evening to their theatrical lodgings, he found her just after she had surprised a burglar, who had fled. Far from being frightened, she was intent on laying hands on the man and acted as if cheated of her prey.

Her attraction for Richardson was immediate; he seemed so clumsy when she was so graceful, she was so instinctive while he was searching, blundering about, making progress almost at random. On the other hand he had charm, humour and an enormous reliability of character lacking in many others of his age—as if, perhaps in contrast to his father, he was going to show he could be trusted. Muriel excited protective feelings in him by her vulnerability and her beauty. He and Kit, as she was called (short for kitten), became friends. From his distance of being almost five years older than she, he enjoyed looking after her, taking her round on the back of his Rudge and later, when he bought his first car, in greater comfort.

They shared professional aims too: Muriel was discriminating and disciplined in her attitude to work—a perfectionist with a dry, almost precise style. Doran was rapidly impressed by her gifts, and as she was thin and boyish at fifteen, he cast her as Puck in *A Midsummer Night's Dream*. However, whether through Irish guile or pure absence of mind, he forgot to offer her a salary. The Actors' Association, to which all the principal actors in the company belonged, were told of this, and a representative went to Doran to object. Being the type of southern Irishman who becomes highly truculent when he feels he is being taken to task, Doran refused to pay her. The Association called the company together and declared that unless the rules were obeyed—one of which laid down that any actor with a speaking part must be paid—it would call a strike.

A strike was unthinkable. Obedience was the company's watchword. Yet support grew for Kit's plight—although she herself was in the unenviable position of causing all this trouble against her will. "Oh please, no," she said. "I don't

want to be paid, I'm a student." The Association had no
desire to consider her wishes in this matter, and even
demanded back salary. Differences of opinion split the
company from top to bottom and in the end Doran had to
cough up. There was no strike.

Richardson kept out of it, as had Kit, although at the
centre of the storm. He was experiencing for the first time
the joys of playing Bottom, having just stepped into this
part which had been vacated by Arthur Young. The tradition of this company was that when you took over a part you
preserved as much of the previous mould as you could, so
Richardson found himself reproducing a characterization
which, he said, became the basis for his several later and
more individual interpretations of the role. At heart a
craftsman, he hadn't much interest in any case in the
political issues. But the morale of Doran's company was
deeply affected by the incident. The names of those known
to have supported the projected strike were soon passed to
Doran, and he stomped about more suspicious than before,
feeling he had been stabbed in the back. As one of the
company who had been prepared to go on strike for her
principles said, "He looked at me as if I was Brutus and he
was Caesar. I kept expecting him to say, 'Et tu,——.'"
Donald Wolfit stated it more bluntly in his early memoirs,
First Interval (1954): "With the incursion of this rigid
registration of artists [instigated by the Actors' Association
as a result of the incident] I believe there came into the
theatre an element of greed and a distrust of the management, and a certain camaraderie was lost for ever."

Many of Doran's fledglings, picked by the master with
such unerring skill, were stretching their wings anyway at
this time, and preparing to fly. Richardson was one. He was
growing restless, after almost three years with the company
in which he had played Shakespeare non-stop. He wanted
to try some modern parts. Wolfit remembered the dance
which took place after the final performance of *The Taming
of the Shrew*, when "the greater proportion of the company
had tears in their eyes". There was a general leavetaking,
and as most of them went their different ways a smaller and

more poignant separation took place: that of Ralph and Kit Hewitt, who stayed with the company.

On his twenty-first birthday, in December 1923, Richardson threw himself on the mercy of the world. He took a little room in London, in Bernard Street, next to the Russell Square Underground, and began making the rounds of the agents. For the most part they were discouraging, or even worse, downright hostile. One, however, took him under her wing: Connie—or Constance— Chapman, of Connie's Agency, observed when she saw him in her waiting room, "Now here's a likely-looking lad."

All Connie could find for Richardson in those first wintry months of 1924 was the part of Henry in a second-string *Outward Bound*, the play by Sutton Vane which had been a success in London and which was being sent out on tour. In one way this pleased him, because it was his first modern play and he could have a shot at acting in the school of du Maurier. But once they opened it filled him with gloom because he found they had no lead "to pull the train along" and he quickly tired of playing the same part night after night. It became in time too simple, for he had no resources of relaxation and self-control, while to be wearing ordinary clothes on stage made him feel naked.

Six months later he was still touring the same play and thoroughly browned off; nothing, either, could make him like provincial theatrical lodgings, though some did improve as the weeks went by. The poky rooms were not to his taste, nor were the shared bathrooms, or the noisy back streets in which most lodgings were to be found. He had none of the romantic feelings about poverty and theatrical companies that writers such as Wells and Priestley made so much of. There was no nostalgia in a lavatory at the end of the garden and having to go through the landlady's kitchen to get to it: "Keep your eyes on your plate," one landlady used to tell her husband when the young actresses traipsed through at supper time. Ralph had seen too much genteel poverty as a boy, travelling with his mother from one makeshift home to another. The theatre was not an end in itself, but a means to an end. He longed for air, for space, and his motor bike became a symbol of his freedom, of taking off for a spin.

During this touring his thoughts again turned to Kit, left behind with Doran, and he wrote to her frequently. His feelings led him to believe that young though they were, she and he might make a go of it together. While he shuffled awkwardly about the set as Henry her absence became less bearable. In an era of innocent romance, of hearts soon broken and even sooner mended, Richardson longed for a steady partner, and the touching fragility and sweetness of Kit became his ideal. At least if he had to go on with touring he would have an anchor.

He both wanted and needed the responsibility of being a husband: the weight. He had already adopted, or developed, from his days in the insurance office, an old-fashioned air combined with an unfailing courtesy which made him seem nearer thirty than twenty. He wore tweed suits, a tie, good solid leather shoes—he made a point of wearing the best leather as if to show that the ancestral Elswick leather works were part of his personality. He learned early, in fact almost at once, to conceal the richness of his temperament.

A sturdy constitution enabled him to mix with others on his own terms—to outdrink them, if need be, to outman-oeuvre them in sport and daring. Among contenders for theatrical glory there is an element of cock fighting, though it may be skilfully disguised and blood, so to speak, is never actually seen—hardly even ruffled combs. Richardson learned the Queensberry Rules of the star system early. As an actor he was also, some might say, fortunate in being just too young to have fought in the war which carried off in death or injury the cream of his generation's talent.

The poetry, the innocence, as well as the wit and playfulness of his character, touched a chord in Kit Hewitt. She was persuaded by Ralph to leave the Doran company, which she did in July 1924. He had left *Outward Bound* to play Fainall in Nigel Playfair's production of *The Way of the World*, then on tour, and Kit was given a role in the Playfair company. On 18 September 1924, Ralph and Kit were married at the Hampstead Register Office. Kit's mother, Maude M. Hewitt, was present. Ralph and Kit were staying near by at 27 Arkwright Road. Richardson was nearly twenty-two while his bride was just nine days older than seventeen. They returned straight away to *The Way of the World*.

8 Descent into solitude

What might have been is an abstraction
Remaining a perpetual possibility
Only in a world of speculation.

T. S. ELIOT, *Burnt Norton*

Today, Richardson is disinclined to speak of his first marriage. Perhaps he learnt early the pointlessness of being preoccupied with any past misfortunate, perhaps far too early in his life the past had become an irrevocable disaster. The pain of his marriage to Kit became something he had to endure stoically and largely on his own. He learnt as a result to contain and support within himself his deepest feelings. Perhaps in that sense Kit Hewitt is still with him, which is why he never wants to speak of her. It may be that, when acting on stage, giving an insight even briefly into pain, into vulnerability, he is allowing a glimpse, even unconsciously, to be seen of Kit. Had she lived she might have become a great actress. Perhaps part of him is what she might have been.

In December 1924 the young married pair joined Barry

Jackson's Birmingham Repertory Company. To ambitious actors and actresses Birmingham Rep possessed, as Eileen Beldon—a distinguished character actress who acted with the company for many years—observed, "the glamour and prestige of the National and Royal Shakespeare Company rolled into one." It was experimental, meticulous in the technical demands it made on its members, but by this time profitable. Often during its heyday it had two plays running at the same time in London's West End, and a play on tour, as well as a production at home in Station Street, Birmingham. The conditions there were a unique blend of intimacy and austerity. The theatre had a steeply banked auditorium, of which Eileen Beldon recalled: "to encounter a wall of pink faces instead of the usual hospitable void on a first night was very off-putting until one got used to it."

Jackson employed Ralph and Kit Richardson on a joint contract which began with a seemingly endless tour of Eden Phillpotts's *The Farmer's Wife*. Ralph found himself cast as Richard Coaker the lovesick young farmer, and Kit played Petronell, a coquettish young woman who makes a habit of refusing eligible young men; she and Ralph shared a scene of delicate homespun charm:

RICHARD: There's a good few very proper men have come afore you with their hearts naked —(*with a change of tone*) and no doubt, to a proud thing like you, 'tis easy to say "no".

PETRONELL: I'm not proud—only self-respecting, Richard.

RICHARD: Don't say "no" too often, however. A girl gets a bad name for it; and then, afore she knows where she is, 'tis out that she's not for a husband, and she never gets the chance of saying "yes".

PETRONELL: I'll not say "no" to the right one.

RICHARD: O-o-o-h! I wonder what *his name* is.

PETRONELL: Perhaps you know it, Richard.

RICHARD: Yes, I reckon I do.
PETRONELL: The men be always after brains they say
              nowadays.
RICHARD: Don't you believe it. Most men take a
              woman—like a girl takes a box of choco-
              lates—for the picture on the lid.

It's not difficult to imagine the subtle range of double
meanings, ironies, flirtatious looks and secret signs the
newly married pair could for their own amusement intro-
duce into this. They opened in Cambridge on 16 February
1925, and for the rest of the year toured the provinces, with
a fortnight's visit to London.

Richardson never worked with Barry Jackson, the blue-
eyed philanthropist who chain-smoked through a cigarette
holder and to whom Shaw, when told Jackson proposed to
do *Back to Methuselah*, quipped, "But are your wife and
family provided for?" (He need not have bothered, for
Jackson had no wife or child—theatre took the place of
both.) But Ralph found Jackson's adjutant, H. K. Ayliff,
much to his taste as a director.

Ayliff was a hard and demanding taskmaster, better
suited by temperament to fostering the slow increase in
Richardson's powers as an actor than the more glamorous
Jackson. For some years Ralph had neither the confidence
nor—in his own view at least—the experience to tackle
big roles, and was content with small gains, the gradual
assimilation and consolidation of what he had learnt. A
stickler for detail, Ayliff was ideal for Richardson, and
directed him in no fewer than 27 plays over the next ten
years.

No other director in the Twenties and Thirties so consistently groomed fine talent as did Ayliff, and he continued
doing so until after the Second World War, when Paul
Scofield and Margaret Leighton were among his protégés.
The Scottish playwright James Bridie wrote of him, "Actor
after actor leapt to the top of his profession under his
command, or as a result of his command. Their illustrious
names are as bright as any in our theatrical history, but the

name of Ayliff is too often overlooked and the debt they
owe him has not yet been paid."

A tall, gaunt man, like a stick of asparagus, with a
tonsured and almost hairless crown (for a time he wore a
wig but it fell off as he was crossing the Atlantic), Ayliff had
an autocratic manner; for an inner circle of actors he was a
father figure. Like Richardson, he wanted to be a painter,
and trained at the Royal Academy School in London, and
in Paris. He was extremely widely read, a deep, pondering
presence who paced the theatre wrapped in his own
thoughts, but who could, when occasion demanded, become extremely angry. Heaven help you, they said, if ever
you gave a shoddy performance. They said that if you were
crossing New Street Station footbridge which overlooked
the green roof of the repertory theatre and Ayliff was in a
bad mood, you could see the roof shaking. Paul Scofield,
who worked much later at Birmingham, recalled:

> He had a terrifying warning signal for the unwary and
> inept—he sat at rehearsal with legs crossed at the knee
> and when displeased would swing the upper leg and foot
> like a pendulum of doom. We all recognized the signal
> and trembled.

Ayliff plotted the actors' moves beforehand; he had an
excellent eye for detail, especially for furniture and lights:
at the time directors did their own lighting, and Birmingham possessed advanced equipment. He worked with a
resident set designer, Paul Shelving, who paid considerable
attention to exact and naturalistic detail, also to achieving a
unified effect. The total impression was one of careful and
unobtrusive quality—an ordinary appearance which on
closer scrutiny one saw was fashioned from the most expensive materials—and as such calculated to appeal to
Richardson.

At first Kit Hewitt was promoted more rapidly than
Ralph. She was, as he said of her later, "the perfect
example of the natural actress. Nothing was any trouble for
her, everything she did was right. Grace in movement with
perfect diction and a serenity unruffled under any stage

conditions." In fact, he seems to have been more enamoured of her talent than of his own; in the reviews he
collected in his scrapbook her name figures more prominently than his. He found himself in the No. 2 team, playing
Dick Whittington at home in Barry Jackson's Christmas
play and, later, Dearth in *Dear Brutus*,* while she gained
more than a foothold in the London side of the company.
Kit made a strong impact particularly with her Ophelia in
the modern-dress version of *Hamlet*, which opened at the
Kingsway Theatre on 25 August 1925. For this she wore
short skirts, light stockings, and the "exiguous shoes of the
moment". Several critics said she was the best Ophelia they
had ever seen, that she made Ophelia real, tormented, and
extremely moving, and high hopes were placed in her
future.

The "*Hamlet* in plus fours", as it was affectionately
called, ran for several months; Colin Keith-Johnston as
Hamlet was quiet and colloquial while Claudius, mag-
nificently played by Frank Vosper, kept a syphon and a
decanter in his prayer cabinet. Separation, then as now,
was not good for acting couples, especially when they were,
like Ralph and Kit, very young. While Kit was rehearsing
Barry Jackson's production of *The Marvellous History of St
Bernard*, by Henri Ghéon, another member of the company, then only nineteen, fell precipitously for her—
having just been jilted by another girl.

It was not the first time the newcomer, who lived in a
bedsitter and dressed in his uncle's suits, had grown
attached in thought to an actress. Nor was it to be the last.
The status of the object of his affections, married or
unmarried, hardly mattered to him, for he was young,
carefree, and endowed with a modernity of egoism and
ambition which would, one day, make him pre-eminent.
But for the moment the limit of his achievement was several
lines as "A Minstrel". Even his appearance was considered

*Kit rejoined Richardson for this, playing the dream daughter. In *The
Birmingham Repertory Theatre, 1913–1963* (1963), J. C. Trewin describes
her as "crying from the impalpable that is carrying her away, 'Come back;
I don't want to be a might-have-been.'"

a drawback: teeth set too far apart, a broad nose and bushy eyebrows—none of the self-fabricated refinements that were later to remould his features—none of the capacity for metamorphosis which he would soon learn to wield with supreme cunning.

Richardson soon knew his rival's name, which was Laurence Olivier. Husband and aspiring lover had a very sticky first meeting two months later in the sublime environs of Clacton-on-Sea where they were closeted together to perform a piece called *The Barber and the Cow*. Richardson was cast as Dr Tudor Bevan in this Welsh comedy whose second-act curtain ran thus:

ACTOR A: The cow has fallen into a coma.
ACTOR B: That wasn't a coma; it was a full stop.

Richardson was reluctant to encourage this upstart who presented a threat to his marriage, and who was also a rival to his career: they therefore got on very badly together. Richardson judged Olivier callow and presumptuous, "a cocky young pup full of fire and energy"; Olivier, in contrast to Richardson, restless for recognition and sensitive to any real or imaginary snub, felt himself slighted by the cast. His view of Richardson was that he was unreasonably ponderous and huffy—and the gap of four years between the two young men further intensified the dislike. Relations were not made easier when, one day, Ralph offered to take Olivier to the next stage of the tour, Bridlington, in his brand-new 1925 Austin 7, just for the fun of the ride.

The Austin was open, and Richardson was inordinately proud of her, "with every spoke of those spidery wire wheels polished". He had driven it on a visit to a rich relation who lived near Wolverhampton and been told crushingly, "Austin 7s are beautiful little cars—we are giving them away for Christmas!" Now, with Olivier and Kit squashed next to each other, and to him, in the front seat, the brave little vehicle was struggling to reach the top of a steep hill and Ralph was growing deeply perplexed.

Would she make it? The radiator gauge registered "boiling". Concern turned to real alarm.

"I think it's overheating," he said as nonchalantly as he could, as they just managed to cross over the brow. He stopped the car abruptly, throwing both his passengers forward, and climbed out of his seat. He noted none too happily that Kit and Olivier, who were laughing and chatting excitedly, hadn't taken a bit of notice of what was going on, being too wrapped up in each other's company. With deep irritation he threw open the bonnet of the car, seized the cap of the domed brass radiator, almost forgetting to arm himself with a rag, and gave it a twist. Steam and water hissed and boiled out of the troubled pipe. Unseen by Richardson, Olivier had hopped lightly down from the vehicle and now came up to him, gesturing that he wanted to ask him something in private. The pair drew off several yards.

"What the devil is it, Laurence?" said Richardson.

"I wanted to ask you, Ralph, if you would mind if I called Muriel, Kit."

Fortunately for future relations between the two men, *The Barber and the Cow* drew no great response, and Olivier was banished to the most remote provinces in the never-ending *The Farmer's Wife*, in the same part, Richard Coaker, that Richardson had played eighteen months before. By contrast with Ralph, Olivier disliked Ayliff, whose high-handed manner reduced him to a state of nervous insufficiency. Ralph and Kit stayed with Cedric Hardwicke, who had also suffered exposure to *The Barber and the Cow*, and it was probably through Hardwicke's good offices that they received joint promotion into the next Eden Phillpotts venture, *Yellow Sands* (a collaboration with his daughter Adelaide).

This was another, and better, *Farmer's Wife*, set by the sea and complete with boat and crab pots from Salcombe in Devon. James Agate's review in the *Sunday Times* exhorted the public with the Shakespearian line from which the title had been lifted: "Come unto these yellow sands and then take hands", summarizing the plot, with succinct wit: "The time is not yet, in the theatre, when we shall cease to believe that a legacy of 4,000 pounds can turn the most frenzied Communist into a rapturous Individualist, bent upon securing a fishing-smack of his own, two coats, and everything handsome about him—including a pretty wife." Kit Hewitt played an eye-catching little serving maid whose fresh simplicity set the keynote of the play—"one will look for her again," said Agate. Frank Vosper impersonated the Bolshevist fisherman, while the down-at-heel, middle-aged Churdles Ash figure in this play was Cedric Hardwicke. Richardson played Arthur Varwell, an amorous young fool who couldn't resist red-headed girls. Of him (and two others) Agate wrote, patting them as one might a friendly dog, "nice things must be said."

Outwardly inauspicious, this small role which Richardson repeated in 610 consecutive performances, including three matinées a week, at the Haymarket Theatre, became the making of him. Up to this point he had always felt of himself that he was undisciplined, tangled, muddled, a disaster of a chap. But now he had to sit on stage for a long time listening to the reading of the will that brought the Bolshevist fisherman the legacy, done with great professionalism by H. O. Nicholson. Richardson assessed the result:

> There I had to sit, day after day, performance after performance—this was torture, but I had to do it. And it gave me the beginnings of the sinews, which every actor must know is necessary, this discipline. I'd played perhaps a hundred parts before that, but never under the iron discipline, night after night, whether you feel like it, whether it's funny, whether you want to go out and play cricket, whether you want to go to the cinema, of having to give a performance of the same part. Those years of grind formed the first thread of nervous tissue connecting what I had in my mind and what I was doing with my body.

A perceptive member of the audience might, on some nights of the play's long run, have noticed strange and

Muriel Hewitt and Frank Vosper in *Yellow Sands*

worrying signs in Kit's behaviour on stage. At one point she might be seen to be blinking several times as if her vision had suddenly clouded and she had to clear it, but it wouldn't wipe clean. At another time she might catch her hand involuntarily trembling as she raised it to another member of the cast. On a third occasion she might feel an irresistible urge to run across the stage when she knew she had to execute a carefully measured walk.

She had been caught in an epidemic of world-wide proportions which before it had finished had taken or ravaged the lives of nearly five million people—and which then disappeared as mysteriously and suddenly as it had arrived. The year she was infected, 1927, was the year sleeping or 'sleepy' sickness, encephalitis lethargica, ceased to spread—so she was among the last to catch it.

9   *The grey mist of movement*

Richardson acted not only in *Yellow Sands*, and *The Farmer's Wife* by Eden Phillpotts, but also in *Devonshire Cream* (with Kit as Beth Widicombe), and in 1928 as James Jago in *The Runaways* (with Kit as Gladys Wonnacott). *The Runaways* failed, and marked the end of a decade of Phillpotts's ascendancy. Ralph had a strong family link with the West Country, where these plays were set, because his father and his older brothers all now lived in Devon.

He visited them in Dawlish and came back with tales of family rows: the brothers were a wild pair and drank a lot and threw things about the kitchen. Neither of them would ever come to see him act. He had not much affection for them, but in time he had grown more tolerant of his father, remembering the look in his eye and the sixpence he once gave him as a child—a rogue, possibly, he thought at the end, but not a wilfully wicked man. In 1928, during Ralph's run in *Yellow Sands*, Arthur Richardson died, leaving his son nothing more than an extraordinary compassion, as yet in its infancy, towards weak men.

Ralph had now embarked on a new phase of his career: creating roles instead of reproducing them, and in the West End instead of the provinces. For the next year or two the parts he played remained on the small side while his reputation was consolidated and he prepared himself for the next surge forward, which came in 1930. In 1928, he and Olivier were cast together in three plays at the Royal Court: with the clouds now forming over Richardson's marriage, the two men seemed disposed to like each other more, though remaining at first cold in manner. No one quite knew who broke the ice first, whether Ralph deliberately took the initiative, whether Olivier had a sudden impulse of friendliness, but reports ("Ralph Richardson, a little surprised, nodded," or, "he invited his young rival to join him") soon have them drinking together over the lunch break in the refreshment room above Sloane Square station.

In the fashion of the time, the rivalry swiftly transferred

itself from women to cars, and one day a little later Olivier drove Richardson's car at fifty miles an hour—almost as much as it would do—over the junction of the Croydon bypass and the Purley road. Richardson was absolutely horrified, for there were no lights at the crossroads, and told him, "If I live to be hundreds and hundreds of years old, Laurence, I shall never forgive you for that."

"Old man," replied Olivier cheerfully, "what are you fussing about? It is a well-known thing that when you get to a point of danger, you must get over it as quickly as you can."

Some time later, Richardson reported, Laurence returned from New York, where he had had a successful run, with a smashing American car. They met in the West End after the show—Olivier had the car with him. "I want you to try this," he said. Richardson got behind the wheel and they drove down Piccadilly. As they passed the Ritz Richardson opened up a bit—"We do eighty-five before Apsley House—sheer madness. Immediately, Laurence says, 'I thought you'd like it, Ralphie.'"

While Richardson became "Ralphie" for Olivier, Laurence never became "Larry" for him, as he did for everyone else. (Indeed, as Richardson grew into his middle years, one has the feeling he liked less being called "Ralphie", his mother's pet-name for him, while he never seems to have cared for the old-fashioned pronunciation of Ralph as "Rafe".) But he found Olivier warm and affectionate, a wonderful companion, blessed with a gaiety of heart, a joyful zest, often saying "I have never ceased to laugh my head off with him."

They had other exciting experiences together. Olivier recalled being at the Richardsons' Bernard Street flat at 3 a.m. when they heard screams outside. A Jewish establishment in Russell Square had caught fire and the occupants were throwing themselves out of the windows into the street below, and in paroxysms of grief, beating their heads with their fists or pounding their breasts. The husband of one woman who had thrown herself from a window tried to shake her back into life.

The disease Kit had caught, encephalitis lethargica, was a hydra with a thousand heads. It was an epidemic, virus-borne, and it was believed she picked it up in Croydon by drinking infected milk. Equally tragically affected was one of H. K. Ayliff's three children, his younger daughter Esther, who remained alive until 1948.

Of those affected, a third died in the acute stage of the first bout of infection, in states of sleeping sickness so deep that they couldn't be roused. Many recovered, but those who had had a severe attack simply failed to regain their original vitality. They would be conscious and aware yet not fully awake, speechless and without motion, vacuous, registering what went on about them with profound indifference. According to Oliver Sacks in his book *Awakenings* (1973), "They neither conveyed nor felt the feeling of life; they were as insubstantial as ghosts, and as passive as zombies."

It was to be some years before Kit Richardson reached this stage of the disease, and some time before she withdrew altogether from active life; but inevitably her illness cast a shadow over Richardson's life. He, of course, remained reserved over it, would never talk of it, never in public quite acknowledge what was wrong with her. Great fear and superstition surrounded the epidemic anyway, and the disease was only diagnosed much later.* While saying that Kit's career was "brilliant but brief", Richardson added that her courage was terribly tested. She fell, he says, under "some rare nervous attack, perhaps akin to polio". His reticence and the depth of his feeling went together.

His own courage was terribly tested as well, though he was too stoical ever to admit to this; but in talking of his career over the next 13 or 14 years, until Kit's death in 1942, one has to remember the background. He was trying to cope, as far as he was capable, with an invalid wife who lived first at the flat they had bought together, and then at various hospitals or nursing homes, or in cottages near by where she could be looked after. He had to support her

*There had been a smaller epidemic in London in 1672–3, described in *Awakenings* as "febris comatosa".

entirely, to visit her as often as he was able to, and to comfort her, in so far as she could respond to comfort in the strange half-life to which fate had committed her. But Richardson would have been the first to claim that his own feelings shouldn't be considered in this tragic event, that Kit's plight was quite unspeakably hard for her to bear, reduced from being so full of life, so spirited, the essence of the *ingénue*, gay and feckless, to being gradually turned into a living statue, an extinct volcano.

These personal trials, never spoken over, apparently endured with severe and admirable pride by both parties, could not but have helped to broaden his character and enrich his work. They may do more than anything else to explain the quality of compassion which came to permeate his acting. Few actors have been better able to engage an audience instinctively with unspoken sympathy, whether it be for pain, for goodness, or for weakness. While one wants in no sense to imply that Richardson used his suffering over Kit consciously—for he like anyone else would have done his best to escape it—there is no doubt that it left its mark, that it came to be an indivisible part of him, and made him more prepared to live near the edge than he might otherwise have been tempted to do. He seemed, additionally, to have found release for something bottled up inside through physical danger: the theatre was not quite dangerous enough; the theatre belonged more to the realm of imagination and conscious craft.

Consolation lay in the world of action; and London instead of Birmingham was now firmly the setting of Richardson's burgeoning talent. A revival of *Back to Methuselah*, with the five parts spread over three weeks and the whole work performed twice in the fourth week, gave him opportunity to shine in Part V as Pygmalion, in which guise he spoke Shaw's long biological prophecy about synthetic life.

A production of Tennyson's *Harold* put him in a role subsidiary to Olivier's first lead, though neither Olivier nor Tennyson received much commendation. It brought Richardson into contact for the first time with George

Howe, whom he worked with later and who recalled going back to their flat and playing classical records with him and Kit. Richardson, as a Sagittarian, having been born under the sign of the Archer, perhaps found a more than passing interest in the part played by an arrow in the action of Tennyson's turgid piece—also in that Halley's comet, which he had seen as a boy, was given dramatic representation.

Everyone appeared to have had more fun with the final production of that 1928 Barry Jackson season at the Royal Court, a modern dress *The Taming of the Shrew*, in which Richardson played Tranio, bringing, as the critic Horace Hornsell wrote, "the refinements of modern cockney to the speaking of Shakespeare's archasims." (Accents have never been Richardson's strong point: one assumes "refiements" to be the operative word.)

Christopher Sly was played by Frank Pettingell, while Olivier languished in the minor role of the Lord in the Induction scene. These two used to sit night after night in a stage box in full view of the audience, Olivier in a silk top hat and morning coat, trying, as Pettingell recounted with great relish, to "do unspeakable things to upset Ralph and make him laugh". They changed make-up, fidgeted, whispered behind their hands, pulled faces, waved—but nothing they could do put Richardson off his stroke. One night, however, they sat absolutely still—elbows resting on the front of the box—just watching him and doing nothing. This began to tease Richardson, make him gradually nervous. He wondered what they were up to. Concentration wavered. What would they be doing next? He kept looking over in their direction. Finally he could take no more—and "corpsed", or doubled over with laughter, in full view of everybody.

10   *A new friend*

Olivier was twenty-one in 1928, and by 1930 had already played a leading role in the West End, albeit in an unsuccessful production. Promotion had come fast for him: Richardson was to wait until 1933 for his first leading role. Olivier's two years with the Birmingham Company had turned him from a juvenile of almost amoebic appearance into a figure of considerable sex appeal. His friend Denys Blakelock pinpointed elements in this transformation in *Advice to a Young Player* (1957)—his hair was now parted, the gaps between his teeth had been filled in, "his eyebrows trimmed and straightened, and he was beautifully and rather gaily dressed. He had stopped short at his nose, though he has made up for this since by remodelling it with nose clay . . . in almost every part he has played . . ."

Another young actor of the highest theatrical credentials —he was a grand-nephew of Ellen Terry—and with classic good looks, a voice of marked lyrical beauty, and an unquenchable charm (the "Terry charm") of which he himself was somewhat distrustful, now entered Richardson's life. John Gielgud, a year younger than Richardson though three years older than Olivier, had made his début at the Old Vic in 1921, at the age of seventeen. Eight years later he was still the prodigy of that same theatre, having, in the course of one season, played Romeo, Antonio, Oberon, Richard II, Orlando, Macbeth and Hamlet, as well as other roles outside Shakespeare.

In 1930 the director of the Vic, Harcourt Williams, decided to take on Richardson to complement Gielgud. He had liked his Pygmalion, enjoyed in particular his dash of impertinence—"one felt his wreath—though meticulously straight—might at any time assume a slight tilt"—and was also to respond to his Roderigo, which Richardson played to Paul Robeson's much-maligned Moor at the Savoy Theatre in May 1930. (This *Othello* also had Peggy Ashcroft in the cast.) Gielgud was inclined at first to question the advisability of having Richardson in The Old Vic company. Richardson, with his usual diffidence, was not only doubtful of his usefulness but also highly suspicious of Gielgud. At that time he avoided Gielgud's acting: it used, he said, to "keep him out of the theatre", and the knowledge that he would have to act with the younger man almost prevented him from accepting Williams's offer. "I found his clothes extravagant, I found his conversation flippant. He was the New Young Man of his time and I didn't like him." "So are many good friendships brought about," commented Gielgud. Almost at once a kind of double act formed, each one playing off against the dominant trait in the other's character, fancifully elaborating differences, spinning yarns and confidences about the other. It was the beginning of what was to be, in many ways, the most significant and lasting relationship in Richardson's life.

Temperamentally the two men could not have been more dissimilar. Clearly there were certain of Gielgud's tastes that Richardson did not share, and which he ignored while seeming to view them with the prejudices of his class and generation. Gielgud, who was shy of exposure of some sides of his life, took care in Ralph's presence not to offend, while conscious of his own love of scandal and indiscretion. So, from the very beginning, in some curious way they complemented one another, more than Harcourt Williams had ever intended, each having for the other the attraction of a total opposite. "I was always rather amazed at him," said Richardson; "—a kind of brilliant sort of butterfly, while I was a gloomy sort of boy." Or, at another time: "he was so brilliant, he shone, he was so handsome and his voice was so splendid." "Unlike me," responded Gielgud, "he is intensely interested in machinery and in all the intimate details of science and engineering"; or, "He is inclined to despise the petty accessories of theatrical life, the gossip, the theatrical columns in the newspapers, which appeal so strongly to me." In *Early Stages* (1939) Gielgud reports that he found Richardson similar in temperament to Leslie Faber, an actor of dark and unhappy mood whose private life never brought him fulfilment, and whose career never entirely generated satisfaction.

The two actors' first play together was *Henry IV*, *Part I*, with Richardson making his Old Vic début as Prince Hal; he and Gielgud (as Hotspur, "vivid and debonair") met on stage only in the final scene. Richardson audibly counted out his fight in numbers (a trick he culled from Mrs Patrick Campbell practising her pistol shots). "All gallant and full of young life," applauded Harcourt Williams later; "a rare moment that is lastingly chronicled in the mind." Richardson made a good impression on the critics, though his qualms at handling a romantic juvenile were so considerable that he brought a bottle of champagne into the dressing room on the first night to give himself some Dutch courage. But he couldn't, he said: "get the damn thing open. In desperation I knocked the neck against the edge of the table and it exploded like a Mills bomb—all over the walls—everywhere." A. E. Wilson wrote in the *Star* that his "madcap Prince is perhaps richer with opportunity than that of the firebrand Percy", no doubt referring to the business Richardson invented of having Falstaff bring him a dish of buttered eggs in their first scene, and, in a later scene, Poins bringing him his shaving water. Wilson added, "his actual elocution was better than Mr Gielgud's." This showed how hard he must have been trying.

Next he was cast as Caliban in *The Tempest*, with Gielgud as Prospero and Leslie French as Ariel. This Ariel was the nearest an audience of 1930 got to seeing a naked body on the stage—Gielgud's great-uncle, Fred Terry, wrote in great outrage to Gielgud complaining of this—and served as Eric Gill's model for the relief of Prospero and Ariel above the Portland Place entrance to the BBC's new Broadcasting House.

Richardson was most uneasy through rehearsals. Harcourt Williams said it appeared his nose was out of joint about the part: "It was like watching an armadillo that had trodden on its own tail." A little while later Gielgud, whom Richardson was treating offhandedly, asked:

"Would you care to run over your scene with me?"

Richardson thought to himself, Not much, and then, grudgingly, answered, "Oh yes, all right."

They did the scene.

"Stop," said Gielgud.

Richardson stopped.

"You know there's something about Caliban, he's much more unhappy than this, he's much more hostile. Try it this way."

Richardson did, and Gielgud was impressed.

"But don't you understand what is so liberating for Caliban—I think if you came up the stairs this way and come round here it would help you, you'd immediately be in the key position for your first line. Why not try it like that?" These and other suggestions flowed like a torrent from Gielgud's lips.

The scales then fell from Richardson's eyes. This chap I don't like, he's a very great craftsman, he's a wonderful fellow. He knows an awful lot about his job.

Williams and Gielgud between them got Richardson to be as nasty as they could. It was neither the first time nor the last he showed reluctance to portray evil with anything less than a human face; and even with his appearance—hair in long strings, tonsured head and a face done up like a Mongolian devil mask (Richardson had sketched the design for this in greasepaint on his dressing-room mirror)— one paper complained he was a "shade too gentlemanly". But he excelled at lines that might have been written expressly for him: "Be not afraid. The isle is full of noises . . . when I waked, I cried to dream again," imbuing them with magic simplicity. The setting, a kind of Japanese bridge with a cave beneath it which Williams had based on the Rother bridge between Kent and Sussex, provoked extreme feeling in one quarter. During a performance Edward Gordon Craig, a cousin of Gielgud's, was seen throwing himself in a frenzy against the emergency exit door: luckily the door gave way with little resistance.

Harcourt Williams had taken over the reins from H. K. Ayliff as mentor of Richardson's career, loosening them in the meantime. Under his sensitive direction, in the productions which followed—*Richard II* (in which Richardson played Bolingbroke), *Antony and Cleopatra* (Enobarbus),

Twelfth Night (Sir Toby Belch), *Arms and the Man* (Shaw came to one rehearsal and told Richardson his Bluntschli breathed too realistically at the beginning of Act I, destroying the rhythms of his prose: "Your gasps are upsetting my stops and my semi-colons"), *King Lear* (Kent) and *Much Ado* (Don Pedro)—Richardson led a charmed life, utterly confounding Gielgud's fears that he would be no good. Williams, like Ayliff an under-rated director, trusted his main actors (Gielgud, Richardson, Dorothy Green and Leslie French), building his productions round them. He had been a conscientious objector in the First World War (said to be the reason why he received no official recognition for his work in the theatre), and his method was the reverse of the bully or slave-driver. Richardson called it a "kind of secret magnetism. He found out what you could do best and brought the two bests together. He himself was a terrible bundle of nerves. He was always eating Bemax [a kind of breakfast food] in the stalls and rushing up and down pulling his hair; but he made us calm, took all the calmness out of himself."

So well did Richardson acquit himself in this first Old Vic season that he was persuaded by Harcourt Williams to return for a second, this time at the head of the company. Gielgud had accepted an invitation to take J. B. Priestley's *The Good Companions* into the West End—no one earned much working at the Old Vic—and Leslie French and Dorothy Green were also leaving. But it was hard to persuade Richardson to stay. Williams later reflected:

> I wonder how many miles I trod in the quiet streets behind the Friends Meeting House off the Euston Road before I had wrung acceptance from him. His mood was diffident, I might almost say obstinate, and he was doubtful of his ability to play such a wide range of parts. He could not believe in the rich humour of his Sir Toby Belch, the virility of his Kent, and the lyric beauty and tragic feeling of his Enobarbus.

August of 1930 saw Richardson engaged for the Malvern Festival, near the Cheltenham of his birth, but in better circumstances than when he left it. And with a car. "Whatever you do, don't let Ralph take you for a drive," exclaimed Gielgud to a third party. The pair, now firm friends after their season together, had met by chance during the summer. Gielgud remembered that

> I had been enjoying myself quietly in my own way, admiring the scenery [in Cornwall] without inspecting any of it too closely, enjoying the air without wondering from which direction the wind was blowing, puzzling over various signs of industrial activity such as slag heaps which I thought added to the picturesque effect though I had no idea what use they were,

when Richardson drew alongside and soon transferred him from his own comfortable car to a

> long, low, wicked-looking racer, and proceeded to rush me through the air at ninety miles an hour. He could never pass a hill without insisting that we should get out and scale it on foot. Once, on the top of a cliff, he immediately decided that we should both struggle down it to the beach. We visited tin mines, salt mines, pottery works, and listened attentively for several minutes [at one of the slag heaps he had noticed] while a workman explained the technical details of his occupation to us. Ralph never seemed to tire of long technical discussions, though I found these matters entirely beyond my grasp and felt painfully conscious of my one-track mind. Although I missed him as soon as he had left, I was secretly relieved when, later in the day, Ralph climbed back into his car alone, and almost immediately disappeared from view like a shell shot from a cannon.

Each loved employing metaphors drawn from the world of munitions. At another time, of Gielgud's manner of expressing himself, Richardson noted that he didn't employ the "precision of the range rifle", but went off more "like a catherine wheel".

11   *The beast in the stalls*

> The fact is, though nobody has perceived it, that a professional play critic is a monstrosity—a sow with five legs or a man with four thumbs. Nature did not intend him, and that is why we have to conceal our repulsion when he confronts us.
>
> CLIFFORD BAX (quoted by James Agate, *Ego 7*)

Richardson's second season at the Old Vic, which opened as Britain went off the gold standard and slid into deep financial crisis, was his greatest challenge yet. His first part was Faulconbridge in *King John* (with Robert Speaight as the King). He followed this with Petruchio, Bottom, Henry V, Ralph in *The Knight of the Burning Pestle*, Brutus in *Julius Caesar*, General Grant in John Drinkwater's *Abraham Lincoln*, Iago in *Othello*, ending with the Ghost and First Gravedigger in an uncut *Hamlet*. It added up to ten major roles in eight months.

Under the aegis of the Old Vic's manageress, Lilian Baylis ("When the world was in trouble one came to the Old Vic for relaxation"), the Sadler's Wells Theatre had been restored and reopened, mainly as a home for opera; *Twelfth Night* had opened there, and now in this new season each production ran two weeks at the Vic, and one at the Wells. The neighbourhood of the Wells did not entirely suit Richardson: he used to complain to his friends about not being able to find a good steak (he would never touch "offal", meaning liver). They'd go down to Kingsway.

His greatest stumbling block in this season, and in the years to follow, however, lay not in any element on his side of the footlights, or in any factor which he could control through technique or interpretation. It lived on the other side of the lights, in the auditorium, in the form of a critic then in his prime and at the height of his reputation: the Mancunian James Agate. Brought up on the genius of Irving and of Sarah Bernhardt (with whom he used to claim a connection through his mother), Agate had never quite arrived at the realization since that time that, in the theatre at least, nothing ever came up to the primacy of one's first impressions.

Agate was in many ways a coarse man; a homosexual, stout in build, he wore, according to Gielgud, check suits "like a bookie", smoked cigars, played golf, and spent money on racing ponies. His great non-theatrical enthusiasm was cricket, which of course he never played. On holiday either at Margate or in the South of France, he sat on the beach in his bowler hat, never removing his shoes and socks. (It was an un-athletic age: James Bridie wrote in an autobiographical note for Malvern, "I have a wife and two small children (starving). I take no exercise.") Agate used to write in bed.

His authority was unquestioned. No one dared take issue with him on the nature of acting, least of all the humble and aspiring actor. Agate was both ogre and god—an illusion he did his best to foster by the series of autobiographical outpourings known as *Ego*, *Ego 2*, *Ego 3*, up to *Ego 9*, published from 1933 onwards, in which he carefully preserved his best critical pieces for posterity—part of the "insane desire to perpetuate oneself", as he dubbed it. By the 1930s his critical megalomania, tempered with wry wit, and his lust for money had reached elephantine proportions: he says himself that for twelve years, from 1921, he penned no less than half a million words a year, to a total of over six million, while Dickens in a comparable period wrote only five and a half (excluding journalism). Or, as Agate put it at another time—by which point he had further augmented his total—he wrote double the number of words in Balzac's *La Comédie humaine*. "Whaur's your Arnold Bennett noo?" he modestly inquired.

He was unfortunately also deeply prejudiced by the time Richardson began to be known (and that he could be spiteful, obnoxious and opinionated, also goes almost without saying).* He couldn't, for a start, waive his view that an

---

*Gielgud recalled that Agate "later in life . . . did a dirty trick; he threw over his trusted friend and companion Alan 'Jock' Dent in favour of Harold Hobson whom he recommended directly to Kemsley as his successor." Hobson himself gives a somewhat different account in his

actor's personality was wholly dependent on his physical limitations. This may be arguable, but in Agate's case the view was carried to extremes: so-and-so could never be Hamlet—he didn't look the part. It was a romantic and homosexual view. Agate's first talk of Richardson after meeting him socially, and lunching with him at the Savage Club in 1932, is significant: "A year or two ago Richardson had the habit of acting all his parts with his buttocks. I cured him of this, and his Henry V had no backside at all, though it reappeared, and rightly, in his next comic part."

Richardson showed, by lunching with Agate at the Savoy Grill, or his other haunt, the Ivy, that he was at least conversant with the diplomatic processes by which one achieved notices. George Howe, who had scrupulously avoided Agate at the Savoy in the belief that actors and critics shouldn't mix, recalled being told: "Ah, you're the young man who refuses to meet me. Didn't you know I never give an actor a good notice unless I've been introduced to him first!" But Agate also took advantage of knowing actors, and could be very indiscreet and embarrassing. Gielgud recalled his coming to his dressing room in 1929, during the first interval of *Macbeth*, and saying: "I have never seen the murder scene better done, so I have come to congratulate you now. At the end of the performance I shall probably have changed my mind, for you can't possibly play the rest of it."

At first Agate responded well to Ralph's promotion. In his notice of him as Faulconbridge he wrote, "Mr Ralph Richardson who a year or two ago was good in a shambling

autobiography, *Indirect Journey* (1979), saying that when Lord Kemsley, proprietor of the *Sunday Times*, "discovered something that was known all over theatrical London, namely, that Agate was a homosexual", he was most upset, and it was only when it was pointed out to him "that Agate was a famous man, the head of his profession, and that many of the world's greatest geniuses had been homosexuals" that the critic was saved from dismissal. Hobson was appointed his deputy and from then on until his death Agate cultivated Hobson's friendship, possibly out of fear. Two topics dominated conversation at their weekly meetings, Hobson noted: the size and colour of his testicles (large as billiard balls, bright orange in hue) and his desire for a knighthood (which he was never to receive).

sort of way, has discarded loutishness and an oafish gait and transmuted these into the sterling of forthrightness and honesty." But then, having fixed, as it were, the outer limits of Richardson's ability with those two words "forthrightness" and "honesty", he would never concede he was capable of anything else.

So Richardson's Petruchio, which he played with panache and debonair skill, dropping down on Kate from a ten-foot balcony, was dismissed out of hand. On the other hand, his Bottom was applauded with the unusual and trenchant perception of which Agate was often capable: "he abandoned clowning in favour of a dim consciousness of a rare world and of being at court there. . . . Shakespeare says he was 'translated' and Mr Richardson translated him."

Even here the praise was grudging. It was the ordinary, prosaic surface of Richardson's character-drawing, his unique power of conveying goodness in an interesting way, that Agate could never bring himself to acknowledge as art. But many other critics, such as J. C. Trewin and A. E. Wilson, and later especially Ivor Brown, responded warmly to it. His Henry V, deliberately anti-heroic, was extremely popular with the public. He injected a hard, almost cruel quality into the part. He excelled in the wooing of Kate, and in the impression of shrewdness he conveyed.

His portrayal of his namesake in *The Knight of the Burning Pestle* was also demolished by Agate. Here Richardson acted on an equal footing with Sybil Thorndike, cast as the Citizen's wife. This was his first chance to play with an actress of her calibre. Five minutes before the curtain rose he wondered if he dare pay court to her and wish her well. He went along to her dressing room, but was afraid to knock in case she was "communing with herself before that big part". Hearing a buzz of talk inside, he plucked up courage—and found her feeding half a dozen schoolgirls with buns.

"Come in, Ralph dear," she told him. "Won't you have a bun? There really isn't time for introductions."

Dame Sybil has commented that "Ralph Richardson was

so lovely as Ralph. He really is my favourite actor." Harcourt Williams found that he romped away with the part of the boisterous apprentice with all the resourcefulness of a music-hall comedian. But, in what was becoming a habit, Agate's pen squeaked in the stalls with its spidery secretions: "His stolid, inexpressive mien, altogether admirable . . . in all delineations of the downright . . . [does] not belong to the volatile mercurial apprentice."

Two productions later Agate followed with a savage assessment of Richardson's Iago:

> Failing supreme virtuosity, what shall the actor attempt? Shall he contravene Shakespeare's instructions and make us despise Othello for being too easily the dolt and gull? Or shall he stick to Shakespeare and present so single honest a face that even the audience can read nothing else? Mr Ralph Richardson chose the second course, and growing more honest as the play proceeded convinced us that he could not hurt a fly, which was very good Richardson but indifferent Shakespeare.

Agate's imagination didn't lend itself to suggestion, and the only meeting ground between him and Richardson were blunt servants and comics: in Agate's canon it seemed all right to underplay comedy, but not heroism or evil.

Towards the end of this 1931–2 season the strain of so many heavy roles began to tell on Richardson. During one performance of *Othello* his voice gave out completely, and after the cashiering of Cassio scene he had to withdraw. Harcourt Williams seized the book and, mastering his stomach nerves with a double ration of Bemax, took his place. By the next production—a revival of *Twelfth Night* —Richardson was well again, and his Sir Toby saw him at the height of relaxed form, drawing from Robert Speaight, who played other leading roles in that season, the tribute: "Richardson has his own way of picking up the whole stage, putting it in his mouth, and chewing it very slowly, like a piece of ripe Stilton."

Although Harcourt Williams would have liked to keep him longer and much regretted the loss of his jovial nature and sheer enthusiasm, Richardson now felt, as he had with Doran, that two straight years of Shakespeare was enough.

12   *A bid for West End glory*

The mood of the Twenties had been symbolized by J. B. Priestley's *The Good Companions* (1929), in which it seems as if, after the terrible bloodbath of the Great War, the survivors were huddling together to provide each other with companionable warmth and nostalgia. The touring players of Priestley's novel (later a play) were a paradigm of all that was best in the rapidly vanishing provincial England, its separateness being eroded by cheaper, swifter transport and communications.

In the Thirties Priestley, together with certain other writers who had made their reputations as novelists, turned to the theatre to provide an analysis of the decaying social order. Richardson, now a rising serious actor, even, as long as it didn't deface his public image, an intellectual one, inevitably became involved with the attempts of such writers to provide more than just the average West End fare of the type of a Wyndham's vehicle for a du Maurier.

Certain West End theatres became centres of radical attempts by Somerset Maugham, Priestley and others to change society. Richardson, like Olivier and Gielgud, began frequently to appear in Sunday-night try-out performances of plays with such titles as *Prejudice*—about the persecution of a Polish Jew in the American Middle West —or *Red Sunday*, by Hubert Griffith. Anti-war sentiments began to rise, as typified in *Douaumont, or the Return of the Soldier Ulysses*, by the German author E. W. Moeller, in which Gielgud declaimed passages from Homer. The radical socialist Bernard Shaw had meanwhile, by delighting audiences with the wit and musical skill of his construction, made his name in the commercial theatre. It was in Shaw's *Too True to be Good*, in September 1932, that Richardson —rejoining the Birmingham Rep outfit—made his first attempt to establish himself in the West End.

This sermon on modern life had first been seen the previous month at the Malvern Festival. Shaw's expanding acts of homage to his own talent had been provoking complaints among critics that they couldn't get away from the theatre in time to write their notices for next morning's papers, so an ambitious publicity director chartered an aeroplane to fly them down to Malvern for a Saturday matinée at 2.30 p.m. The cast duly assembled on the terrace to watch the little plane come down from the skies. All waved and cheered wildly—but the plane passed over, disappearing in the direction of Hereford. Well past 3.30, when the audience had lost hope, a bus arrived and a cargo of critics spilled out of it looking pale and wan. The pilot of the plane had lost his way in the mist. The sight of the critics, looking "so very human and like I feel on every first night", recalled Eileen Beldon, for once endeared them to the actors. But, she continued, the "cold collation was wasted and the notices were not very good". Subsequently the London production lost money and put Barry Jackson's company in financial jeopardy.

Agate for once was full of praise for Richardson. Of his Bunyanesque Sergeant Fielding he wrote: "The piece was run-away-with, in vulgar parlance, by Mr Ralph Richardson, who spoke the long speech with a medieval forthrightness and controlled passion beyond all praise." It should be noted, though, that once more Richardson was allowed only to excel within the limits imposed by Agate.

Richardson celebrated the significant advance in his career with a typical gesture: he acquired an antique clock, his very first. It is, he has said, still my best friend; it is a long case, with oak sides and a pine front. It was once decorated with Chinese lacquer, the proportions are graceful; there is a second dial and a date slot, which is easy to adjust, something not too common; it is a gallant goer with no tantrums, it clears error on striking 12; it has an "anchor escapement" by Gill of Clerkenwell *circa* 1738. I bought it from Davis in the Tottenham Court Road on 5 December 1932; I have his receipt pasted behind the clock case door: there are two tuppenny George V stamps written across; the first is for £5 which was a deposit, the second is for £7/12*s*. "gratefully received 1939". In those days 12 guineas was not always on the ready.

He followed *Too True to be Good* with Maugham's *For Services Rendered*, in which he played Colin Stratton, the returning naval hero. Stratton tries to run a garage in the country where he settles, but falls into deeper and deeper debt, and is given little help by the upper-crust set who were quite happy to put up with his protection during the war. In the end he shoots himself.

The first-night audience coughed and fidgeted in the key scene Richardson played with Flora Robson, when, as the hapless spinster Eva, she proposed marriage to him. The actual proposal, blurted out with suppressed emotion, caused laughter, at which Robson experienced discomfort, while Richardson, as she later reported, left the stage looking doleful. The audience reaction, however, wasn't mirrored in the reviews, but even with these, this bitter wintry piece lasted only six weeks. Richardson and Flora Robson played together again in *Head-on Crash*, by Laurence Miller, in early 1933; none of the cast saw a full script of the play until five days before the first night—they rehearsed from separately typed parts—and the whole proved a disappointment.

As Maugham's character Stratton it was, Harold Hobson commented, for "his quality of stillness" that Richardson was memorable—so much so that it led Gielgud, later in the year, to offer Richardson his first leading part in the

West End. Gielgud, who had been approached by Bronson Albery to direct Maugham's next (and last) play, *Sheppey*, asked Ralph to play the name part. Sheppey, a hairdresser's assistant, wins £8,500 in a sweepstake; spurning the more obvious gratifications, he decides, in a Pauline-like act of conversion which is accompanied by some form of seizure, to take the harlot and the thief from the gutter to his heart. Gielgud found that the character needed clarifying, and in vain sought hints from Maugham himself, who had been writing successful plays for nearly thirty years. By contrast the theme was vividly clear, and the action, for the two acts out of the three at least, progressed by virtue of Maugham's craftsmanship.

But the breadth of vision Maugham opened up in the play was artistically and possibly spiritually too exacting for this essentially lightweight writer to build on. Had he done so he might have given the young actor, testing his range, a chance to transform a sound portrait—which with an artist's patience Richardson built up stroke by stroke, employing both realism and restraint—into something more: a rare form of vision, perhaps, a dream or nightmare. Instead, relying on a well-seasoned power of bitter observation, Maugham showed Sheppey's family trying to have him committed for insanity. The result was an ordinary success which ran three months. The portrayal by Richardson of human goodness, of a saint with his feet on the ground, was much liked and he was thought to be better than the play.

But *Sheppey* was as soft fruit to the scorpion attacks of Agate's pen and Richardson, for Agate, spoke too finely to be a hairdresser.

13   *Great Britain, Ltd.*

He turned next to a far more ambitious author: J. B. Priestley. Priestley wrote plays to a pattern, one with which Richardson at once found himself in sympathy. He had fixed his prose style early on and would spend some time thinking out a play before dashing it off, taking usually not more than a week to write out a first draft. He did not like having too fixed an idea, considering that if you had too solid a scheme you would only ever write with the front part of your mind, not with the whole of it. With *Eden End*, set before the First World War in the house of a Yorkshire general practitioner, Priestley realized one of his most complete pictures of English society. The part Richardson created in 1934, that of Charles Appleby—an actor down on his luck but buoyed up by inner confidence and often pleasurably blurred in his sense of ill-fortune by his predilection for alcohol—was in the line of the Churdles Ash characters Cedric Hardwicke had portrayed so successfully.

Appleby was for Richardson the best shorter part he ever played, full of "wonderful jokes all set to music—what more could one ask?". The music, of course, was the melody of Priestley's deceptively simple prose, which, with its calculated hesitations and doublings-back of thought, looked as if it might have been penned with Richardson in mind:

WILFRED: And I didn't know you existed.
CHARLES: Didn't you? Dam' shame. But there you are, you see. Here I am. And here you are. Having a drink together. Everything's quiet. Women asleep upstairs—or hope they are. Your governor out there somewhere— helping some poor devil out of the world—or perhaps helping some other poor devil into the world—and here we are. And you'll go back to Ceylon—
WILFRED: Africa

CHARLES: It's all the same, old boy. This isn't geography. And I'll go back to town. Get a job. Go on tour again perhaps. People will come to see me. I don't know anything about them. Never mind. Perhaps I make 'em cry. Perhaps I make 'em laugh. And, mind you, old boy, give me a part with a ghost of a bit of comedy fat in it, and I can make 'em laugh. I can make 'em yell. Weedon Grossmith—Weedon Grossmith, mind you—once said to me: "You've got a touch, Appleby old boy. You've *got* something." And I have. The trouble is—and this is where *luck* comes in—most of the time I've had to make something out of nothing.

Robert Speaight had already noted, at the Old Vic, how every piece of stage business was for Ralph a jigsaw puzzle which he would sit down before his dressing-room mirror to solve, smoking one of the Charaton pipes which lay in a bowl on the table. A peep into Richardson's meticulous, loving method with a modern play is also given by the actress Fabia Drake who, after one run-through of *Eden End*, found herself going backstage through the pass door to collect tickets for the first night. There, on the darkened stage lit only by a working light, she discovered him as Appleby:

a figure in the gloom which rose from a table, moved unsteadily towards a door up-stage and passed, or rather tottered, through it. I reached the box office where there was a sizeable queue, and after about half an hour collected my tickets, and, returning through the pass door again, crossed the stage. The figure was still there, still moving unsteadily across the room, still "weaving" out of the door.

On their first meeting Priestley found Richardson "quite mannered" but felt beneath this surface the richness of his personality. He assessed him: "I always see Ralph myself not as a down-to-earth character but as if he is about to float away somewhere. He could be terrifying at the end of a day's rehearsal. You could have a few drinks and then he would invite you to go for a drive. After a while I began to dodge going round to the bar."

Richardson's next Priestley part, in 1935, was much longer, the name part of *Cornelius*. The play, which was dedicated to him, was a somewhat flimsy attack on the decline of capitalism in England, symbolized by the firm of Briggs and Murison, of which Cornelius is a partner. It was directed by Basil Dean—tall, bald, bespectacled, almost a civil servant type (he began life in a City office)—who, as a brilliant manipulator both of people and of scenic effects, was for Richardson as much the New Director as Gielgud had been the New Man.

While *Eden End* ran for nearly six months, *Cornelius* ran less than two. But the production, with its efficiency and ruthless drive, held high possibilities for the future. Richardson wrote to Dean immediately it had opened: "My dear Basil, Last night amid some licquor and distraction I tried to say how grateful I was to you. Now I would like to say it again." He has never had such direction from anyone before, he goes on, and earnestly hopes "I may be able to work with you again, for I don't know where else I shall find it."

Something more than a merely professional interest in Priestley's plays cemented their friendship. One day Dean expressed the intention of buying an Aston Martin, and Richardson wrote off to him at once: "If you are interested in cars for their own sake I am sure you will have a great deal of pleasure out of the new Aston. You are going to buy the long chassis, personally I would rather have the short. I do not think the proportion is so good in the long and the cornering will not be the same."

Advice continued in this vein, which appealed to Dean's methodical and analytical nature (he had had leanings at school towards chemistry). Richardson suggested visiting the works at Fulham, "before they start making it for

With Lydia; 'My mother was my first love'.

The high-spirited schoolboy, aged fifteen. *(News Chronicle)*

Kit Hewitt as Ophelia in the
modern-dress *Hamlet* of 1925.
*(Birmingham Repertory
Company)*

As Bill Sikes in *Oliver Twist*,
1921. He also played
Mr Bumble. *(Birmingham
Repertory Company)*

With the Birmingham Rep as Ben Hawley in *Aren't Women Wonderful?* *(Birmingham Repertory Company)*

With the Birmingham Rep as Arthur Varwell in *Yellow Sands*, pinned to the ground by brother (Frank Vosper). *(Birmingham Repertory Company)*

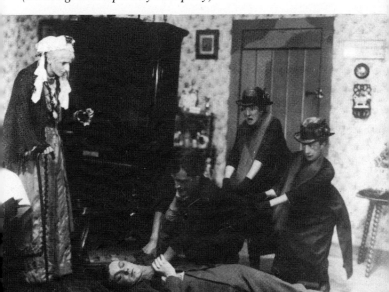

Early film roles: as Nigel Hartley in *The Ghoul*, 1933. *(The Rank Organisation Ltd)*

Early film roles: as the villain Morell, cornered underground by Jack Hulbert in *Bulldog Jack,* 1935. *(The Rank Organisation Ltd)*

Richardson at the Old Vic, 1930-32: as Henry V. *(The Mander and Mitchenson Theatre Collection)*

Richardson at the Old Vic, 1930-32: as the First Gravedigger, with Robert Harris as Hamlet. *(The Mander and Mitchenson Theatre Collection)*

At the Old Vic, as Iago with Edith Evans as Emilia. *(The Mander and Mitchenson Theatre Collection)*

In *Cornelius,* with James Harcourt as Biddle. *(The Mander and Mitchenson Theatre Collection)*

In Priestley's *Eden End: (left top and bottom)* as the amiable drink-addicted Charles Appleby; *(right)* with Stella Kirby (Beatrix Lehmann). *(The Mander and Mitchenson Theatre Collection)*

The landowner Carne in the film of South Riding, 1938, encountering the schoolmistress (Edna Best) and the left-wing Councillor (John Clements). *(London Films)*

Othello, knife poised over Desdemona (Curigwen Lewis), at the Old Vic, 1938. *(The Mander and Mitchenson Theatre Collection)*

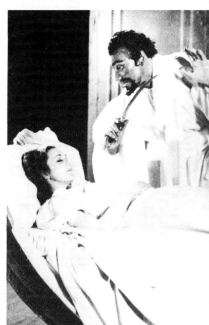

you—": "They will take a great personal interest in you, and in trying to please you, and this is one of the greatest advantages in getting their cars. You can talk to Bertelli the coach man and to Sutherland and Brand and they will do anything for you if they think you are interested." He advises Dean to have a Scintilla magneto and not a Lucas, "which is about as much use as a Stilton cheese for the purpose", and gives him the serial number for the sparking plugs. The only gadget he reveals to Dean which he himself has is a Bosch fog lamp, which he calls "splendid". Richardson the inventor now came to the fore, modestly listing his achievements (something he never did with acting): "Some little improvements I have suggested to them they have put into practice generally. I have for example designed a new exhaust box so that I am rather in their good books and you might tell them I'll kill them if they are not good to you."

A pleading reply issued from Dean next day: "Could you possibly find time to come with me?"

Cedric Hardwicke, whom Richardson visited at Mead Lodge, commented on the compulsion which the internal-combustion engine exerted on his fellow actor:

This addiction at Sunny Mede [a previous address of Hardwicke] had taken the form of buzzing the house in an aeroplane with Bob Pickard as co-pilot. . . . [Now] it took the form of racing whatever car he owned on the London Road. Where cars were concerned, he suffered from a peculiar form of madness which drove him to favour rare and exotic makes. So long as there were no more than half a dozen of his favourite brand in London, he was content. Let them begin to gain ever so slightly in popularity, then he started to find things amiss in the function or design, until he felt compelled to trade the fallen idol against some new and more récherché line. He would have me take the wheel and pelt down the road as he yelled, "Go on, faster, faster. You're not frightening me yet."

Richardson liked Basil Dean more than most actors did,

and not only because they shared a passion for cars. Dean was, as Ayliff had been, a keen disciplinarian. "Actors hated his guts," said Priestley, "for he could be very sharp-tongued and sarcastic." Looking to the future, Richardson saw that the actor-manager's days were numbered. Basil Dean was the first of the new breed intent on imposing his own stamp on each production he did. According to James Dale, an actor of an earlier vintage than Richardson or Olivier, who lived on into the 1980s, this new form of direction "drove the public away, and it drove the prigs in."

14   *The image of ordinariness*

The failure of *Cornelius*, and a lull in 1935 before his next West End engagement, gave Richardson his first opportunity to appear in New York, as Mercutio in the revival of a *Romeo and Juliet* in which Katharine Cornell played Juliet. This season Maurice Evans was making his début as Romeo in the production. He and Richardson appeared to be "a shade harassed", as the *New York Times* remarked—perhaps by Forty-Fifth Street, where the Martin Beck Theatre was situated, and "its similar tenants of a year ago". But "that wore away," the review went on, "and the Messrs. Evans and Richardson were voted in."

Richardson didn't take kindly to New York, and was unnerved by customs prevailing in the theatre there, such as applause on certain actors' first entrances and exits, and the blaze of publicity that followed Cornell everywhere. "I hated New York," he commented. "I was in fear. I loathed it," adding, when reminded of his love of climbing round high buildings on the outside, that the ledges of New York were a "bit high, outside my gambit or range." But he saw the Lunts in *The Taming of the Shrew*, and they were magnificent.

Next, he visited Paris, where Gielgud had recommended he pay homage to the art of Louis Jouvet. He didn't care much for what he saw. Gielgud recalled Richardson telling him of his reaction: "Every time Jouvet turned his back to the audience, which he did frequently, Ralph moved a seat nearer the exit, until finally he slipped out unnoticed into the street. Good enough reason, he would always say, not to act with your back to the audience." Richardson responded much more to Sacha Guitry whose *bon mot* about acting he later quoted: "Acting is a trick."

Back in England, in February 1936, Richardson's next venture was Henry Bernstein's *Espoir*, translated as *Promise*, in which he joined a cast "with which a box office might conjure"—including Madge Titheradge, Edna Best, Ann Todd and Robert Harris. Richardson played the part of Madge Titheradge's husband Emil with tenderness and discrimination, bringing to it an "unspectacular authenticity", as Charles Morgan noted in the *New York Times*. Titheradge was far more demonstrative as the selfish Thérèse and, when overcome at last with remorse at how badly she'd treated him, in Richardson's description, "thunder-striking". On the set everything appeared to Richardson quite different from the effect about to come:

> I was on the stage alone before she entered for her magic moment. Now, I have always been very sensitive about noises off-stage—and there was Madge off-stage chattering, giggling, she was practically dancing. I would remonstrate afterwards. "Oh you poor lamb," she would say, "I'm so sorry. I'll be like a mouse." She was like a mouse for the next night and the next, and then her gaiety and irrepressible high-jinks would simply bubble up and burst in a Vesuvius of laughter.

Although he was now something of a West End star, and authors wrote with him in mind, popular success obstinately eluded Richardson. He had no great instinct for vulgar acclaim, didn't feed off the applause of the gallery, and with assiduous care and devotion he kept himself out of the gossip columns. He was sometimes referred to as an intellectual actor, though when he became aware of this he strenuously did his best to avoid giving an impression of intellectuality; that wasn't considered healthy or sane at the time, and he took refuge in numerous hobbies and pastimes instead, cultivating vigorously an image of ordinariness.

During these years he gave many interviews, but there was no romance in his private life for newspapermen to seize on. The sad personal story of Kit was simply not mentioned. More often than not a reporter who visited him backstage would find this very staid individual smoking a pipe. He presented himself as a creature of earnest good sense, upright and devoted to his work: a character that accorded with the mood of the times. None of the eccentricity lurking in the background was in any way then evident.* To his hobbies of flying, painting and fast driving, he added fishing, golfing, squash, tennis, modelling, collecting and literature, but the imaginative leaps, the intimacy and quirkiness were submerged in a straightforwardness whose very efficiency and impact might have led the perceptive observer to wonder how ordinary he actually was. That person might well have come to the conclusion that the ordinariness was a skilful feat of engineering on the part of an extremely individual and extraordinary man whose conflicts, tensions, miseries, slights and anger he was endlessly resourceful in covering up and keeping hidden from the world—and as such they were a direct source of power both to his work and to himself.

---

*Or scarcely. In Liverpool in 1929, when he was an understudy in a musical comedy, *Silver Wings*, in which an aeroplane crashed on stage into the interior of a house, Leslie Sarony remembered him knitting in his dressing room. He had some odd practices, too; sometimes, in order to get in the right mood, he would pretend to be a bee; never a confident 'study', he'd scrawl out his lines in coloured chalks.

What made him so ordinary in appearance, so unspectacular, was his capacity for self-presentation. Everything, from the clothes he bought to the clubs he frequented, the careful remarks he made which might pass as clichés if they hadn't had an edge of something different about them, served to reinforce this. The articles he contributed to programmes, to acting journals, and the talks he made on the radio about contemporaries, all served to disguise himself, to remove himself from the too-eager grasp of publicity. He left the limelight to his more ostentatious friends, Gielgud and Olivier, and yet in many significant ways, as the other two would perhaps acknowledge, he was the most extraordinary of the three. But while in fact larger than life, he was intent on showing himself to be less large—and not until in old age, and almost out of an instinctive sense of tact, would he allow his full dimensions to be seen and then only partially and intermittently. He was incapable of outrageousness, of the boldness expected by the public from a profession which by its very nature was bound up with harlotry and exposure.

15 *Light relief*

In circumstances which were extremely distressful, Richardson had organized care for his wife short of the full hospital treatment which became necessary in most cases of the disease from which she suffered. They were now living apart, she in a flat in the Gloucester Road with her friends Violet and Hugh Pearson, a devoted couple who did their best to help her physically to relieve the effects of the rigidity caused by encephalitis and to keep up her spirits. Among the symptoms of her affliction, which was related to Parkinson's disease, were exaggerated movement, a blocking or periodic freezing of all energy, forms of mania and depression and abrupt changes in character—though all these might remain dormant for as much as nine months at a time. Kit, well rooted in reality, withstood the onset of these symptoms with remarkable bravery, but there was no understanding of the disease, and no foreseeable hope of cure.*

To assuage his loneliness and maintain an ordinary life Richardson, whose work-load as an actor was, and would remain, consistently heavy, turned to lively and consolatory companions of his own sex, to reading and drinking, and to club-land; he now belonged to no less than five clubs, the Athenaeum, the Green Room, the Beefsteak, the Cumberland (a tennis club) and the Savile. One day Priestley asked Richardson to meet him at the Duchess Theatre. He failed to keep the appointment, and when Richardson enquired for him, "Oh," they told him, "he's over the road." Richardson went over and found Priestley playing squash. He was "absolutely fascinated", he said; "it opened up a great vista," for he had never played games as a child. From this he was to claim that Priestley introduced him to racquet games, though Priestley said much later, "I don't remember Ralph as a tennis player."

Olivier and Richardson still shared many experiences, even when not playing together. They acquired a reputation for high-spiritedness, each trying to outdrink or outdrive the other. They were together in January 1936 when they heard of the death of George V, and both were strongly affected.

*It was not until 1960 that the drug known as L-Dopa was developed, which replaced the loss of nerve-transmission power that was at the root of the various symptoms. When over subsequent years this drug was administered to the remaining sufferers, the results showed an unparalleled and extraordinary—if uneven—restoration of vitality in some cases lost to the patient for as long as fifty years.

Maurice Evans told Olivier that when Richardson played Mercutio in New York he had introduced some little jokes into the part. Olivier wanted to know them, as he was doing Mercutio at the Old Vic. "My dear boy," wrote Richardson from Boston, where he was on tour with *Romeo and Juliet*:

I can't tell you how to play Mercutio; you should be much better than me—don't forget you could colour Bothwell which drove me right out of the stage door.* But as you ask me I will tell you my experience of it. Be careful not to hurry the "Mab" speech, as I did at first from over-anxiety to be bright. It is a speech that depends on detail and if all the points are made will seem enormously brilliant, but if slightly rushed is just dull.

The second scene plays itself. I play it with a sort of lazy humour and come on yawning and blowing pip-squeaks after the party—but don't forget the sudden delicacy of "if love be blind, love cannot hit the mark". The next scene you should do extremely well—here I am as rapid as I can be—the real "Mercutio" tremendously smart and as full of full-up light and life as I can make him.

You should try to produce a different key every time you come on—and wear your clothes in a different way. I have a tremendous circular scarlet cloak of fine red flannelette; this I can do a great many things with.

I hope you are not very bored with all this my dear boy—but one thing more—the greatest difficulty is to keep sober enough in the one hour twenty-five minutes wait you have before the end to take your call without falling into an orchestra-pit. This takes years of skill and cannot be overestimated, as much of the effect of the poetic "Mab" speech may be lost by such an incident.

*A reference to his withdrawal in 1934 from *Queen of Scots* by Gordon Daviot (a pen name of Josephine Tey): he had been cast as Bothwell but found himself unable to meet the romantic demands of the part, so had withdrawn before the first night, suggesting Olivier take his place. The role had been Olivier's first undisputed success, though according to John Cottrell in his biography of Olivier, it was "more Hollywood than Holyrood".

I am writing this in my wait in a dressing-room in a hot—you know how hot—theatre with no window or ventilation whatever.

Goodnight, my dear fellow.

RALPH.

After *Promise* closed, the two friends came together in May 1936 as joint stars and directors of another Priestley play, *Bees on the Boat Deck*. Basil Dean had turned it down and Harold Hobson succinctly summed up the run: "the bankrupt firm had become a doomed ship; and Olivier and Richardson went down with her after four weeks' struggle." Ivor Brown in the *Observer* (10 May 1936) more kindly called it "a grand partnership . . . Continually these two by delicacy of inflection or business win their author an uncovenanted benefit of laughter." The play had a sentimental interest for Olivier: one afternoon during brilliant weather Vivien Leigh came to a matinée with Ivor Novello and sat prominently in a box. "Stop groaning, Ralphie," Olivier had during Act I to hiss at Richardson, who had by now become bored and depressed with the play. Richardson sensed there was someone out front his friend wanted to impress, and managed (according to Felix Barker, first biographer of the Oliviers) with great difficulty to restrain his irritation until the interval, when he asked, "Shall we stop now?"

16　*The dream controller*

"In 1933," wrote the film producer-director Herbert Wilcox, in *Twenty-Five Thousand Sunsets* (1967),

> Cedric Hardwicke told me of a young friend of his who
> was as exciting an actor as he had met. Not only that, but
> he was a very fast driver of very fast cars.
>
> I was about to produce a film on the life of Sacha
> Guitry, called *The King of Paris* with Cedric playing
> Sacha, and he suggested we give his young, fast-driving
> friend the second lead. My director Jack Raymond, and I
> met him—and I must say he was no Jack Buchanan or
> Ivor Novello to look at, but I had a feeling that he was a
> mystic. I exerted my influence and persuaded Raymond,
> saying: "Cedric would not have suggested him if he did
> not really believe in him."
>
> We started the film with a most unenthusiastic director
> —until the day's rushes were shown.
>
> "Don't understand it," said Raymond, "on the floor,
> gives nothing—on the screen, he's terrific!"
>
> "That's where the public will see him," I replied.
>
> And in the most difficult, nondescript part of a Parisian
> artisan [he] was superb.
>
> Whenever Ralph scored an outstanding hit after-
> wards, which was often, Cedric's only sly comment
> was—yes! "Herbert—I told you so."

The King of Paris was Richardson's sixth film. He had
appeared as Nigel Hartley in *The Ghoul*, then as the
schoolmaster in *Friday the Thirteenth* (when he worked for
the first time with the director Victor Saville), in *Java Head*,
and as Hugh Drummond in *The Return of Bulldog Drummond*, before he met Wilcox. He also excelled in his next
film, *Bulldog Jack*, as the French villain Morell, equipped
with eyeglass, bushy eyebrows and white wig, and speaking
most uncharacteristically in a foreign accent. Everything he
did even in this early film was distinctive and individual,
even though the character was involved in the most banal of
adventure stories. *Bulldog Jack* ended in a mad melod-

ramatic chase on the London Underground. Richardson, his crime unmasked, his eyes popping and with white wig streaming in the wind, drove the tube train to the end of the line where, just short of the buffers, he was overpowered: a memorable image. His clarity and power of projection quite outclassed the hero of the piece, played by the long-jawed Jack Hulbert.

His first picture for Alexander Korda, the great Hungarian producer-director who settled in London in 1930, was *The Shape of Things to Come*, scripted by H. G. Wells from his own book. Korda had asked Richardson to play the name part in *Sanders of the River* but other commitments had ruled this out. So it was in 1935, as the Mussolini-like Boss, that he first savoured the delights of the picturesque Korda empire which had just been raised in white-painted concrete at Denham, in Buckinghamshire. The art deco palace had swans imprisoned on its ponds, which were built too short for them to effect flight (to keep swans, London Films' historical adviser, Winston Churchill, had obtained royal assent—Churchill once said of Korda's extravagance, "He would make a good Prime Minister of Hungary, as long as he had Rockefeller at the Exchequer"). The studio also had massive hangar-like sound stages (they were nearly 100 yards long and 50 feet high) which enabled shooting to be carried out in all weathers. Denham became a second home for Richardson. With Korda, in his sleek and exotic surroundings—he had fresh flowers in both offices and home changed daily—he formed a strong and lasting bond. "His manner to me," said Richardson, "was mostly one of ironic weariness. He gave me the impression that I slightly bored him—very likely I did—but at the same time he drew me towards him . . . Though not so much older than I am, I regarded him in a way as a father, and to me he was as generous as a prince."

Korda and Wells had divergent aims over *Things to Come*, Korda being more idealistic than Wells, who wanted more than anything else to provide a good night out. Richardson's own first encounter with the author of *Kipps* confirmed very much his expectations in the meeting the author-hero of his early reading. Wells was a short stout man; his shoulders sloped, his head was large. His smile was benign and vital. Richardson recalled:

> I came very close to Wells. Adored him. I was a very young man and indeed a rather gauche boy, and remember very well going to a very smart party and taking a cigarette and dropping it. The hostess swooped over and shrieked "What have you done?" and Wells, of course, he was her prize guest, stooped down and picked it up and said: "Madam, I dropped it."

Reactions to *Things to Come* were mixed, but Richardson's own impact was unforgettable. "I was a picture of Mew-soh-lini. Because there was no dictator before Mew-soh-lini. He invented the whole thing." So near to the bone did it prove that Il Duce himself, when he saw it, was outraged and all showings of *Things to Come* were banned in Italy on his personal order.

Richardson thereafter seized on and responded to the essence of Korda's mid-European power, to "his gift of charm—and strength of personality that could be described as hypnotic." Using this gift, Korda propelled Richardson gently but firmly, in the work he began to do for London Films, towards parts Korda saw as right for him. Sometimes Richardson baulked at this:

> Alex could be maddening too, and one could be tremendously exasperated by him. Those moments came, I think, from the fact that he had an enormous number of sides to his nature—like an enormous crystal revolving on its orbit—and one never knew which facet might present itself. After struggling with a problem, one would be stunned to find the edge confronting one would be completely at variance with one's own ideas based on a previous discussion. Instead of a helpful reaction to one's thoughts one found only a refraction . . . the hardness of a glass wall and a consequent frustration of mind that set it splintering into a thousand fragments of rage. One would be left feeling like that for a while and

then would realize that Alex had cast another aspect, more enlightened and more original and helpful to one's problem. Alex always understood.

He summed up on another occasion without employing metaphors: "Alexander Korda continuously makes people do things against their will but seldom against their interest." Test cases for this astute observation were Richardson's next films—one in particular.

The most remarkable revelation of Richardson as an actor of inner feeling came not in any play he acted in at this time, but in *South Riding*, the film based on Winifred Holtby's novel, and directed by Victor Saville. Korda's genius for picking subjects to make his stars reveal themselves, and in particular the vulnerable sides of their natures which would awaken sympathy in their audience, was never displayed more perfectly than in his casting of Richardson as Councillor Robert Carne.

Carne, an increasingly insolvent landowner, is at the centre of Holtby's compassionate picture of regional life. His incurable wife, played by Ann Todd, is in a private mental home, whose bills are draining his resources, while on the local council, of which he is a prominent member, the socialists are coming under the grip of the heartless and cunning property exploiters. Carne, in spite of the reactionary posture he adopts, is the hero of the story, the archetypal Englishman who transcends politics because like a figure in pre-revolutionary Russian literature he belongs to the land which belongs to him, and is close to the traditional values of his race. "Aren't we teaching people to rely on others instead of on themselves?" he asks when opposing the local communist with a tubercular cough who (played by John Clements) stands for a more protective egalitarianism. In between the two is the schoolmistress, Miss Burton, played by Edna Best, who is entrusted with the education of Carne's teenage daughter. Carne fears his daughter will become wayward and mad like her mother.

Richardson's underplaying of Carne's tragic dilemma over his wife when faced with his love for Sarah Burton is registered with deep and sensitive feeling. It may be reading too much into the film—which was released in 1937—to see him projecting into it some of his thoughts over Kit, in particular in the scenes which deal with Carne's sick wife. The schoolmistress comments on the wife's portrait which, as in Daphne du Maurier's *Rebecca*, hangs over the main staircase in Carne's manor: "She's the most beautiful woman I ever saw." To which Carne answers, "You wouldn't think so if you saw her now." "You mustn't torture yourself like this," she tells him. The insight into the pain of Carne's predicament remains memorable, for, by seeming so outwardly unmoved, Richardson managed to bring out all the more emotion from within the part.

At the end Carne cannot escape his debts for being trapped by his wife's tragedy, and goes with a twelve-bore shotgun into a dark wood intending to shoot himself, but is found and saved by Sarah Burton. He tells her, "My unhappiness is on my own head: I can't burden you with it." By this point in *South Riding*, Richardson has completed a moving definition of the self-reliant and high-principled Englishman (who in spite of being a landlord and a Tory is ordinary and representative), who would die rather than face dishonour, who is committed to a national ideal of what any decent Englishman who found himself in his shoes would do.

17   *A success and a failure*

It may be exaggerated to speak of Richardson himself being rescued from suicide by his friendship with a fellow actress,

Meriel Forbes. When he appeared on stage with her in *The Amazing Dr Clitterhouse* in 1936, during the filming of *South Riding*, he was not a bankrupt landowner without prospects but a thriving and successful actor near the peak of his profession. But there was undoubtedly an aspect of salvation in the part played over the next few years by this pretty, vivacious and gifted comedienne, who brought some light again into his life. A spirited companion, Mu, as she was called, took Richardson's mind off other matters. "I like that one," he said of her when, with another girl, she auditioned for the part of Daisy, the gangster's moll, in *Dr Clitterhouse*.

Her full name was Meriel Forbes-Robertson. She had been born in Fulham in 1913, the daughter of Frank Forbes-Robertson, the actor-manager, and Honoria McDermott, and grandniece of the great Sir Johnston Forbes-Robertson. Her first appearance had been in York in 1931, in *The Passing of the Third-Floor Back*, and while her range was never as wide as that of her great-uncle ("never as good an actress I don't mind telling you," said J. B. Priestley), yet within her limits she was extremely good. She had joined the Birmingham Repertory company in 1931 and for the next five years had gone from one light West End show to another. At one time she was engaged to Robert Morley: this lasted until she went on a long tour in a play with Robert Donat. Morley is reported to have told her, "You'll never succeed." "Why not?" she replied. "I'm never out of work." "That's true," he answered, "but you have no ambition."

By some irony, *Dr Clitterhouse* was to run almost as long at the Haymarket as *Yellow Sands*, in which Richardson had appeared with Kit Hewitt ten years before, and as with the earlier production it was to create stability for him, though more private than artistic. Barré Lyndon's play was no more than an ingenious thriller, hardly likely to advance his career. In it, a psychologist turned criminologist, wanting to study the moment-to-moment reactions of those committing a crime, takes to robbery himself, being well placed to dispose of the fruits of his experiments.

Richardson as Clitterhouse was able to combine a phlegmatic self-examination with impudence in the character's high-handed dealings with the most influential and the seediest in the land. He also delighted in the Doctor's quizzical observation of his guinea pigs' symptoms in the heat of their chosen trade. Mu's Daisy one reviewer described as "dark and spirited and smartly dressed". Although the ending narrowly skirted melodrama as Clitterhouse turns to murder to escape being incriminated, Lyndon—it was his one outstanding success—brought the play to a satisfactory close. It lasted 497 performances, which meant that Richardson with 5 per cent of the weekly takings, as well as his generous contract with Korda, could comfortably maintain a high standard of living.

Critical acclaim, however, stubbornly eluded him. Agate was there again to pass sentence of death on his next play: "Nov. 17 1937. Went to *Silent Knight* by Hungarian author, Eugene Heltai, translated into English verse by Humbert Wolfe. Bored to catalepsy."

After *The Silent Knight*'s demise Richardson, neatly side-stepping down, re-surfaced almost at once as Bottom in Tyrone Guthrie's Old Vic production of *A Midsummer Night's Dream*, in which Vivien Leigh played Titania and Robert Helpmann—like "some strange sinister stag beetle" —Oberon. This much-praised *Dream* was remarkable for more than its artistic brilliance (choreography by Ninette de Valois, sets by Oliver Messel). Just prior to it, during the run of Olivier's *Macbeth*, Lilian Baylis, dubbed by Agate "a Magnificent Tyrant", died. Queen Elizabeth (now the Queen Mother) had promised Miss Baylis that the first Shakespeare production her daughters were taken to should be in one of the Baylis theatres. On 12 January 1938 the Queen duly took Princesses Elizabeth and Margaret Rose to the Old Vic to see the *Dream*.

Now came Richardson's first attempt to play one of Shakespeare's great tragic four: his ill-fated Othello, in which he was joined by Olivier as Iago. The double act began full of confidence in spite of Richardson's fears that he hadn't the strength or energy to fill out the character

Richardson as Bottom with Titania (Vivien Leigh)

from within: feeling he had in plenty, but was more doubtful about his capacity for fury. To some extent he had been
reassured by a try at *Macbeth* made for radio in 1933, in
which his impact had been strong, growing in stature as the
play progressed; also by the "darkie" he had played in
Southerne's *Oroonoko*, done at Malvern in 1932.

In their dressing room at the Vic before one dress
rehearsal (based on interviews given to the press):

RICHARDSON: It's funny about *Othello*, I know the play
so well. I've played Roderigo and Iago
to Wilfrid Walter's Othello at the Old
Vic. When I hear people speaking my
old parts, it's like hearing ghosts. I want
to stop and correct them.

OLIVIER: It's Othello's play. Iago speaks in short
passages. He hasn't any of those
tremendous speeches, and emotional
climaxes. Iago doesn't rival Othello in
importance.

RICHARDSON *(removing pipe from mouth and turning
his sombre, coffee-coloured face towards
Olivier, and fixing his large mysterious
eyes reprovingly on him):* I don't know
about that. Iago speaks in short bursts,
but he's whirring all the time—like a
sewing machine. He's a man of great
nervous energy

OLIVIER: —who might have been great. He has
been perverted and frustrated by
jealousy at being passed over for the
captaincy. It might happen to anyone.
Suppose Ralph and I were condemned
to play film extras all the time. We
should either have to put on plays for
ourselves, or go mad like Al Capone in
prison. If it hadn't been for jealousy,
Iago might have been a great man.

RICHARDSON: All Shakespeare's tragedies deal with

greatness misdirected or destroyed through a frailty. Mr Gielgud, who, of course, has a great understanding of Shakespeare, suggested to me that Othello is a saint overcome by villainy. But I don't think Othello was a saint. Despite his greatness I think that jealousy was in him all the time. I admit that there's an objection to that. In almost his last speech Othello speaks of himself as "One not easily jealous".

OLIVIER: Not *easily* jealous. But capable of jealousy.

RICHARDSON: Yes. I think he's a more tragic figure like that. If you regard him as a majestic oak, and Iago a little fuse niggling away in the trunk and finally blowing it up—well, where's the tragedy? A big tree has been knocked down. We say: Tut-tut! It's a sad accident! But it's not a tragedy.

Clearly both were more than a little confused as to who was to be jealous of what. And this confusion was thickened before the play opened by a number of secret visits paid by Guthrie and Olivier to the Hampstead house of Dr Ernest Jones. Olivier, with his unerring instinct for changes in fashion, had already discussed Freudian interpretations of *Hamlet* with Dr Jones; now Freud's biographer was consulted on a possible Freudian basis for Iago's jealousy of Othello, namely unconscious homosexual love. Richardson, who remained always rather more circumspect about sex as a driving force in the human psyche, was neither consulted nor informed about the visits.

As they left Dr Jones's house after their first call, Olivier asked Guthrie what he thought of the theory. "I think it is inescapable of course—on an unconscious plane, of course." "Oh, of course," echoed Olivier and added, "I don't think we dare tell Ralphie." He felt rather guilty about such treachery. In fact, as Guthrie revealed later, they spent two long evenings with Dr Jones, "evenings of the greatest interest and excitement. But Richardson would not go along with us." In practical terms Olivier and Guthrie wanted the climax of the Iago–Othello relationship to be created with explicit intent; assertions such as

> Witness that here Iago doth give up
> The execution of his wit, hands, heart,
> To wrong'd Othello's service

and "I'm your own forever", became tantamount to declarations of love:

"There came a moment in rehearsal," Olivier later said, ". . . I don't remember this, but this is the story that is told—that losing all control of myself, I flung my arms round Ralph's neck and kissed him. Whereat Ralph . . . sort of patted me and said 'Dear fellow dear boy,' much more pitying me for having lost control of myself than despising me for being a very bad actor."

Another dialogue with the trio at a tavern in the Waterloo Road:

GUTHRIE: Undoubtedly it is worse to be betrayed by a best friend. If one is betrayed by a casual stranger, one merely loses one's wife. If one is betrayed by one's best friend, one loses one's wife, and one's best friend as well!

RALPH: Ah! (*banging the table*) that's the beauty of the play to me!—the magnificence of its rhetoric. Never mind your psychology. Leave me my "monumental alabaster".

GUTHRIE: You keep your "monumental alabaster". It's your business as an actor to speak the rhetoric. It's my business as director to look after the psychological balance. So we can both be happy!

The muddle of intentions continued, with Richardson still believed to be ignorant of the smiling antics and unconscious—and even conscious—revelations of Iago's love for him, until the first night. It is much more likely that he chose to continue to ignore these excesses, as he preferred to avoid all fuss and confrontation, keeping behind his façade of infallibly courteous rectitude; but inwardly he was insecure about his performance. "The more psychological Iago became, the more embarrassed became poor old Othello," observed Guthrie; "I think a good row might have cleared the air. But everyone behaved too well. Each of us thought that by the next day the clouds of misunderstanding would lift and all would be well. Friendships remained unimpaired but the production was a ghastly, boring hash."*

Agate interred this production. His cruel but highly readable review was headed "Othello without the Moor: Iago takes a holiday". In it he compared Richardson to one Monsieur Talbot of the Comédie-Française, an admirable portrayer of the humble character and the rustic, but who on a visit to London in 1879 was thrust into the part of Théramène, for which he was singularly ill-suited. So courteously did Agate go about his ritual dismemberment ("I am to assure Mr Richardson here that it is as painful for me to write this as it would be for him if he should read it") that one could almost forget he was dealing with a living reputation and a breathing human being. "The pity of it is that this Othello begins and ends so well," he continues, until having cut off all possibility of escape he turns to the kill, even entering, with a touch of devilry, the preserve of Richardson's hobby:

He is like a chauffeur at the starting-handle wrenching his arm off but getting no spark because the engine is so cold. The truth is that Nature, which has showered upon this actor the kindly gifts of the comedian, has unkindly refused him any tragic facilities whatever. His voice has not a tragic note in its whole gamut, all the accents being those of the sweetest reasonableness. He cannot blaze.

*Another less charitable explanation might be that Guthrie's forte was not the well-constructed dramatic masterpiece, though he excelled at the poetic and the spectacular.

He saws away at his nether lip with the enthusiasm of a Queen's Hall fiddler or a maniac reducing a torso to its minimum.'*

Richardson, who as a motorist could dismiss Agate's metaphor as nonsense, meekly agreed, as the actor on the spot, that the description was just. He was perhaps only too ready to admit his shortcomings. Olivier, whose performance was equally scorned by Agate ("a super-subtle dilettante", "as though a light tenor should be cast for the part of Mephistopheles in the opera"), was never going to allow any critic, and certainly not Agate, to dictate to him his limits. He is reputed once to have punched Agate on the nose. But to say Richardson was too deferential is again simplifying a paradox into one broad proposition, though the view was undeniably forming in his own mind that he was not an actor fit for the "first division" and that he rightly belonged in the "doomed second".

Any thoughts he had in that direction must have been bleakly confirmed by his next, almost innocent appearance, for one performance only, as Thomas à Becket at the Irving Centenary Matinée on 23 May 1938. About this Agate wrote that Richardson clearly had not seen anyone's Becket, never mind Irving's. What had happened to all the subtlety and pride, he demanded to know, and how could Richardson hope to replace it by honesty and forthrightness? Of course there were at this matinée none of the elaborate trappings on which Irving relied, such as the hurry music, with its sink and rise, nor the long intervals and elaborately painted sets. The whole occasion was, according to John Gielgud, very ineffective.

*There were, of course, other views: Harcourt Williams judged Richardson's performance as "one of great dignity and restrained power. He did not tear a passion to tatters, but one was never in doubt that a reserve of great power was held in leash. I found his Othello more moving than any I have seen." In 1973 Sybil Thorndike compared Richardson's Othello favourably with Olivier's. ". . . I think Larry missed the deep agony of the part. I don't think he can ever do agony. . . . Now Ralph Richardson can get it. And he did years ago, incidentally, when Larry played a wonderful Iago to him."

18   *The doomed second*

At the beginning of 1939 Richardson's reputation as a stage actor stood lower than it had seven years before, at the end of two excellent seasons at the Vic, the second including an Iago of which he remained justly proud. Being a successful Korda star in his mind never quite counted—the actor in films is "passive material", he was always saying, or, his often quoted, "I don't like my face at all. It's always been a great drawback to me." It was to Priestley that he turned once again, the Priestley on whom Agate, with his ceaseless drumming home of the supremacy of the classics over the contemporary, had pronounced; "Obviously Irving would have ruined a play like, say, *Eden End*; mark, however, that Irving would have remained intact, the only thing in smithereens being Mr Priestley's play."

Priestley's new play for Richardson was a bold experiment for which the author later claimed he was never given enough credit. Presented this time by Basil Dean's own production company, it had begun rehearsals in late 1938. "When he handed me the script of *Johnson over Jordan*," Dean wrote,

> a modern morality, in which the outstanding events in a man's life flit through the middle years of temptation, thence to unsullied youth—a life history in reverse order as it were—I realized that it would afford some opportunities not only for the display of Ralph's gifts, but also give me a chance to resume my experiments in new production methods.

Benjamin Britten was asked to write the incidental music, while the setting, consisting of two cycloramas and a bare stage—revolutionary for the time—was designed by Edward Craig, the son of Gordon.

The small audiences gave the play a standing ovation every night of its three-week run at the New Theatre: much of the stir was caused by the final moments when Johnson, carrying umbrella and briefcase, began his ascent to another world. Here Richardson would turn up his collar and walk out into something quite unknown, very huge and very cold. Britten's thrilling music, added to the blue immensity of Dean's two cycloramas, never failed to bring down the house.

But, for all its innovations in terms of crowd scenes and time-juggling, the script was deficient; the character of Johnson was too generalized for even Ralph to flesh it out with his own idiosyncrasies, although the quality of the music in his voice made Harold Hobson, then a young critic with an attitude to Richardson very different from Agate's, want to cry. Agate, predictably, responded adversely, though not without some grain of sense: "I disliked it not because the presentation was new but because, while pretending to be new, it was, or seemed to be, a mish-mash of *Outward Bound* and *Liliom* done in the demoded Elmer Rice manner."

Perhaps Priestley might have done better by trying to show ordinary qualities through the depiction of an extraordinary man. But the director, author and leading actor were totally committed to the play. When it closed at the New they were determined to move it to a smaller, cheaper Saville theatre, and the owner of the Saville gave them favourable terms. They evolved an experimental contract in which Priestley and Dean each took half-royalty, while Richardson agreed to receive no salary for a certain period and then to split with Priestley on a fifty-fifty basis any receipts over the production costs. The latter rewrote some passages in the play, in particular the Act II scene in Hell, trying to spice it up with some sex. A classic rejoinder to one of his lines came from the Lord Chamberlain's office, to whom the second version of the script was submitted in conformity with the law at the time. The Lord Chamberlain, it seemed, was prepared to issue a licence provided that, on page 15 of Act II, the following words were omitted: "As the bishop said to the actress!"

However, neither Priestley, nor the Saville, nor Richardson tinkering with his own performance, could save *Johnson over Jordan*. After a few weeks, during which Dean began preparing other work, Richardson sank into a state of deep despair. Dean had left behind him a certain residue of ill-feeling because of his obstinacy over changes and his refusal to spend more money out of his own pocket on further rehearsals. After one Wednesday matinée Richardson wrote from Portland Place:

My dear Basil,

I do most urgently beg that you will find time before you go away to help us with our second act. It is terrible as it is—it all wants setting and pulling together—we are sunk unless this is done. You did say you would help us with the alterations we would make. I never wanted help more than now.

I know that you have felt that I have interfered too much—where I have been wrong I am sorry. If I have done or said anything to hurt you I am sorry—if you will let me say so. I have great affection for you personally; anything I have done is for the show, which we are all agreed could be altered for the better, but I have been over anxious and tactless I am afraid, but do not let us have any bad feelings, do forgive us and let us work together and get this second act right.

Yours ever
RALPH RICHARDSON

My voice is simply awful—lord knows how it will be tonight.

Johnson over Jordan also left Priestley pugnacious and hurt in mood, particularly towards Agate with whom he continued a bitter controversy for years. "Pretty stupid remark about the nose," he said of Agate's comment on Richardson's "funny round nose" (viz., "The nose . . . was a considerable handicap in the matter of his Othello, his Iago, his Henry V, and that silly Silent Knight of Humbert Wolfe's").

As for Richardson, he seemed only too painfully aware of his limitations. First there had been the long struggle to win the power of concentration; but now this had been achieved—as painstakingly he wrote out in different coloured inks each part he learned, turning it into a calligraphic marvel in order to focus his attention wholly on the words—he was saddled with a whole new set of difficulties. "To be frank, Richardson has never moved me as an actor. Whereas Irving . . ." Grudgingly, Agate had praised him for the quality of his defects. Like Kean, he said, Richardson could present in coarse form a simple image, but there was "no subtlety of sympathy, no nicety of observation, no variety of expression". He excelled at serving parts, which could be played "without elevation".

THE MICHAEL PARKINSON SHOW (BBC TV), 25 November 1978:

On his entry Richardson is described appropriately, in a paraphrase of the words of the late critic Sir Desmond MacCarthy, as being able as an actor to do what no other actor in the world can do, make a good man interesting; he can do more than that, says Michael Parkinson, the show's compère; he can make him "fascinating, exciting and profoundly moving". (The actual quotation from MacCarthy runs, "Once again [Richardson] shows a rare understanding of human goodness, and a rare restraint in expressing it.") Ignoring this, Richardson eases himself in with the studio audience, consisting largely of North Country people, as if lowering himself slowly into a swimming pool of indeterminate temperature, evaluating the effect on every inch of his skin. "Three or four hundred good wishes to all of you—well—I have to go now," he says confidentially, turning round to face Parkinson.

The other guest on the show is Barry Sheene, the world's champion motorcyclist. Richardson is entirely at his ease with him. He finds motor-bike talk fascinating and slips easily into the mood of innocent sharp brightness set by Sheene, who tells vividly of his near-fatal crashes ("Travelling at 140 miles an hour, I hit a concrete curb with my knee: sometimes it gets to you a little bit . . . if I'd got thrown up in the air I'd have been history").

Speaking of risk, Richardson starts telling Parkinson, in his most benign manner, that he would not like to be an interviewer:

RICHARDSON: I think you have the most dangerous job in the world.

PARKINSON   (*after a few moments of being submerged in confusion, resurfaces—this is all conducted with good humour, with much laughter at Richardson's unexpected sally*):   You're a marvellous interviewee—even if you do tend to take over. You have to have confidence.

RICHARDSON: I haven't come here to do your job. You're wonderful at it.

PARKINSON   (*turning the tables*):   Do you really lack confidence, is that what you're saying?

RICHARDSON   (*guard dropped, as if one has got very near to him—though it will soon be seen to be only an illusion*):   Yes . . . mmm . . . I think I do . . . a bit, yes, mmm.

PARKINSON: In what way?

RICHARDSON: Well I don't know . . . I do rather lack confidence, I think . . . I don't lack it always, or I wouldn't be able to do my job. . . .

Everyone edges forward in his seat in expectation that this sudden baring of the heart will continue. This is television at its most unrestricted: a gladiatorial medium for raw sights of action or the inner man. Richardson without a flicker of change in his expression or a modification of tempo, goes on: "I was driving along at 85 miles an hour, rather fast for me. . . . I felt very confident. . . . And the whole thing happened very . . . I had a wheel wobble. . . . Have you ever heard of a wheel wobble? . . . A wheel wobble is simply . . . Have you ever had a wheel wobble?" The audience, far from feeling cheated as they well might at total evasion, are delighted at the sleight of hand, and rock with laughter and recognition as they realize they are now back to Barry Sheene and dangerous moments. Also Richardson's comic sense of timing is masterly: he underplays the last line, as if in refrain, "Rather brought my confidence down as a matter of fact."

Having set the carefree tone, as well as the range, Richardson feels safe. He goes on to tell of his flying experiences ("But where I have got a lot of confidence is in the air . . . when I came down to ground, the aircraft fell to bits . . ."), to being a super-salesman for Concorde ("It takes off twice"), and then indirectly, but now very much on his own terms, back to acting ("I'm still learning, thank God, otherwise I'd cut my throat. You learn to explore yourself as a writer learns to balance and explore his vocabulary").

Now, having done what everyone wants of him, which is to talk about his work—to give the viewer a privileged peep behind the curtain—he can withdraw the privilege. He starts on Parkinson again, asking him about the music and cricket writer Neville Cardus, with whom Parkinson worked on the *Guardian*, and about cricket. Parkinson responds, gives him his head, then in a little while coming back to acting. Richardson pays a warm-hearted tribute to Priestley. Here again he seems to lower his guard and to show vulnerable inner feeling—"I like him very much." Parkinson sees his chance. "Why do you like him?" Bland, put-down reply: "Well, he's a Yorkshireman!" Delighted laughter from North Country audience.

Skilfully, one might even say doggedly, Parkinson keeps at it. This may well be one of the best interviews of his long career: instructive, revealing—up to a point; wildly entertaining. He draws Richardson away again from motor bikes, back to his peers. After establishing that Laurence Olivier and Richardson both had bikes during the war, Parkinson prompts Richardson to tell how he has taken John Gielgud on his pillion: "I don't think he likes it. He didn't like it. He's not a car or bike man." The interviewer sees his opportunity:

PARKINSON: What's the difference between your acting and Gielgud's?

RICHARDSON: I'd say he's a much better actor than I am. I admire him so much, his range is enormous. Richard II, Richard III* . . . he's a great speaker, the finest speaker of verse in the world today.

PARKINSON: Aren't there parts that he can't play that you could?

RICHARDSON: Well I wouldn't like to talk about that. So complex . . . let's talk about motor bikes.

PARKINSON: Stop looking at your watch.

19   *One woe upon another's heals*

At the beginning of 1940, as World War II began, Kit Richardson moved to The Old Cottage, Wivelsfield, East Sussex, with Hugh and Violet Pearson who had now been living with her and taking care of her for 11 years. For some time the more active symptoms of sleeping sickness had

*In fact Gielgud seems never to have played Richard III.

been dormant, and she had been able to care for herself. Unlike many other sufferers from the disease, she had not been isolated. She looked younger than her years, half sleeping and dreaming her way through life, half claimed already by another world. Richardson, by then in the Royal Naval Volunteer Reserve, saw her regularly.

It was in early 1942, on one of his trips either to or from Wivelsfield, that he had the near-fatal crash he was to describe some 36 years later on the Parkinson show. He was riding a big Harley Davidson and wore goggles and a service cap (crash helmets were not then compulsory). About a mile from his wife's cottage he was travelling so fast the bike got into a speed wobble. ("Have you ever heard of a wheel wobble . . . a wheel wobble is simply . . . have you ever had a wheel wobble . . ."). Then, as John Burrell (who later joined him to help run the Old Vic company) wrote, "not long afterwards came the smash which projected him on a parabolic curve that hit the ground forty feet away and desposited him on his head with a force that would have killed a lesser actor" (or, presumably, man). He lay by the roadside stunned and barely breathing. Some minutes later a member of the wartime Reserve Police Force found him and summoned an ambulance. Richardson was rushed off to hospital at Haywards Heath, and from there, still unconscious, transferred to Southampton. The policeman (by coincidence he was the father of the actor Donald Sinden, then beginning his own theatrical career) had the onerous task of pushing Richardson's heavy bike to safety.

Richardson's recovery was slow and he remained in hospital for several weeks. Kit was able to visit him there. "I've been very close to death," he said later. "It's like dropping into an abyss—very drowsy, rather nice." (And, after an even greater lapse of time, to Parkinson: "I was in hospital for quite a long time. Rather brought my confidence down as a matter of fact.")

Later in 1942, on 3 September, Kit Richardson went to call on her doctor, C. F. J. Smith, in Haywards Heath, complaining of intense pain in the back; this was diagnosed as a lumbar puncture, signalling a turn for the worse in her post-encephalitic condition. The pain did not respond to treatment and when on 9 September, her thirty-fifth birthday, she called on Dr Smith a second time, she felt more desperate. Her state was exacerbated by the onset of compulsive and involuntary movement, and she asked to be taken into Hurstwood Park Hospital.

Kit had gradually been growing weaker, and recently the Pearsons had had to extricate her from difficult positions —Violet often had to help her when she had fallen. By now the whole muscular system of the body had become rigid and she had difficulty in making certain movements, such as dressing, owing to stiffness. Dr Smith, who had treated Kit for three years, diagnosed that the disease had again entered an acute phase, and told Richardson when he visited her in hospital, that "we can't do any more for her."

On 3 October Dr Smith discharged her from hospital. She seemed in reasonable spirits, appearing to the doctor generally alert and plucky, though occasionally depressed. However, on the following day, Monday, 4 October, she again felt very low and told Violet that she did not think she could bear the pain any longer. In the evening she complained of feeling sick and went upstairs early to bed. Violet stayed with her until 10 p.m. and then said goodnight and left her listening to the wireless.

Kit was more helpless in bed than elsewhere and if she slipped into an uncomfortable position, had to be lifted up. She was particularly sensitive to draughts, and often wore a scarf in bed. When Violet came in to see her the next morning at 7.15, she found her almost on her face in bed. The light was still on from the previous evening. The pillow was rather high, and her head was pressed back, her face being buried in the pillow, her arms folded under her chest. As the *Mid-Sussex Times* reported later (14 October 1942), a soft scarf of red silk was tied round her neck with a half-knot, directly over her thyroid, and had seemingly caught on the bedpost. There was a slight swelling above the scarf. She had apparently suffocated.

At the subsequent inquest Violet and Hugh Pearson,

P.C. Jeremiah Coghlan (who had been summoned to The Old Cottage), and the doctor all gave evidence, attesting to Kit's great courage. "Taking it all round," Violet Pearson said, "she was wonderfully cheerful." The Coroner, E. F. Hoare, observed, on being told that on her return from hospital Kit had declared she wanted to kill herself, that "she had talked rather wildly under the influence of great pain", but that he did not attach importance to it. He recorded a verdict of death by misadventure.

On Friday, 8 October 1942, the funeral service took place in the simple Norman church at Wivelsfield. Many of Kit's and Ralph's friends from London were present. Richardson himself attended in naval uniform. Following the service, interment took place in Wivelsfield churchyard, among box cypresses and cedars of Lebanon, with a fine view over the valley.

Richardson had specified a simple gravestone. On one side was engraved, "In Loving Memory Muriel Richardson 9 September 1907–4 October 1942". On the other, bordered by Plantagenet roses and leaves carved in the stone, was the simple epitaph:

A

LOVING WIFE

A

CHARMING ACTRESS

Kit's last appearance on stage had been with Ralph in *Yellow Sands* at the Haymarket Theatre nearly 14 years before.

TWO

Middle Layers

1942–1949

Some months after our first meeting, having duly digested all he has lent me, I return to Chester Terrace. This time a cheerful housekeeper opens the doors and says, "Sir Ralph's in his study." She motions me towards the lift, a novel way to make my ascent of the three flights. Richardson greets me on the landing, a mischievous grin on his face.

"Out of breath? Quite a climb, isn't it?"

We go into his study and he bids me be seated. He offers coffee with transparent crystals of pale brown sugar in a silver bowl. I tell him I have written a synopsis, which I am about to hand over to the possible publisher.

"Read it to me," he says.

I hesitate, taken aback. This is the last thing I have expected. But there's no escape. I begin by reading my introduction. My heart is in my mouth.

"Sir Ralph Richardson, who was knighted before Laurence Olivier and before John Gielgud, has been a pillar of the English theatre for over four decades. All through his varied career he has moved uncannily onwards, not without setbacks, to determine a shape to his professional achievements which few in any walk of life can rival, and even to this day he continues to ripen, expanding both in uniqueness and eccentricity. While the peaks of tragic drama eluded him . . ."

At this point I feel somewhat weak at the knees, and stop for breath, snatching a look at Richardson. But he sits quite still, unruffled. I clearly haven't offended him yet.

". . . for as Tynan has written, 'his voice is most delicate; breathlight of texture . . . a yeasty, agile voice. Where

Olivier would pounce upon a line and rip its heart out, Richardson skips and lilts and bounces along it, shaving off pathos of great flakes,' he still is arguably the greatest poetic actor alive, successfully conveying what he has called 'the theatre's most powerful asset, a sense of mystery'. His most famous roles divide almost equally between the classical and commercial theatre: Dr Clitterhouse in *The Amazing Dr Clitterhouse*, Charles Appleby in *Eden End*, Peer Gynt, Falstaff, Dr Sloper in *The Heiress*, from James's *Washington Square*, the Father in *Six Characters in Search of an Author*, Cherry in *Flowering Cherry*, Jack in *Home*, John Gabriel Borkman, Hirst in *No Mans Land*.''

The going is easier here: but I wonder how he will react to the next bit. I take another good breath and proceed:

"Behind the hundreds of film and theatre roles Richardson has played lies a complex, many-faceted individual, one side cultivatedly bluff, another, paradoxically, almost spectrally distant. At various times no one could be more genuinely shy, more artful at self-concealment, more innocent, warm, and revealing, or more cold and ruthless. Perhaps he has in him much of Ibsen's character Peer Gynt."

Not a flicker. I begin my chronological synopsis. Birth. Family background. How the shadows of his first marriage are all the more deep and moving in contrast to the buoyancy, the astuteness, the luck. How he was born a Sagittarian, an expansive sign, denoting an exploring and adventurous spirit. Sagittarians were supposed to have a hearty handshake, slap their cards on the table, but tended to be euphoric.

As I read on I gain more confidence; delivering the whole 14-page synopsis takes roughly half an hour. All the while Richardson has been listening attentively, puffing at his pipe, and every now and again either nodding or making a small comment on detail.

"Always interesting in the beginning—the expectation

—the obstacles," he says when I have finished. I see that he views the whole prospect with complete objectivity, or at least this is how it appears. He has eaten and digested his own myth. Narrative is his prime concern. "It's the later period that worries me."

He then abruptly changes the subject and tells me about the progress being made with Storey's play *Early Days*. He begins reading from the part he hopes to play: "'I was remembering my childhood a moment ago. One's childhood is the profoundest of one's life; after that comes anti-climax. After the age of twenty-one nothing happens again.'" He turns over some more pages of the text and takes another passage: "'Travelling broadens the mind . . . [No] it narrows it. Jesus never travelled; not more than a hundred miles; Michelangelo, Rembrandt, Milton: they are people who made a journey of scarcely any consequence at all and subsequently never travelled further. Travel is for people without imagination: dullards, clods; those who need to animate the landscape otherwise they see nothing there at all.'"

"It might make an ending for you—if it comes off," he adds, returning at last to the synopsis.

20   *Parachute Maintenance Officers ahoy*

The eve of the outbreak of World War II, 2 September 1939, had found Richardson dining at his club with Gielgud and Agate's secretary, Jock Dent, discussing what an actor would be most likely to keep when ordered to the front:

"His bibelots and bric-à-brac, his Matthew Smiths," noted Agate in *Ego 4*, "all these may go up in smoke—excuse the wartime metaphor!—but not his uniquely valuable possession, his book of old press notices."

Neither actor was ordered to the front, but Gielgud joined ENSA, the Entertainments National Service Association directed by Basil Dean, and with Beatrice Lillie toured garrison theatres in Noël Coward's *Fumed Oak*. Richardson attended one of ENSA's first concerts, in October 1939, and wrote to Dean, "though regrettably not with us yourself, your wizardly touch was felt by me, in the organization with which your people folded themselves up and stole away not in silence, but with cheers and thunderous applause."

Richardson himself had a quiet war. He joined the Royal Naval Volunteer Reserve in Eastleigh with the acting rank of sub-lieutenant, moving about later to other south coast stations. In the service he took up painting again, making friends with L. A. Hart, known as "Boy", who also painted. Before the war Hart had been a solicitor, and after it entered the banking profession. Later the pair shared a studio in a mews off Harley Street. In 1940 they had the job of looking after the secret files at Eastleigh: "Secret books," said Richardson, "sounded exciting, romantic, perhaps they might even be a little naughty." During the threat of invasion they had to prepare to destroy these valuable documents by fire. "Our little community regarded our activities at the incinerator with acute interest. We were like the little couple in a Swiss barometer, popping in and out to indicate 'wet' or 'fine'." Grim-faced, laden with volumes, they would lurch towards the incinerator; a few hours later they could be seen, "taking all the books out of the furnace with fatuous grins on our faces."

Later Richardson was promoted to the rank of naval commander and worked in the Admiral's office at Lee-on-the-Solent. There he served successively under Admirals Bell-Davis, VC, Dennis Boyd, later Second Sea Lord, and C. B. Robinson. Richardson was put in charge of aircraft movements and would allot aircraft to stations as they came off the line. On the wall he had a big board and was able to evolve his own operational system. As a perk, or reward, he could fly from time to time to the stations to check on progress.

The flying put danger in his path. His first mission was to carry a wireless telegraphist 200 miles on a North course. But navigation was not his strong point: when the time came to make his turn the sun was dead low on the horizon and he couldn't see a thing. On this occasion he and the passenger got safely back, the Blackburn Shark almost nosing, as he put it, "her own way back to the stable." At other times he was less lucky, acquiring the nickname "Pranger" Richardson, until the toll became so great the Navy was only too happy to let him go. According to John Burrell, he survived "several Walruses . . . an Albatross." In May 1940 he made a forced landing on Nora Baddeley Common in Hampshire, climbed out of his plane and was faced by villagers who were armed with shotguns, scythes and clubs. "I was very lucky not to be killed," he said. "I had some narrow escapes. Old planes, especially the Albacores, just falling to bits . . . one burst into flames just after I landed." The worst that happened was that he tore a little rent in his trousers.

He couldn't be prevailed upon to stop. Flying held as strong a romantic appeal as ever: before the war he had owned a Gypsy Moth. Motion brought an intoxication, one went faster in bursts, like a daring amateur—speed was still a gentlemanly pursuit for those so inclined. In the Strand one day he bumped into an old friend, Jeffrey Quill, a test pilot but recently assigned to work in the Admiralty. Richardson asked how he was getting on. "Oh," Quill told him, "I don't know, not very well—I'm no good without my daily fright."

Richardson was also parachute maintenance officer. Olivier, who had been in the States but had now returned, was posted to Worthy Down in May 1941, and Richardson was instrumental in having him, too, appointed Parachute Officer. After Olivier had been in the job a while Richard-

son, the senior, thought he would go and see how his old
friend was getting on.

I had not seen him for a while, not since his recent
promotion to Lieutenant. He looked fine, his natural
perquisite of good looks went well with his uniform. The
uniform was perfect: it looked as if it had been worn long
on arduous service but had kept its cut. The gold wings
on his sleeve had no distasteful glitter; only the shoes
shone. The hair under his cap had a touch of debonair
cheek, being perhaps a quarter of an inch longer than the
dead correct. His manner was Naval, it was quiet, alert,
businesslike, with the air of there being a joke somewhere around. . . .

Parachutes need to be unpacked from time to time and
hung up; the big white silk canopies with white silken
cords hang limp and motionless from rafters in the tower,
taking their air—they are strangely beautiful. Later,
they are taken down and laid upon the long, narrow,
green-topped tables, where the workers, in overalls, fold
them, with the help of wooden spatulas, into their packs.
This work must be very carefully and precisely done: it
could take me the best part of an hour to pack one, for I
had to learn how it was done. They must so lie in a small
space as to be ready, at an instant, to spring out into
life-giving embrace. . . .

Lieutenant Olivier's parachute section was clean as
well as being quiet, I found no fault at all; it surprised me
that he had, in so short a time, got such a hand of the
work, but what surprised me more was the way he had
with the workers . . . as we went round he spoke to
Wrens and seamen and sometimes introduced me, he
never made a mistake, and in this case most were in
overalls with no distinction showing.

This little tour over, Richardson took his leave. "I walked a
little way down the asphalt path," he said, "stopped and
looked back at the building. 'Larry did that very well
indeed,' I said to myself; I walked on. Then a thought
crossed my mind: 'I wonder if he rehearsed it?'"

At other times the two men would, as when younger, go drinking together. Both had been discouraged from taking a more active role in the war, and both were pretty fed up. One night they drank rather too much and decided to call on Frank Duncan, who was acting in *Night Must Fall* at Winchester. They tried to get on to the stage and had to be gently dissuaded, causing a stir backstage. Richardson looked genuinely aggrieved when told of this many years later by Duncan on a chance meeting at the BBC Television Centre. "Of course Laurence never had a head for drink," he told Duncan. "I think he looked up to me. I was his senior. He came up to me one day and said, 'The trouble with you, Ralph, is that you can't hold your liquor.' And he fell flat on his face." Richardson then demonstrated how, falling flat on his face in the bar where he was talking to Duncan.

Not only was Richardson growing restless—he, too, like Jeffrey Quill, needed his daily fright.

21 *Admirals and arc lights*

Korda was very generous to Richardson during the war, keeping him on half-salary, as his RNVR pay was £38 a month, and later refusing when Ralph offered to repay him.

The two film roles Richardson played just prior to the war had been among his best. In *Q Planes* (1939), as Major Hammond, the master spy, of uniquely eccentric but fundamentally British traits, he was unrivalled, even by Olivier, who played the dashing test pilot. The performance was bursting with wonderful comic exuberance, both in the Thirties jargon whose delivery Richardson had perfected, and in elaborate Tati-like flourishes of stage business. "Would you like your whisky neat?" someone asks. "Very neat," he replies. And on introducing the test pilot: "Come and meet Blenkinsop—he's a perfect swine."

In *The Four Feathers* (also filmed in 1939, but not seen on general release until after the war), Richardson played the equally English though very different Major Durrance, who defined as had Hammond in *Q Planes* a fundamental heroic spirit on the eve of the war. It needed, perhaps, a foreigner like Korda to distil the essence of being British; as R. C. Sherriff, whom Korda set to work adapting *The Four Feathers* for the screen, wrote in his autobiography, *No Leading Lady* (1968), "He had decided to be an Englishman, and wanted to find out everything he ought to know." *The Four Feathers* was Korda's exhortation to the English to be brave. The sequence in which Durrance goes blind in the fierce Sudan sun and is led to safety, after the massacre of his company, by Captain Faversham (played by John Clements) disguised as a mute native slave, has something almost abstract about its resonance. If human will as Schopenhauer defined it is the strong blind man carrying on his shoulders the lame man who can see, in this case the mutilated coward Faversham is keeping the blind and suicidal man alive to prove his ultimate courage. As a character remarks elsewhere in the film: "There's no place in England for a coward."

The film critic C. A. Lejeune recalled visiting Richardson one afternoon at Denham, when he was making *The Four Feathers*:

> While the big blue cyclorama was being lit for Durrance's blind scene, he showed me a picture postcard from his friend Olivier.
> Olivier was playing on the New York stage, commuting at weekends to California, where Vivien Leigh was at work on *Gone with the Wind*. . . . He sounded light-

hearted and gay, and urged Ralph to come out and enjoy the climate and the absurd luxury of Hollywood.

I asked him if he meant to go, and he replied firmly in the negative.

Subsequently Richardson, in the extended process of cooling his heels in the Naval Reserve, engaged in what were more specifically propaganda exercises: as the Wing Commander in *The Lion has Wings* (1939), which Korda without any government aid completed in less than two months by cashing in his life-insurance policies, and which apparently made Hitler threaten to bomb Denham studios; in Thorold Dickinson's *The Next of Kin* (1942); as the Narrator in *The Biter Bit* (1943). He also made two films with naval subjects: *The Silver Fleet* (1943), about the Dutch Navy, in which he played Jaap Van Leydon, a hero of the Dutch underground; and *The Volunteer*, a Ministry of Information film shot in the Mediterranean, in which he played "himself". This last was shown to the Lords of the Admiralty in the tiny cinema under Admiralty Arch, with Richardson in attendance, together with Michael Powell who had directed the film, and Emeric Pressburger, who had written the script. Richardson commented on the response:

> They sat through it in silence, after which the Sea Lord got up and—while we had stood up to be presented —walked straight past us in silence . . . not a word . . . till he came to the exit door by the projectionist's box. He stopped. In his glass box the projectionist, rather a naughty chap, pulling faces, cigarette dangling from mouth, was winding the film back by hand. The Sea Lord spots him and goes straight over. "Very fine," he says, "wonderful film—congratulations," and shakes him warmly by the hand. I think he thought the projectionist had done the whole damn thing.

He also joined, early in 1943, in an impressive display of solidarity with the Soviet Union, a salute to the Red Army. In the Albert Hall, against a huge formalized backdrop of

Stalingrad, Lieutenant Laurence Olivier, RNVR, began with a stirring speech from Eisenstein's film *Alexander Nevsky*. This was followed by the Royal Choral Society singing the "Volga Boat Song". John Gielgud, as the voice of Radio Moscow, delivered a panegyric to the heroic defenders of Stalingrad. Powerful arc lights criss-crossing from the domed ceiling picked out the face of Lieutenant-Commander Richardson. He wore a gold costume, a high-peaked helmet and his face was covered in thick gold paint, hiding the scar of his motor-bike accident of the year before.

> Come up here, you seamen of Britain—
> You who have kept the route open to Russia,
> You who deliver the goods

A single rank of merchant seamen filed down to form a blue line across the mighty arena; they were joined by naval ratings in arctic equipment. Richardson hailed them: "Ahoy there Jack!"

"Ahoy," answered one, played by John Laurie.

"Everything under control sir."

"Right. Steer to close."

CHESTER TERRACE, *9 October 1979:*

> PLAYER: We're *actors*—we're the opposite of people! . . .
> Think of the most . . . *private* . . . *secret* . . . *intimate*
> thing you have ever done secure in the knowledge of
> its privacy. . . . *Well, I saw you do it!*
> TOM STOPPARD, *Rosencrantz and Guildenstern are*
> *Dead*

The synopsis is duly presented to the publisher, a most
genial and courteous man. "Ralph's main fear," he im-
parts, "is that he has had a dull life and is not interesting to
write about." He suggests I write a chapter or two, as a
sample "to show to Ralph."

The subject chosen for the sample is the Old Vic seasons
at the New Theatre, 1944–9. Richardson consents to be
questioned directly. At his house a few days later, I start
with a general enquiry. He begins: "Tony Guthrie, who
had run the Vic through all of the war, wanted to step
down, so he wanted me to come along, you know, be a
daddy. I had worked with Guthrie before the war as
Bottom in *A Midsummer Night's Dream* and we got on
well. But there was a snag. I was still in the Fleet Air Arm
and I'd made my contract with them for the term of the
war. . . ."

In talking of himself Richardson is careful and selective;
he fluctuates between two forms of self-presentation: either
he is ordinary, prosaic, with much the same feelings as
everyone else; or he is eccentric and sees the humorous
sides of a situation. There is never any reference made to
motive, and revelation of what might have been driving
him, of ambitions yet unfulfilled, of ideas or plans being
laid down for his return from service into civilian life, of
contacts being maintained or parts being read.

Above all he keeps the canvas of self-representation a
small one: it is as if he likes to look at himself through the
large end of a telescope, as if, if he were to catch a glimpse
of his full size, he might shy away. Other accounts of him
always loom twenty times the size of his own. But he has

always had a dark side, and has admitted on occasions to being "a very cross man". Again, he compares Gielgud favourably with himself: "I can never get him to lose his temper." He has never gone along much with Freud, as witness his Othello: in Tynan's *New Yorker* profile he is quoted on the subject: "I've always been intrigued by [Freud's] picture of life—the sex down here, the caretaker up here. But I wouldn't put sex ace high, not the thing that winds up the whole clock. I think murder is more basic. Before you get the woman, you must kill the man who possesses her."

Sensing that his mood is relaxed and co-operative, I now begin recording his words in a notebook:

"'I'm not going to ask to leave the navy,' I said to Guthrie. 'If you'd like to ask for me, that's a different matter—'"

At this point he turns to me. "Remember," he says, his eyes lighting up with humour, "the Japs had not yet been beaten and, you never know, they might still have wanted to kill the Emperor of Japan. But they were glad to let me go."

The tone becomes higher, almost unearthly. "They had a lot of younger men coming along now. . . ."

22   *Gathering up the threads*

> All the time I told myself . . . if I came through I was going to
> make up for lost time.
>
> TREVOR HOWARD

In the 1930s Richardson had been making progress towards
the summit of his powers and his achievements, but every
time it looked to be within his grasp, he seemed to lose his
way or mistake his own dimension. Now, suddenly the
mists cleared. Instead of seeing around him the same
landscape as before, he found himself resting on the very
peak, all he ever wanted within his grasp. From an actor of
solid middle rank he passed in the next two years into
undisputed joint leader of the theatrical world. The man
responsible for his appointment at the Old Vic, and who
aided him to secure his new eminence, was as much potential enemy as friend: Tyrone Guthrie.

When, early in 1944, Guthrie had approached Richardson to lead the Old Vic company, Richardson said the Old
Vic should ask the Sea Lords to release him. He also
wanted Olivier to join him in running the Vic. (He asked
Gielgud, but Gielgud declined the invitation.) Lord Lytton, the agreeable and partly deaf chairman of the Vic's
Board of Governors, a descendant of the Victorian novelist
Bulwer-Lytton, wrote to the Admiralty pointing out the
indispensability to the theatre of the two men, and their
outstanding reputations, and saying how important they
could be to the rehabilitation of the Old Vic which he hoped
would be regarded as nationally important. The Sea Lords
raised no objection, releasing both of them with an alacrity,
Olivier commented, which was almost hurtful. After the
number of written-off or badly damaged old planes attri-
butable to the pair, the Navy seemed only too relieved to
see the backs of them.

Meanwhile on the personal front, with the trauma of
Kit's death and his own near-fatal motor-bike crash reced-
ing into the past, Richardson had remarried. At noon on 26
January 1944, in the Chelsea Register Office, he and Meriel

Forbes were married, with his wartime companion Boy Hart and his wife as witnesses. The wedding was widely reported in the press, pictures of the bride showing a slim and attractive young woman—Mu was thirty years old—of petite, even French appearance. Similarities were inevitably noted between her and Kit: both were good at detail, commonsensical, slight of build; both, coincidentally, born under the sign of Virgo. Mu, having been an actress for more than ten years, knew the theatre backwards and accepted its demands. Her background recalled strikingly that of Priscilla, wife of the great actor John Philip Kemble. Kemble's niece Fanny said of Priscilla, that she was "quick, keen, clever and shrewd . . . with the air and address of a finished woman of the world". In particular she was of amenable disposition, willing to submerge her own interests in those of her husband. This became true of Mu as she grew to respect and protect Richardson's needs.

When they were married Mu was about to open in *A Soldier for Christmas* by Reginald Beckwith, at Wyndham's. When she did, in the following month, Beverley Baxter devoted a whole column in the *Evening Standard* to her playing of the housemaid Milly Smith. Later in the year *A Soldier for Christmas* became one of the first productions to tour Europe. It stopped off at Dieppe and Rouen, where with the front line only 26 miles away, some performances were given without electricity.

To help him and Olivier run the Old Vic, Richardson had requested a third person, John Burrell. After training with Michel Saint-Denis before the war, Burrell had joined the BBC. There he had worked on the 1943 radio production of Ibsen's *Peer Gynt* which Guthrie directed, with Richardson as Peer. The broadcast had been Richardson's largest dramatic effort during his years in the RNVR; it therefore came as no surprise when, with Burrell and Guthrie as part of his production team at the Old Vic, he chose *Peer Gynt* as the first play of the 1944 season.

Burrell, a good ten years younger than Richardson or Olivier, might well be thought of as a Lepidus figure to their

Antony and/or Octavius, unable to stand up against the powerful personalities of the other two. "He hadn't got the guns," someone said of him: a "very good office boy", or the "timekeeper", as he was variously labelled; it was far from the truth.

Burrell was steely-willed, ambitious. As a small boy he had caught polio; with irons on one leg, a surgical boot on the foot of the other, he hobbled along on two sticks. "You never thought of him as a cripple," observed Kate Ashbury, his former secretary. He would pull himself up ladders, or hoist himself on to the stage to give notes, by the strength of his forearms alone. He had Scotch-blonde hair, a crumpled pinkish face with a broken nose. Sometimes, to younger members of the company, or to the office staff, he could be a fearful practical joker. In the triumvirate he was in fact the pivotal pin on which the larger-than-life pair turned.

Richardson and Olivier already had a rich and compatible friendship: they had known one another since April 1926, nearly twenty years; they were equals; they greatly respected one another. "I wasn't greedy, nor was Laurence," explained Richardson, "so we balanced everything out well." They still kept up their wonderful high-spiritedness together. ("My dear old Cocky," effused Olivier on Richardson's seventieth birthday, "I wish I could convey my feeling of warmth and surge of gratitude . . . gratitude of marvellous friendship.")

The three directors were full of excitement when they met together at Denham to discuss plans for the Old Vic. Before their eyes, in the office, was stretched the model of the Globe Theatre in 1589 surrounded by whole areas of Shakespeare's London which Olivier was using as the basic setting for *Henry V*, which he had been filming, on leave from the Navy, when the Old Vic invitation came.

King Henry V was not a part he had looked forward in the slightest to playing, until he received some invaluable advice from Richardson. This advice, showing as he said "Ralphie's gift for summarization", he was now busy putting into effect. It stemmed from Richardson's own experience in the part 14 years earlier: Henry, he noted, "you might say was a cold bath king, that he was a scoutmaster, yes. But you must remember he is the *exaltation* of scoutmasters." No phrase describes better Olivier's great performance in the film.

At later meetings of the triumvirate, Richardson used to take Burrell's two sons in his grey Rolls for a spin round the block by the Mercury Theatre (the Burrells lived opposite), while Burrell and Olivier got down to serious discussion. But plans were slow to materialize. By the middle of April 1944 they still had no theatre, for the Old Vic had been damaged in the war, and Bronson Albery had not taken kindly to the suggestion that the company should take over his New Theatre. Burrell wrote to Guthrie how "pretty nebulous" it all seemed and asked, "Are we and the scheme more important to the Vic than Bronnie?" They had not been able to get CEMA's attitude into focus (CEMA, the Council for the Encouragement of Music and the Arts, forerunner of the present-day Arts Council, had intimated that it might risk £5,000). He could not ascertain what the attitude of the other Governors would be if Albery were to resign from the Old Vic Board.

Richardson was crucial to subsequent developments. He had just the right way of dealing with Albery, who had been left the New Theatre by his mother and who was a firebrand of the old school, shrewd, ruthless and fairly eccentric. Richardson's pocket diary for 12 May 1944 has two entries —entries of any kind being rare. "Commission resigned. Lunch with Bronson Albery." Even though Albery agreed to go along he was dubious about the triumvirate's long-term plans, remarking ominously, "I have earned a good deal of money for the Old Vic, but now they're going to lose it all."

The company they picked was a strong one, in spite of subsequent charges to the contrary. Wisely they left out Vivien Leigh, by now married to Olivier but subject to nervous crises, and in any case heavily committed to film-making. She had been turned down by Guthrie earlier in the war when she had wanted to work for the Vic, on the grounds that the Vic was a repertory company and (according to her biographer Anne Edwards) because her "star status would off-balance the productions". Instead Richardson and Olivier had a remarkable notion of where to look for a leading lady. They would telephone their old headmaster to see if he had any ideas.

"I think there might be," answered Sir Barry Jackson, to the question they put. They set out at once and drove to Birmingham, parking their car opposite the theatre and walking round to the stage door in Hurst Street. Immediately they set foot in the theatre they bumped into Martha Jordan ("Jordie") the last old usherette of the pre-war rep. "You boys have done well for yourselves," she greeted them, and showed them to their seats. They had come to see *Six Characters in Search of an Author* which had the seventeen-year-old Margaret Leighton playing the Stepdaughter. H. K. Ayliff was the Producer, portraying himself with a delicious sense of mischief, moving furniture round the set in meticulous fashion, as he did in real life. (Of Leighton and Ayliff, Paul Scofield recalled, "Hers was a formidable combination of talent and beauty. I think she assimilated from H.K. a kind of female version of his towering qualities and his authority.") Richardson and Olivier sat two-thirds of the way back in the house seats. The auditorium was by no means full, those who were there apparently more intent on craning their heads round to watch the distinguished visitors than on following Margaret Leighton.

Afterwards Richardson and Olivier went round to Jackson's offices on the first floor over the stage door. Margaret Leighton was told to take off her make-up and come downstairs. When she did they told her they could offer her a place in the Old Vic company, and the parts of Raina in *Arms and the Man* and the Green Woman in *Peer Gynt*, at a salary of £17 a week. She thought this was spectacular and could not believe her luck. After they had returned to London she walked along the footbridge over New Street Station: "I walked over saying to myself out loud, 'I'm going to London, I'm going to London!'" Someone heard her, and called out "Platform five, dearie."

Besides Leighton, they succeeded in engaging Sybil Thorndike, who with her great prestige and her experience of the Old Vic in its halcyon pre-war days became, like Richardson, a figurehead for the company, and the Irish-born Joyce Redman, to form an irresistible trio of leading ladies. Also from the pre-war Old Vic came their old director, Harcourt Williams, though now as an actor. And despite the wartime dearth of male actors—there were, according to Kenneth Tynan (also from Birmingham), only two kinds available: the elderly, suffering from thyroid deficiency, and the very young, affected in the opposite way—the company included Nicholas "Beau" Hannen, George Relph, Michael Warre, Peter Copley, Sydney Tafler and Frank Duncan.

23 *The cryptic as king*

In June 1944, in a large empty hall in the National Gallery —stripped of its paintings which lay safely hidden in the Cheddar caves—the Old Vic company assembled for the first time. The hall was poor in acoustics but equipped with rostra and a supply of useful props; the New Theatre round the corner, the company's ultimate home, was still full of the Old Vic Opera's scenery. Younger members were agreeably surprised to find themselves warmly greeted —"I'm Richardson," "I'm Olivier"—by the two senior directors, who were approachable and quickly became popular with the rank and file. War had been in terms of the star system a leveller. Tony Guthrie started by showing the scenery changes for *Peer Gynt* on a model stage.

The company's initial euphoria was short-lived, for on 14 June the first V1 flying bomb fell on London, to be followed by 8,000 more V1s and V2s. Of 36 shows open at the time, all closed except Ronald Millar's *Zero Hour*, about D-Day, which opened on 14 June, took £9 and closed on the 17th. Reactions of the cast rehearsing *Peer Gynt* varied between merest hesitation, as a flying bomb passed overhead, to utter panic, as actors took shelter under tables when one seemed to be heading straight for them. Burrell, undaunted and brave, would forge, amid total desolation, a slow and painful progress up St Martin's Lane, unheeding of the wardens' cries to make for the nearest shelter. Richardson and Olivier were observed by Diana Boddington, the stage manager, never to duck or flinch. "It was shaming," wrote Guthrie, "how relieved we all felt when a bang, and the ensuing shattering of timbers and glass, would proclaim that someone else had 'had' it."

Arms and the Man, directed by John Burrell, his professional début as a stage director as well as for the company, opened in Manchester in late August, enabling the company to play itself in and gain confidence before the London season began with *Peer Gynt*. Before the company left London it nearly lost Joyce Redman, who was cast as Louka in the Shaw play, and as Solveig. Being young and inexperienced, she had prayed for some release from the terror of two consecutive first nights opposite, first, the daunting Olivier as Sergius Saranoff, then the equally daunting Richardson as Peer Gynt. While walking in Croydon on the way to her home, a flying bomb fell only feet away from her and exploded. She was rushed to hospital but found, amazingly, to be unhurt. Subsequent to this, she said, "I approached the performances with almost supernatural confidence—but several nights later in Manchester collapsed from delayed shock."

Richardson's Bluntschli was, from the start, a pleasure to watch—he had made a success of this part in 1931—while

Shaw's cynical as well as high-spirited comedy about soldiering hit a new peak of popularity. In numerous different productions it became a favourite entertainment of the troops and was played all over western Europe in 1944 and 1945—at one time near Caen up to a mile from the front line, where its designer Rex Whistler was killed by a shell. But it was hardly breaking new ground for Ralph, though he definitely relished playing opposite the tall and beautiful Margaret Leighton. Highly strung, with a shimmering quality, she was inspirational and could be, off stage, very funny.

Richardson said of his performance in *Peer Gynt*, which opened on 31 August 1944:

> I don't remember . . . it's a funny thing about acting, I have nothing to say about it at all which is a bit odd because one does take such immense trouble to try and find the character, to create the character, that it is rather as if the memory vanishes. Perhaps it's rather a painful experience, really, and one forgets pain very easily, thank heavens.
>
> Given the part on paper; what on earth does this man look like, you ask yourself, how does he speak? And all day long you're thinking, nagging this problem, and you're looking at people consciously or unconsciously, and you're finding a little bit—look at that man's eyes. He's perhaps like that . . . But when it's over, we bundle the clothes back into the wardrobe and we forget them and they go back into the laundry basket and you've nothing to say or think about afterwards.

Peer Gynt is Everyman (as well as no man), and the part is one which, as Richardson said in an article in the *Radio Times* (on the occasion of the 1943 broadcast), knocks hell out of the actor; but the play was "the greatest poetic drama of modern times".

The reasons why he came to play Peer Gynt go back to the spring of 1940 when a listener, a Mrs Meard of Bexhill, had written to Freddie Grisewood of the BBC with a request to hear "The Death of Äase" from *Peer Gynt*, with Grieg's music, as it was appropriate to Norway's dark days, and King Haakon's exile in England. Nothing happened. The letter was passed to two other producers who tried to mount the whole play though without success. But in 1943 Guthrie approached the BBC producer Val Gielgud to put it on, suggesting Richardson, and this was agreed. The broadcast, transmitted on 10 August 1943, proved enormously successful.

From that earlier radio version it is possible to get some idea of Richardson's stage performance. With the youthful Peer the voice he adopted was highish, conveying in every line a sense of wide-eyed, cheeky humour, of delight and playfulness, of buoyancy, with Ibsen's imagery trimmed down (in Norman Ginsbury's version) to make it down-to-earth and intimate in appeal. Lying in the heather, watching the sky, Peer sees his mother in a passing cloud: the dreaming, disembodied quality could not have been better rendered. The speed with which Richardson delivered the lines has an anticipatory, almost faster-than-thought quality. Peer's imagination seems to expand, then suddenly retract as Richardson pulls it in, dragging the character back down to more mundane reality: "see a pine like a knight in armour—I'll bite through you: you're an outlaw." In spontaneity the mood is never deficient. The range of feeling, too, is registered in subtle shades of sound as the voice darkens and deepens to indicate the transition to middle age. Vanity, mystification ("must find a way roundabout . . . confess yet conceal, speak yet be silent"), the cynicism, too, give way, in the scene with his dying mother, so movingly played on stage by Sybil Thorndike, to the keenest sense of poignancy. Richardson's tenderness is so patent, so heartfelt that when, later on, Peer's search for himself ultimately yields nothing—like the onion whose successive layers of skin are peeled in the search for identity: "this layer so soft and immaculate is the man who lived for gaiety; black brings both parson and negro to mind. When am I going to get to the heart? There isn't one? Right through the middle with layers getting smaller—nature is witty!"—a rare concentration of poetic statement has been achieved, as well as a rare identification of player and part. For Peer's essence was much the same as Richardson's own: the dreamer, the romantically creative personality, the poet who was "everything and nothing", the unfixed wide-ranging being whose very centre reveals an enigmatic lack of substance. So he had at long last been able to realize the poet in his personality with fullness and conviction. He had learnt to play himself.

Rehearsing the long and difficult part with Guthrie that summer as the bombs fell on London, Richardson sometimes felt, he said, as if he were trudging through the desert accompanied by a watchful parrot. After hours of toil, suddenly a gleam of water. The parrot would drink the water—at the same time giving you a sharp nip.

Richardson thought Tony Guthrie the most extraordinary and stimulating man of the theatre since Granville-Barker.* Guthrie put leading actors on their mettle, frequently giving the appearance of not liking them. It often seemed, Richardson said, as if he were trying to take the scene away from the leading actor and give it to the man who carried the spear.

With Guthrie's direction, which had assistance in movement from Robert Helpmann, the Old Vic *Peer Gynt* was a triumph, swift in action and simple in design. The part, calling for so many alterations of mood and tone, was richly rewarding. Though he had been terrified of it, after such a long spell of not acting, the part became Richardson's favourite, as much as any part could be said to be that.†

To the critics of the time, and to London audiences,

---

*Guthrie lived at this time in five rooms in Gray's Inn, which Richardson described as a tremendous muddle of kittens and socks. "And in the bedroom there was a great double bed with a label on the end. What could it be? I looked: Carter Paterson, it said—the removal people, who must have delivered the bed years before. But amidst all this he and his wife gave everything an air of tremendous distinction so that it might have been in the grandest Paris salon."

†But he never played it again, though years later he contemplated doing Parts II and III with himself as Peer in middle age while his son Charles, by this time interested in acting, would play the young Peer.

starved of good quality for so many years, nothing in the production could be faulted. Even Agate lauded it, having previously said Richardson would never be any good in Ibsen:

> In plain English I thought that the production was superb, that Ralph Richardson was excellent in all three phases, and that everybody else died or got married or went mad more than competently. But it was one man's evening as in the case of this play it always must be. Here is the actor's dream fulfilled: to be always on the stage and never stop talking. I left the theatre murmuring
> When Richardsons begin to Peer
> With heigh! the doxy over the dale.

"Richardson stretched the wide octave of Peer's life with great skill," wrote Harcourt Williams, who with his one fifteen-minute scene as the mad doctor, Begriffenfelt, and as a former Old Vic director, was in a good position to judge.

> He and Sybil Thorndike played the death scene of Äase superbly. A perfect duet. His old Peer was strange, unearthly and a little terrifying. At first I used to long for something more on those last lines:
> My mother! My wife! You holy woman!
> Oh, hide me, hide me within your love!
> I had a notion, that he was holding back the emotion because he was fearful of becoming sentimental, but after he had played the part for some time the real feeling came.

This appreciation showed how well Harcourt Williams knew his Richardson.

Olivier put in a brief but chillingly effective appearance in *Peer Gynt* as the Button Moulder, but in Burrell's production of *Richard III*, with Olivier as Crookback, Richardson appeared not quite so comfortable in the small part of Richmond. He didn't look right, for a start, in carrot-coloured wig, and the makeshift, stage-convenience character sat ill on his shoulders, even though from the front it glowed "like plated Mars". Often his personality, with its own peculiar and individual facets, could not be wholly subdued to the role, especially as the new, film-conscious West End audiences insisted on recognizing the actor before the character. A rippling murmur would greet his entrance: "Oh look! There's Ralph Richardson!" Richmond's identity came a bad second.

It struck some participants—including Peter Copley, who arranged the sword fight which Olivier transformed into legend—that Richardson was disinclined to join in whole-heartedly. "Do you really need to go so quickly, old chap?" he would ask as Olivier wildly chopped and slashed. As protection from this Richardson arranged a set of metal clips which he would fit over his knuckles under his gauntlet; underlining his discomfort, perhaps, the programme listed him as appearing as "Earl of Richmond, after King Edward VII".

It was not only by taking on blunt Richmond, perhaps too much of an old persona of the Thirties now left behind in his new subtlety of range, that Richardson shiningly demonstrated the duty-sharing spirit of this company. One night a pallbearer of Anne's failed to turn up. At a moment's notice Ralph took his place, slipping on a monk's cowl and cloak, but failing to remove his distinctive brogues, made specially for him by Mr Cleverley* of Clifford Street, which protruded from under the habit.

---

*Just the shoemaker one might expect Richardson to know. Mr Cleverley was a Czech refugee. The shoes were made to the customers' specifications and lasted thirty or forty years. Their renown spread to such a degree that down the steps to the basement where he had his business would come Olivier, Gielgud, Guinness—all queuing for Mr Cleverley's shoes.

24   *Anglo-British relations*

When innocence is present, it is possible to tame. Hence there
follows The Taming Power of the Great.

I Ching (Book of Changes)

On 1 January 1945, the Richardson's only son, Charles,
nicknamed 'Smallie', was born in a London nursing home.
Priestley became his godfather. "I didn't want to have a
child," Richardson told Angela Huth, the playwright and
novelist, in 1981; "I can't stand children. I was playing the
night he was born. I went along to the nursing home
afterwards. Oh God, I thought, it will be awful. But then I
saw this beautiful thing. I couldn't help lifting it up in my
arms. I loved it at that instant."

The family had now moved to Bedegars Lea, a handsome
mock-Queen Anne house on the edge of Hampstead
Heath, close to the Spaniards' Inn. Here, in a long attic
room, Richardson could, when not working, pursue his
hobbies: these were now his ferret, Eddie, toy theatres
—he had bought an interest in Pollock's, the famous
London toy shop—and antique clocks.

His Vanya in Chekhov's *Uncle Vanya*, delayed in its
opening until early 1945, was Richardson's first attempt at
Chekhov. It was not altogether convincing. He tried to
approach the character as if, given the chance, Vanya
would have been a "Schopenhauer or a Dostoevsky", as
Chekhov had declared. But the underlying nature of the
man was that of a failure, and, whatever his circumstances,
he would have remained the same. This Richardson had
not accepted. Some who saw him sensed a reluctance on his
part to identify with Vanya as a failure; others felt he held
back, even feared being laughed at, and didn't fully understand the part. Some critics held that he and Olivier, who
played Astrov, should have changed roles. But the play's
designer, Tanya Moiseiwitch, daughter of the pianist
Benno Moiseiwitch, who had emigrated from Russia—for
authenticity's sake she even used in her set the curtains the

family had brought with them—found herself watching Richardson through "a mist of tears".

Even so, contradicting Albery's gloomy prediction, the Old Vic venture at the New Theatre, using the continental repertory system of rotating four plays, was flourishing. A four-week provincial tour followed the season at the New. Then, as the war in Europe was at last ending, they set sail in mid-May 1945 from Tilbury dock for a six-week tour of the newly liberated areas.

Handed identity discs, and life-belts with an electric torch attachment, the company were crammed into a troop ship. They numbered 66; the general manager, Laurence Evans, had to arrange transport across the pitted and scarred countryside for 20 tons of scenery and 58 padlocked hampers of costumes and personal effects. Finally these went in special RAF lorries used for salvaging crashed planes. Every member of the company had been given the honorary rank of lieutenant, and wore uniforms with ENSA flashes. Richardson and Olivier affixed wings over their breast pockets; Richardson wore a peaked cap, Olivier a beret. At one rehearsal Beau Hannen had the temerity to sport a white shirt with his uniform. Richardson, a stickler for military etiquette, ticked him off. The Old Vic actors were part of what was virtually a second invasion. More than 60 theatrical companies were touring Europe. When the trains stopped they would get out and talk to each other, leave each other notes at the digs.

In Antwerp they played *Arms and the Man* and *Peer Gynt*. There was no viable theatre in Brussels so they journeyed by bus to nearby Ghent, where the Burgomaster requested a special performance of *Richard III*. Richardson found the theatre was made entirely of wood—acting there was like playing a violin: the best setting he had ever spoken in. Then, in four 20-seater aircraft, they flew from Brussels to Hamburg.

There, according to Basil Dean, "The streets stretched endlessly through acres of desolation, in the ruined dock basin ships lay bottom up in the fairway to bear witness to the power of British blockbusting." But the revered and ancient Staatliche Schauspielhaus still stood and, with its efficient stage staff, offered better facilities than the New. From up to fifty miles around, in jeep and lorry, the troops of the 21st army poured in, till they seemed to be hanging from the chandeliers. A sergeant told Jeffrey Segal, "You know I've never been to the theatre before, but I'll tell you what my favourite play is, it's *Peer Gynt*. It's smashing. After that comes *Richard III*."

None of the company was allowed on the streets after eight at night, as there was still danger of sniping from unrepentant Nazis. But in the hotels celebrations went on till all hours, while at weekends the younger and more attractive ENSA "lieutenants" such as Margaret Leighton and Joyce Redman were invited by officers to outlying schlosses where champagne and wine from the cellars flowed freely. No one was allowed to 'frat', even with waiters in the hotel, and when on a drive in Schleswig-Holstein, Sybil Thorndike admired one of the traditional long, horse-drawn carts, and chatted with some peasants, she was sharply reprimanded by an Intelligence officer. She could not think of these people as "enemy civilians".

Off the stage, Richardson, when not reading voraciously as usual, might join in a drink with the 'boys'; but he was always sensitive, mindful of social disturbances, perhaps of some particularly disagreeable barman, and could suddenly take against a place. "Come on, let's get out of here," he would declare abruptly. But if he liked his surroundings, as he did the dark Rembrandtesque bars of the Low Countries, he almost consciously savoured them and soaked them up, even indulging in ribald talk. "Have you ever had a black girl?" he asked Peter Copley. "You know, if you stroke the skin one way it's very smooth, if you stroke it the other way it's rough!"* Undoubtedly he spoke from experience. In Copley's presence he held forth to a well-endowed woman behind the bar, richly elaborating on her natural charms. Fortunately she did not understand a word.

*He told this story again nearly forty years later to a member of the company rehearsing *Early Days*, possibly having been reminded of it by reading through this account.

In June, on the invitation of the English doctors in charge of the camp, they gave a special matinée of *Arms and the Man* at Belsen. The 250 British troops stationed there, with 250 French troops had the job of guarding the 40,000 inmates who were still barely alive, and the 10,000 bodies which were rotting in the sunshine. Before the performance, Margaret Leighton, Joyce Redman and Sybil Thorndike were, on their own request, shown round the camp; they found an old lady sitting up in bed, wrists like matchsticks, her face all eyes, her body almost a total skeleton. One tuft of hair stuck up from her head, "with a red bow tied to it," said Joyce Redman, a grotesque testimony to the power of vanity. The old woman died shortly afterwards. At lunch, which none of them could eat, they met Mervyn Peake, then an Official War Artist, who was sketching the dead and dying.

On the final leg the company played Paris. Here 60 per cent of the population was underfed, surviving usually on dried beans or boiled potatoes. *Arms and the Man* was staged at the Marigny; then they moved to the Comédie-Française, whose wider stage was necessary for both *Richard III* and *Peer Gynt*. On the first night of *Richard*, so carried away was the audience by Olivier's spectacular death convulsions, that when Richardson, as Richmond, came to place his foot on the dead king's neck and declare, "God and your arms be praised . . . the bloody dog is dead", it gave him no chance to speak. Annoyed at the reaction of "the damn Frogs", he had to content himself with one blunt Anglo-Saxon expression.

The Paris critics delighted in the precise technique of the Old Vic troupe, its colourful and strong diction. "Where do we have actors as good as these?" they asked. The theatre, besieged with every kind of celebrity, became a rallying point for French cultural self-esteem. The company was even accorded the honour, unique for a foreign troupe, of playing at the Comédie-Française on the Quatorze Juillet, when the performance was by tradition free. This being the first 14 July since the Liberation, the crowds danced all night.

In the hallowed Comédie building the English players were allotted the dressing rooms of the life-long *sociétaires*. Some impish *spiritus loci* must have been at work. Olivier found himself in the luxurious boudoir of a comédienne who, judging by the décor, still fancied herself a *grande cocotte* intent on stimulating her lovers' attentions with every kind of enticing frill and allurement. He threw up his arms. "I can't act in all this!" he declared. "I shall end by playing Richard as some effeminate woman." Richardson was accommodated in some elderly actor's suite, with leather-backed armchairs dotted around; the sumptuous velvet-papered walls were hung with exquisite eighteenth-century prints which, on closer scrutiny, revealed themselves as pornographic.

Invited to address an august Anglo-French literary society, Richardson, mounting gingerly on a rickety little chair, began: "Ladies and gentlemen, we're here today to celebrate a very dear and important thing—Anglo-British relations. Now where would we be without Anglo-British relations?" The audience remained respectfully silent while he continued eccentrically in this vein, ending, "Ladies and gentlemen, here's to Anglo-British relations!"

25 *The revived humour of Sir John Falstaff*

> The great actor is more exalted than the great poet, on to whose shoulders he climbs, shutting himself up inside a great basketwork figure of which he is the soul.
>
> DIDEROT

In middle age Richardson looked very ordinary, very middle-class. His face was the face of everyman. The man about to impersonate Falstaff, Shakespeare's "huge hill of flesh", one of the "greatest men in the realm", in the New Theatre's next production in the autumn of 1945, wore more often than not a grey suit and would have passed for a nondescript businessman. Now he had entered his forties his lack of physical glamour began to seem less important.*

But he did feel he had none of the necessary proportions. He felt extremely diffident. "Not until you play Falstaff do you realize how small the mere actor is. . . . It's like trying to play a huge organ with too vast a keyboard to reach the steps up at the top and down at the bottom at one and the same time."

This time it was Olivier who gave him encouragement: "Laurence suggested Falstaff—'Let's do the two parts of Falstaff,' he said. I said I think it will be too much. Olivier told me, 'There are no great parts. Some are a bit longer than others, that's all'". Richardson remembered that one of the first auditions he ever gave was as Falstaff. Growcott had commented, "That is quite awful. It is shapeless, senseless, badly spoken, you don't even know it very well, and I can't think why you chose the piece you did because

---

*Richardson does admit, at this time, feeling a strong, one-off pang of envy of Olivier. In a warm tribute to his friend on the occasion of his retirement from the National Theatre in 1973, he remembered an occasion when the pair were about to lunch together at the Arts Club in Glasgow: "Some Celts possess a mystic, extra-sensory cognizance. Now, a very fine-looking Celt came suddenly out of the door of the club. . . . 'Hey,' he seemed to ask. 'Richardson,' I said; this failed to interest. He fixed his gaze upon Laurence. 'But that man,' he said, 'I tell you that that man has the eyes of a poet.' . . . I must confess that I was miffed."

you could never be any good as Falstaff." This no longer
disheartened him: "I thought about it. I have a certain
alacrity in thinking that might help me with the part. My
wife encouraged me. 'It isn't an impossibility,' I told Laurence."

Richardson knew he was approaching a role in which it
was notoriously hard to win acclaim. Memorable Falstaffs
in this century had been few: G. R. Weir, in Frank Benson's company at Stratford; the comedian George Robey
who was, as the *New Statesman* critic wrote in 1935, "the
old soak rather than the fallen gentleman"; during 1942,
Robert Atkins at the Westminster Theatre, who had delivered the role in a quiet, elegiac way. Perhaps fortunately,
Richardson had seen none of these. It made it a lot easier,
he believed. He had seen Roy Byford play Falstaff in *The
Merry Wives of Windsor* at Stratford in 1931, prompting
him to observe, "Falstaff, well he's a little bit of a gent. If
he's vulgar it's no good. If you're put into a laundry, it's not
funny unless it's an indignity."

He found, when considering them years later, a deep
contrast between Falstaff and Hamlet, Macbeth, Othello
and Lear, deeming the latter the "Sputniks" of
Shakespeare's imagination. They took their course outside
the rule of our nature. Like rockets, too, they moved
through the plays at an enormous speed. Too fast for him,
he thought:

> Now, the player of Falstaff is relieved of the special
> technical difficulties that surround the tragic four; unlike
> them, he [Falstaff] is permitted to retain and enjoy his
> basic character without terrible "translation". Unlike
> them, he is not projected at breathless speed to his doom.
> Falstaff proceeds through the play at his own chosen
> pace, like a gorgeous ceremonial Indian elephant.

His idea, therefore, was to make Falstaff the very opposite of coarse. He decided not to belch, not to galumph or
heighten the crudity of the horseplay, or the language: he
wanted it to become a performance pre-eminently of theatrical taste and cunning selection in which the innocent, the

lover of anarchy, the visionary who tries to impose his lordly vision of himself on a disrespectful world, would impose coherence, illuminate the earthy side of the play with an unusual delicacy. He would show there was no viciousness in Falstaff's mind.* Dignity, knighthood would come first. He would carry the weighty man lightly on the balls of his feet, give him a springiness, a loose-limbed resilience, to suggest the energy within. The childish idealism, the heartfelt romanticism, would make his Falstaff akin not only to Peer Gynt but also to Don Quixote. The sensuality, the boozing, the roguery and trickery were to be but metaphors for this inner vision: he could be Falstaff at one and the same time as being himself.

A great amount of planning went into the visual presentation of the character. Richardson's bulk was built up ingeniously. Next to his skin he wore a suit of Turkish towelling material, and over this a light mackintosh. The outer padding was made of horsehair, which, without the protecting mackintosh, felt "like an attack from a swarm of bees". The bulky gnarled and varicosed legs were, on Richardson's prompting, sculptured in silk quilting by costumier Alix Stone, and covered in light red stockings. The traditional leather boots were spurned.

Henry IV, Part I opened on 26 September 1945 and *Part II* a week later. More than 200 people hired stools and queued for the first night of *Part I*. Meriel Richardson came, escorted by Gielgud. The critics were unanimous in approval; and after them flocked the public, needing to refresh its imagination after the war years. They were no longer afraid of imaginative stimulus as they had been in

---

*Tynan in his profile of Richardson quotes W. H. Auden's view that Falstaff is a comic symbol of Jesus Christ. Perhaps, though, Richardson's sympathetic portrayal of Falstaff's weakness shows more a breadth of charity than a Christlike virtue. Another view is that of Stephen Dedalus in *Ulysses*. Speaking of Shakespeare, Stephen says: "What do we care for his wife and father? I should say that only family poets have family lives. Falstaff was not a family man. I feel that the fat knight is his supreme creation."

the 1930s. Richardson's unusual approach won laughs all through in unexpected places.

Perhaps the most striking paradox of Richardson's Falstaff was that while he had not the rhetorical cut-and-thrust to make the complex imagery in the Shakespearian verse as effective as some, he nevertheless now had the experience to free the prose for its most poetic possibilities. As an actor he had progressed to the point where he could make a character appeal to the imagination, he could get at the hidden poetry of a part. He could release, as he had in playing Peer Gynt, the unrepentant boy with his childhood dreams intact, for while his powers as an artist had matured, he had preserved within himself that unrepentant boy, those childhood dreams—one result, possibly, of having had such a sombre and restricted childhood.

As for the critics: the spirit behind the rotund nobility, wrote Tynan in *He That Plays The King* (1950), "was spry and elastic. . . . Each word emerged with immensely careful articulation . . . in rage one noticed a slow meditative relish taking command." "It was the only three-dimensional Falstaff we have ever seen," commented Edwin Schloss, when *Henry IV* moved to New York:

> whether philosophizing in the tavern scenes, bragging and quaking on the battlefield, cozening the recruits on the village green, or in the final tragi-comic scene where his old companion the Prince disowns him, Richardson's Falstaff had the breath of life and the dimensions of reality. A feat all the more remarkable because it triumphed over the low comedy aspects of the role—the puns, the sometimes laboured wit and galumphing horseplay so side-splitting to Elizabethans and so unfunny to a modern audience . . . a great performance.

Averred Priestley bluntly, "Best Falstaff there ever was."

Michael Warre, who played Prince Hal, found himself so deeply affected by the final scene in which Falstaff receives his icy rebuke, that on leaving the stage he regularly burst into tears. Richardson had a trick of being able to turn his face red as he was seized by irrepressible tics of fury. Orson Welles, himself a good Falstaff in his 1939 production of *Five Kings* (and later in his 1966 film *Chimes at Midnight*), told Richardson when he went round after one performance: "Thought I'd done all right as Falstaff but the thing I must say, Ralph, I never matched you at the end. I could never do that because I haven't got your blue eyes." Welles, his own eyes resting on Ralph's face, paused a moment. "By God," he then said very quietly, "you haven't *got* blue eyes."

26 *Top boy is either*

In his pyrotechnical display as Saranoff, in *Arms and the Man*, Olivier had introduced New Theatre audiences to an unusual line in plastic noses. In *Richard III* the long sharp proboscis coupled with the lank black hair, its ends tinged with red as if dipped in blood, made fellow members of the company give him a wide berth, even in the wings waiting to go on. In *Henry IV, Part II*, equipped as Justice Shallow with a sharp, blade-like construction of putty, he was not of the earth but a rarefied clownish creation, in Priestley's beautiful phrase the "shrunken cylinder of a planet" to Sir John's "great round roaring sun". The recruits, Mouldy, Shadow, Wart, Feeble and Bullcalf, played by younger actors, keenly following Olivier's extra-terrestrial example, would also adopt every kind of facial disfigurement to call attention to themselves—blackened teeth or fangs, huge whiskers, warts with bushy hairs. One night before they were about to go on Ralph stopped and, looking them over critically, pronounced, "You know, when I was a young actor, I had some very good advice given me by an old actor: 'If you're playing a character part,' this actor told me, 'just before you come down to the stage, take one last look in your dressing-room mirror and ask y'self, "Is it human?"'" Shallow's recruits stood reproved.

Olivier's comic business as Shallow grew with each performance. He would take off his hat, a bee would land on his head, he would put his hat back on—"farcical character", one critic called it, sounding a "discord as if the first violin in the orchestra was allowed to jazz Elgar's *Enigma Variations*." But for Tynan, whose love of the shocking and outrageous was then at its most restrained, these scenes remained even thirty years later the highest point in his theatre-going. "If I had only half an hour to spend in theatres," he wrote, "and could choose at large, no question but I would have these."

By the end of this massive and ambitious undertaking of *Henry IV*, the triumvirate remained intact, with the inexhaustible pivot, John Burrell, not only supporting the two colossi, but being himself responsible for some remarkable and unobtrusive direction.* At curtain calls Laurence would hold the curtain for Ralph, Ralph for Laurence. Outside in the streets crowds mobbed the leading actors. They chanted "We want Larry, we want Ralph." One reporter wrote: "Top boy is either. You may call him Laurence Richardson or you may call him Ralph Olivier."

Like Olivier and Richardson, Michel Saint-Denis, who joined the Old Vic company to direct Sophocles' *Oedipus* in W. B. Yeats's translation, had spent the war serving his country: he arrived in London after the fall of France, joined de Gaulle, and engaged in propaganda directed against the Vichy regime. A stocky, earthy character both

---

*Though he saw his role as director as subservient to those of his leading actors, Burrell's productions, built as they were round the capacities of the cast acting in them, stood up much better to long runs and touring than those of Tyrone Guthrie.

in appearance and flavour. Saint-Denis had a broad Burgundian accent, smoked a pipe, and often had a merry twinkle in his eye, especially when talking to women. As "Jacques Duchêne", broadcasting frequently over Radio Free French, he had a price on his head, for his function was to pass on coded information to Resistance workers, he was also responsible for other items such as an ebullient interview with Churchill, conducted during an air raid, in which both men, clearly affected by the red wine they were drinking, were audibly being pounded with bombs.

Saint-Denis lacked a heightened sense of selectivity, an eye for editing and consolidating a performance for the public's benefit. But with Olivier as Oedipus, the supreme self-editor of performance, and Richardson as Tiresias, blind and Blake-like in dimension, his abrasive censure of Oedipus delivered with quivering control, there was little cause for worry. In fact *Oedipus*, the most popular production he ever directed, became for Saint-Denis one of several notable exceptions in a line of critical disappointments, and helped establish him as a teacher, in which capacity his influence in post-war theatre was considerable. To the Chorus, whose effect in *Oedipus* was much admired, Saint-Denis gave only two notes, sucking his pipe between words: "Perhaps today zere vas not enough emotion. Go avay and rehearse." And, "perhaps today zere vas too much emotion." Though once he did remark to them, "You look like a lot of dirty old men pissing against a vall."

Preparations for *Oedipus* had begun with Tyrone Guthrie as director, but then Guthrie heard it was to be part of a double bill with Sheridan's *The Critic*, with Olivier as Mr Puff. His reaction to this had been "Over my dead body!" Though he had been instrumental in appointing the Old Vic triumvirate, he found himself overridden; so he not in the best of moods, for New York where he directed, appropriately enough, Andreyev's *He Who Gets Slapped*. When he returned in the latter part of 1946, his attitude had hardened further against the triumvirate, or the "directors-in-triplicate" as they became known in office memos.

In Miles Malleson's production of *The Critic*, officially

his play off, Richardson took the part of the thoughtful Burleigh who appears only in one scene, a miniature play-within-a-play. Holding the centre of a crowded stage, he gave a silent comic performance which had everyone in hysterics. Olivier as Mr Puff, sporting yet another piece of nasal engineering, performed acrobatic feats which on several occasions nearly cost him his life, and once left him stranded high above the stage clinging to the fly gallery.

The contrast between these two actors' methods was never better illustrated than by the plays of this 1945–6 season. Richardson was the watch-maker, the engineer, the selector, the distiller, the endless worrier and seeker who only by painstaking effort (like a dog turning round and round in its basket, as Peter Hall said of him later) —would slowly find his truth in performance, truth meaning what lay just beyond what was natural. All the time he kept his sensitivity well guarded, well concealed, retaining within himself the mystery of his extreme sensitivity, this retention being the source of his hypnotic power: holding the crystal ball up to nature as well as the mirror. So he remained and would remain pre-eminently the actor of suggestion, stimulating the beholder into doing the work with his own imagination, finding hints, leads, clues to make contact, to touch some deep subconscious source which would subject the beholder to his influence.

Olivier was virtually the reverse. Flashy, almost vulgar, spikey, erupting like a volcano—"I haven't got his splendid fury," said Richardson—into every possible virtuosity of effect, he kept nothing back, he was totally *there* in every nerve, sinew and blood vessel. Acting was for him a driving life force, the only element in existence which ever made him feel truly alive. He was the kind of actor, even person, you might dislike the idea of until he took on form in front of you, larger than life. "I hate him," was how Richardson expressed it, "until I see him. Then he has more magnetism than anyone I've ever met."

Outwardly confused, vulnerable, indiscreet, up-and-down in mood, and while disliking publicity unable to stop it blazing forth the passions and upsets of his private life,

Olivier's talent manifested itself beyond the ordinary bounds of nature. He wasn't so much the actor holding the mirror up to nature, as an extraordinary manifestation of nature itself.

Harold Hobson pinpointed the contrast in his monograph on Richardson. During the run of *Oedipus*, Hobson called on the two actors in the dressing room they shared:

> Richardson sat in a corner, puffing away at his pipe and talking quietly and calmly. Olivier burst in, a wild look on his face, peered at himself in the looking glass, shrieked in a distraught voice, "It's a rotten shame," and then, red paint pouring down from his eyes, groped his way along the wall to the door. A moment later there rang through the New Theatre Olivier's tremendous cry of horror and distress as the self-blinded Oedipus. These proceedings somewhat distracted me, but on Richardson they had no effect whatever. He just went on talking quietly, the apparent essence of an ordinary man. But of course, only an extraordinary man could have contrived to behave ordinarily in such curious circumstances.

On the last night of the London season of 1945–6, St Martin's Lane was blocked for an hour as 2,500 fans shouted for Olivier and Richardson, the pair finally, with the help of police and stage hands, boarding a taxi from whose roof they made short and incoherent speeches of farewell. Next day, with Vivien Leigh accompanying them (but not Mu, who stayed behind with Smallie), they boarded the "Old Vic Clipper", a four-engined Constellation, at Hurn airport. Over the Atlantic they were served lobster cocktail, grilled Shannon salmon and "undercut" (entrecôte?) steak. Diana Boddington remembered vividly the frayed cuffs of Olivier's shirt.

The opening of their New York season a few days later at the Century Theater on Seventh Avenue was emotional. The audience rose and cheered before the first scene of *Henry IV, Part I* could start, and Nicholas Hannen as the King, "So shaken as we are," forgot his opening line. There had been much advance excitement over the arrival of this first British company to visit America since the war—they were a symbol of more than the plays they presented—and for the most part the reviews echoed the audiences' warmth. But one or two critics, deciding to be contrary, denounced the productions. Wolcott Gibbs, in *The New Yorker*, while praising the acting balked at the slender scenic resources, and stated, "I'm afraid that I was seriously disappointed in the Vic's first two offerings." The *doyen* of American drama critics, George Jean Nathan, in vituperative mood aimed at the snobbish New York notion that English actors were best, wrote: "For one English actor like Richardson or Olivier in this Old Vic Company, there are three or four whose sharply clipped speech and corrupt pronunciations are absurd and even slightly painful to any American ear practised beyond an appreciation of burlesque shows and Midwestern stock companies." He cited examples of diction which "chafed" his ear, and went on to claim the company was

> built mainly around a star actor and that actor is Olivier. In the five plays it has shown, Olivier has been the star, in the Broadway sense, in all but one. Though Richardson is the star in that one, the second part of *Henry IV*, he plays second fiddle to Hotspur in the first part, second fiddle to Astrov in *Uncle Vanya*, since the doctor's role is theatrically much showier than the name part, third fiddle as Tiresias in *Oedipus* to Oedipus, and tenth fiddle as Lord Burleigh in *The Critic* to Mr Puff.

But the audiences thought very differently: a single ticket on the black market fetched $50; by the end of the six-week run 87,000 people had bought tickets and 31,000 had been turned away.

Richardson's and Olivier's names had at first been billed above the rest of the company on the Century Theater hoardings. This was soon changed. Richardson told an interviewer, William de Bois, "We've had our theatrical tradition in the past. And we've had our actors. Irving, Tree, and the rest. But when they died they were finished. With us, the continuity of the achievement comes first." He also delivered himself, to Otis L. Guernsey, Jr., of a dictum that subsequently became proverbial: "Acting is merely the art of keeping a large group of people from coughing."

In his room in the Algonquin, away from all the fuss and the extraordinary, almost disgusting, state of plenty everywhere, Richardson resumed his old hobby of oil painting. It was from here one day that his New York agent received an urgent call: "Can you send someone round to the hotel to help me hear my lines," he asked her, adding, "and would she mind posing in the nude?" A member of the company calling later found a sheet firmly over the easel, masking whatever it was he was painting.

With probing interviewers Richardson displayed the same mastery of self-concealment: on this, his second visit to Broadway, he refused to be drawn other than to comment how quietly audiences sat, or to voice future aspirations, like "I would like to play Australia on the next tour. They sent us fighters during the war, and now I think we should loan them what they lack—a company like ours, a symphony orchestra, a ballet company and all the pictures in the National Gallery." To the kind of personal questions American journalists usually ask, he would answer: "I don't know myself very well—I'll have to ask myself that question one day and if I tell myself something I'll let you know."

He did, however, outline his intention of alternating three years of Old Vic work with two years of filming, an ominous statement in view of what was to happen in eighteen months' time.

27 *Peacetime in St Martin's Lane*

In the summer of 1946 the Richardsons motored down to Buckinghamshire to spend the weekend at Notley Abbey, the fifteenth-century abbot's lodge the Oliviers had recently bought. Richardson remarked to Mu before they began the ascent to the house (according to Kenneth Tynan, both recalled his exact words): "I hope to God I don't put my foot in it this time." He was referring to a previous visit to Olivier and Vivien in 1937, on Guy Fawkes night (5 November), when Olivier had just bought a house in Chelsea, Durham Cottage, which had deep carpets and a spiral staircase, used by him in practising for that year's *Macbeth*. There are several accounts of this visit, notably one in Jesse L. Lasky, Jr.'s *Love Scene* (1978):

> Ralph entered bearing under his arm something that looked dangerously like a rocket . . . Flourishing it like the mighty claymore of Scotland . . . [he] bore it into the garden where the launch was toasted with a round or two of drinks . . . In the split of a roaring second, the monster firework spurted up, trailing a stream of sparks. Then it whirled into a loop-the-loop and was returned to sender like a fiery boomerang. As everyone in the garden ducked, it swept across a flower bed, smashed through the drawing-room window, and exploded in the delicately appointed room, scattering guests out of its path . . . Screaming with laughter, Larry clapped his deflated pal on his sagging shoulder. "Do it again, Ralphie! Encore."

After that, Tynan speculated, "purely social contacts between the two couples" had remained "minimal" because of a "lingering sense (on Mrs Olivier's part) that there was something 'inherently hazardous, almost poltergeistic' about Richardson's presence."

But the day at Notley passes well. They dine. They discuss the future. Richardson "conducts himself with extreme caution, a man walking on eggshells." Then Olivier suggests they view some "frescoes painted by the monks on beams in the attic". Mu declines the invitation; Richardson accepts.

The men having left, the wives chatted over their coffee. Mrs Olivier felt obscurely uneasy, but after five, ten, fifteen minutes had passed without incident, she was ready to scoff at her qualms. At this moment there was a prolonged splintering noise from above, followed by a colossal crash that made the whole house shake. The women dashed upstairs, where, in the main guest room, lovingly decorated under Mrs Olivier's personal supervision, they found Richardson on his back and covered in plaster, in a bed that had collapsed under his weight. Above it there was a gaping hole in the ceiling, through which he had evidently fallen.

Could one believe 13 stone of Ralph Richardson fell 8 or 9 feet, breaking 4-inch rafters as it crashed down? Tynan's report is reminiscent of an attempt made by Thomas Carlyle in 1853 to have a soundproof room constructed on his top floor: workmen fell through the ceiling into Mr and Mrs Carlyle's bedroom, one narrowly missing Mrs Carlyle's head. The tables and chairs all had their "legs in the air as if in convulsions".

A possibly more reliable account: The following Monday morning saw Richardson arriving at the New Theatre offices in Goodwin's Court off St Martin's Lane. "I've done it again," he told the secretaries, Vi Marriott and Kate Ashbury.

Then, before everyone's eyes, he began to act out the whole scene, using chairs and tables; how he and Olivier left the two ladies downstairs; how Olivier in the course of showing him the attic, said, "You must keep to the beams, dear chap, keep to the main beams." Of course he hadn't. But all of him hadn't gone through the ceiling by any means. Just his leg. Rather easier if it had, because he had great difficulty in getting his leg back. "Quick," said Olivier. "We won't tell her—we must tidy it up." So they'd rushed downstairs to the bedroom, picked up what broken plaster they could, then stolen downstairs and unseen by their wives collected buckets and water, creeping back through the flower beds under the drawing-room window: then desperately tried to get the room straight again so Vivien shouldn't explode. All this Richardson enacted for the New Theatre staff by crawling about on hands and knees on the floor of the Goodwin's Court office.

Tynan's account next has Mrs Olivier "foaming with rage, like a Cassandra whose prophecies of doom had gone unheeded." Ralph was said by Tynan to have told him later, "There was a rational basis to Vivien's fury, which we must salute. If you prod a tigress twice in her lair, you must not expect her to purr."

Other versions of these stories exist (there are at least 15 books about Olivier), each elaborated according to the character of the story-teller, each in its own way showing how the actor cannot avoid offering himself up to a myth-ologizing process he can do little or nothing to stop. He cannot have too exclusive a view of himself. To repeat what Richardson once said: "We don't know who we are, do we? We hardly know anyone else, really completely. We none of us know when we're going to die. . . . We're a mystery to ourselves, and to other people."

Guthrie and the Old Vic Governors had originally asked Richardson, Olivier and Burrell, to run the Old Vic com-pany until one year after the war ended. Before the expiry of that agreement they had extended the run of the direc-tors-in-triplicate to five years, while they expanded their responsibilities to include all Old Vic drama activities. In particular they developed a twelve-year plan for a National Theatre tie-up with the Old Vic. The Governors also initiated a school and committed Michel Saint-Denis, George Devine, Glen Byam Shaw and Hugh Hunt to deep and long-term involvement with Old Vic activities. Many leading actors and actresses had come forward expressing their desire to work at the Vic. But a permit had still not materialized to begin reconstruction work on the Old Vic Theatre in the Waterloo Road, whose roof had been extensively damaged in a bombing raid. The company still depended on the goodwill and support of Bronson Albery, who owned the New Theatre.

Plans for the 1946–7 season had been made by the triumvirate before the company went to New York. The plans for 1947 and for 1948, which were being formulated during the summer of 1946, gave Richardson, as he had wanted, time off to make several new films; the first, *Anna Karenina*, was due to be filmed in London in the summer and autumn of 1947. He was also to direct a play at Wyndham's in the spring of 1948. Above all he needed a rest from playing Shakespeare, of whom—not for the first time—two concentrated years at a time seemed enough.

It had also been planned that in 1948 Olivier would take an Old Vic company out to Australasia, a goodwill gesture to which Richardson had made reference in New York. This was part of the long-term plan to develop a second company. The tour had been fixed to depart in February 1948 and to return in November, and for it Vivien Leigh had been engaged, with the parts of Lady Anne in *Richard III*, Lady Teazle in *The School for Scandal* and Sabina in Thornton Wilder's *The Skin of our Teeth*. The choice of these plays caused consternation to at least two members of the board, one of them being Tyrone Guthrie. After a long rest in New York from his previous exhausting spell with the Old Vic, Guthrie's proud eagle-like intelligence was surveying the London landscape, only too keen to take back authority from Olivier and Richardson.

He was still harbouring a grudge against the directors-in-triplicate over *Oedipus* and *The Critic*: everything had shown his objection to the double bill was misjudged, but Guthrie frowned somewhat on commercial success, he was in certain respects a prophet of subsidized theatre.

Meeting Burrell in the Lace Curtains Café in Holborn, he made known his strong objections to the directors-in-triplicate's forthcoming schemes. Burrell then offered him the directorship of the 1946–7 season but he refused, saying he didn't want to be responsible to Burrell, Richardson and Olivier. A new proposal was made, namely that before they picked the company for Olivier to take on tour, Guthrie should form a second company, with Alec Guinness at its head, for the 1947–8 season. In the meantime he was offered the autumn 1946 production of *Cyrano de Bergerac*, as guest director, which he accepted.

While Guthrie objected to the pair of actor-manager stars at the head of the company (only one instance is known of Richardson calling himself an "actor-manager" and this was on the birth certificate of his son Charles), the more hard-headed and commercially-minded Bronson Albery was letting it be known in martinet terms that he viewed the forthcoming absences of Richardson and Olivier (which had been leaked in a story to the *News Chronicle*) with grave misgivings. Albery wrote Burrell on 30 September that he had met Mr Richardson "and the information I received was of a decidedly disquieting nature." However, a fortnight later Albery appeared to have been placated. A meeting with Burrell ended, in the latter's words, "in an aura of beaming satisfaction, mutual back-slapping, hand-shaking and uproarious cordiality."

In the same period death intervened in the Old Vic affairs, carrying off the genial Lord Lytton, aged seventy-one. Lytton had been benevolent and sympathetic towards the triumvirate, but his ultimate replacement—his immediate successor, Lord Hambledon, was to be rapidly struck down—the icier and more ambitious Viscount Esher, became, though for different reasons, an ally of Guthrie's. Esher's long-term aim was also for the Old Vic to be the seedbed for a National Theatre, but to head this he had in mind others than such self-willed upstarts as he considered Richardson and Olivier. So it was with Esher, already chairman in all but name of the Board of Governors, that Albery met in early October.

Albery pointed out that by not taking part in *Richard II*—which Richardson was directing, while Olivier was on leave filming *Hamlet*—Richardson and Olivier were breaking their contract which stipulated that one or the other should be in the cast of every Old Vic production. Albery suggested that André Obey's *Noah* should be added to the end of the 1946–7 season, with Richardson in the name role and Saint-Denis directing. Eventually Richardson agreed to take the part of John of Gaunt in *Richard II*.

But objections were also raised to the plan to have a second company headed by Guthrie for the 1947–8 season. As it was pointed out by Barbara Ward (later Baroness Jackson of Lodsworth), another member of the Board, it would—given that Olivier was already leading a second company in the antipodes—be a third team. A sense of crisis was rapidly developing over the 1947–8 season, when both Richardson and Olivier would be absent. Directors had also to lead in the present, as well as plan successfully for several years in advance. While Barbara Ward suggested all kinds of compromise solutions, some of them very sensible, to avoid a deadlock, she too held the belief that the director of a National Theatre could not be an actor. The suspicion was forming that the two great stars were using the Old Vic to serve their own selfish ambitions. And there were, as someone said at the time, too many white ties in the stalls. The director should be someone outside the profession, a City man, or a politician.

Perhaps one can see in all these rising difficulties no more than the euphoria of peace giving way to the harsher post-war realities. But for all Britain's austerity, seats at the New were cheap. The company was still fulfilling its pre-war function of providing a theatre for the poor (as the Old Vic Theatre's original founder, the social reformer Emma Cons, had specified); half of the seats were sold at prices ranging from 1/6*d*. to 4/6*d*.—about the cost, at the time, of between 10 cigarettes and 40. The New York tour had realized a gross profit of $300,000, most of which went straight into the British Exchequer.

28 *Dominant features*

Versions differ as to how Richardson and Olivier settled between them the roles of King Lear and Cyrano de Bergerac, the two productions that opened the Old Vic's 1946–7 season at the New Theatre. Richardson, really wanting to do Lear, is believed to have voiced in round-about, Peer Gynt fashion, a first preference for Cyrano, hoping Olivier would immediately want to play the role himself. But Olivier was apparently not to be drawn, so Richardson was left in possession of Cyrano (though one might ask how Olivier could have passed up without a murmur of regret the false nose to end all false noses). Richardson could presumably, being the elder and in the directorate, more senior, have made a strong bid for Lear, but as he said of himself, with justification, he was not greedy. Still, the role could not have been far from his mind, in spite of his diffidence over the tragic Big Four, for a few months before, in November 1945, James Agate had thoughtfully dispatched to him a cutting from The *Illustrated London News* of a wave dashing against a breakwater, "forming a magnificent picture of Ralph Richardson as I see him in the role of Lear." This would seem to have been a genuine suggestion, to which Richardson replied courteously.

By the time *Lear* opened, on 24 September 1946, Agate had changed his tune. Why not Richardson for Kent? he asked. Why not indeed? But since the New York tour a slight disengagement of the two friends may be detected. Never again did they act together on the same stage; they now headed separate casts within the same company, and while they still shared a dressing room, they were now never there on the same night. The game-playing grew more elaborate, barely able to contain Olivier's expanding ambition. The two might well have reforged their partnership—and they never stopped being the best of friends—had the company been allowed to continue; future plans included a James Bridie play about Sir Lancelot, with Olivier as Lancelot and Richardson as Merlin. But in 1946, in spite of the success of *King Lear*, the euphoria was not quite as great as in the previous season. Demobilization had flooded the labour market with deserving and talented young men, with experience they could turn to good account on the stage. The realities of peacetime, the unpleasant re-awakening of cut-throat competition, wrought a different edge to friendships.

Olivier's Lear, popular with the public, was seldom given a high critical rating. Peter Hall (who was later to ask Richardson to play Falstaff again) thought it misfired. Agate compared it unfavourably to Wolfit's Lear, "a ruined piece of nature; Olivier's is a picture of ruins most cunningly presented." The performance which everyone acclaimed without reservation was Alec Guinness as the Fool. Olivier never again attempted on stage to play Lear. Richardson never attempted it at all.

The triumvirate's policy was to present new plays as well as classics and on 1 October 1946, Priestley's *An Inspector Calls* received its first performance in England, Priestley having waited faithfully for Richardson to be available to play the Inspector. *An Inspector Calls* had already been done all over the world, including two productions in Russia, and temporarily Priestley, in the afterglow of his triumph, joined in the chorus of praise for Russia. "The real advantage the Russians have," he divulged, "is that their theatre is properly organized. Ours is usually a chaos. The exception . . . is the Old Vic company, which is well organized. That is why it is so successful." Even Shakespeare was enjoying popularity in Russia. As a journalist at the time wrote, *Romeo and Juliet* was being deployed as part of the campaign for better family life:

> The Soviet State could then maintain
> That Blackguard British Bourgeois Bard
> Had not lived utterly in vain.

An Inspector Calls was dazzlingly cast and brilliantly directed by Basil Dean, who spent an undue amount of time shouting at his wife, Victoria Hopper, who was in the cast; but was not quite the success with the London public it should have been. A thriller set in 1912, with many triggers of suspense and surprise buried in its central enquiry into a young factory hand's suicide, *An Inspector Calls* contains a socialist message, to which the Inspector at the end tries to give a universal context. But the overt political intention somehow dogs the thriller aspect, and Priestley lays the cards of universal brotherhood too quickly on the table. Ted Willis, writing in the *Daily Worker* under the headline 'Priestley's Indictment' invoked a concept of Lenin's: "The old society was based on the principle: 'rob or be robbed; work for others or make others work for you, etc.' which the play brilliantly illustrated." Priestley shows, he continued, "the greed, jealousy and moral degeneracy which springs from the profit motive in that society."

Richardson can hardly have believed he was delivering a Leninist tract. He had always, one might suppose, rather more than supported the profit motive: both he and Olivier voted Conservative in the 1945 General Election which had brought Attlee's Labour Government to power. It was the high order of Priestley's craftsmanship which appealed to Richardson, and the fact that as Inspector Goole, the avenging, more than ordinary policeman, he could bring a poetic dimension to the prosaic qualities of the character. In his performance Goole's authority, his integrity, the flash of anger, the glint of irony, were invested with strangeness, with a not quite human quality; though he seems not to have responded to the Inspector's lack of humility. This was the last play of Priestley's in which Richardson appeared.*

The third production of the 1946–7 season, *Cyrano de Bergerac*, was a favourite with French actors but a rare import into England; it encouraged the drift towards poetic

*Many years later, appearing on the BBC's Parkinson show, Richardson was questioned about Priestley: "It's a lovely spring," he remembered saying one day to Jack Priestley. "The primroses are out, . . . I don't like the spring, Ralph," replied Jack—Richardson catching the Yorkshire accent perfectly (he is usually no good at accents). "The spring succeeds, grows old and ugly. I like the autumn when you can see the skeleton of life itself. No, I don't like the spring."

drama, as if in the face of the drab social realities colourful language and metaphor could inject delight and a sense of luxury. Or, as Henry Jame wrote in his story "A Landscape Painter", "When people have to economize with the dollars and cents, they have a right to be splendid in their feelings." It was the same impetus which had brought Shakespeare and Marlowe to the forefront in just as bleak a time; but the poetic drama of Eliot and Christopher Fry —Cyrano is the prototype of Fry's Thomas Mendip, in *The Lady's Not for Burning*—waned in the prosperity of the late 1950s, achieved with so little real effort.

The romantic, poetical side of Richardson's personality was in its element with Cyrano, the hero who is both poet and swordsman: the composition of a poem, the craftsmanship of a duel, are to him one and the same thing. The insurmountable ugliness of his monstrous nose brings universality and pathos to his hopeless love for Roxane. In the famous Act I speech he laments his deformity:

For example, thus—
Aggressive: I sir, for example, thus—if that nose were mine,
I'd have it amputated—on the spot!
Friendly: How do you drink with such a nose?
You ought to have a cup made specially.
Descriptive: What is that receptacle—
A razor-case or a portfolio?—
Kindly: Ah, do you love the little birds
so much that when they come and sing to you
you give them this to perch on?

In New York Richardson had met the American actor Walter Hampden, who played Cyrano many years before: "He gave me his nose, nice old chap," Richardson told Michael Warre, cast as Christian, Roxane's lover, at the New.

Audrey Williamson, who wrote a full account of these Old Vic seasons in her book of 1948, was one of a dozen critics enamoured of Richardson's Cyrano, claiming it was as great as, if not greater than his Falstaff. She found his suspense and hope during the early part when Roxane speaks of her unnamed love, and which he conveyed almost without motion, quite unbearable. When he received news of Christian's death, she says, "from that round disfigured countenance, with the questioning witty eyebrow one saw the humour and eager passion slowly drain right out, leaving it blank, sad-eyed and desolate, like the face of a deserted child." When Cyrano dies she departs into pure hyperbole: "This had the pale flame of absolute genius; the light was unmistakeable. The man was like a white plastered tree torn up by the roots, yet still miraculously upright, magnificent in dissolution." Everyone agreed with her—and even Agate said Richardson's death scene was better than Coquelin's.

It is widely held that Richardson at this time was more than half in love himself with his Roxane, Margaret Leighton, 24 years his junior, confusing the reality with the dream; if so, it gave an added poignancy and sense of danger to his performance as Cyrano. Tyrone Guthrie, who sometimes showed little interest in rehearsing principals except to give them, as Richardson put it, those parrot-like sharp nips to keep them awake, sent them off to a corner of the rehearsal room to work out their long scenes by themselves.*

The non-poetical, paradoxical side of Richardson's character also came into play during *Cyrano*. On one occasion Frank Duncan, as a minor character in Guthrie's vivid Hôtel de Bourgogne tableau, bumped up hard against Cyrano's dominant feature. At the interval he went round to Richardson's dressing room to apologize. "Do watch it, dear fellow," Richardson told him, finger wagging in slow metronomic fashion; "If the old conk goes it rather buggers up the piece."

As a token of the deeper tension that was rising in the company between its star and the director—and the

---

*Interviewed in 1973, Margaret Leighton spoke of the "tremendous admiration" she had for Richardson's acting "because it was immaculately truthful and immensely moving; yet it was technically concealed and subtle—more than Olivier's was then, or so I thought."

nearest Richardson had ever been in his career to a public quarrel—at one dress rehearsal Guthrie rounded angrily on him from the darkness of the circle.

"For God's sake, Ralph, play the scene!—play the play!" Guthrie, as his biographer James Forsyth records, was always on the move at rehearsals, up and down the stalls aisles, or between stalls and circle. Now, Forsyth says, "All action stopped on stage. In the stalls we sat up, shocked and expectant. Here was to be the big row."

Richardson, who had been, as was his habit, feeling his way round the Tanya Moiseiwitch set, touching the wood, came to the downstage edge of the stage, "peering, gimlet-eyed from both sides of the great de Bergerac nose up to where Guthrie stood."

"I was brought up to find my lights," he said. "And I'm finding them, and for the first time in your production. So . . . don't call me a bloody fool—old cock . . ."

This clear and cold reaction of anger from Richardson made everyone even more tense. But Guthrie, Forsyth says, withdrew from the brink.

"Raight!" (clap of hands). "On we go!"

This was the last time Richardson and Guthrie worked together, but he bore Guthrie no ill will. When Guthrie died in 1971, Richardson delivered, on the telephone to the *Sunday Times*, an impromptu tribute:

I remember Alec Guinness once giving me a fascinating glimpse of Guthrie in his Irish home. Guinness was staying there, went out for a walk after dinner, in the dark. He wasn't too sure where the front door was, found himself looking through the drawing-room window. There sat Guthrie, that tall great man, that eagle profile, towering over a card-table; and three elderly female relatives, all, because the old ladies had poor sight, holding enormous playing cards seven or eight inches deep. That shows something of the sweetness in him.

It was not the sweetness that Richardson and his fellow directors were to see in the following year.

29   *The parfit gentil knight*

There was a developing sense of crisis all through this autumn. But the season had its lighter moments. At a meal break during rehearsals Burrell, Richardson and Olivier arranged to meet at the Salisbury in St Martin's Lane to discuss some momentous decision or other. They had only an hour. On their way into the pub Richardson was waylaid by a little man. Seeming to recognize the man, Richardson said to the others, "I'll join you in a minute." Five—ten —fifteen minutes passed. It was nearly half an hour before Richardson finally rejoined the others. Olivier was in a rage. "Who the fucking hell was that?" "Oh," answered Richardson, in that high, far-away tone, "Don't know. He thought he'd seen me somewhere before and I was trying to help him remember where."

At the beginning of November 1946 Richardson and Olivier attended the opening night of *The Taming of the Shrew*, with Patricia Burke and Trevor Howard, and later in the month Olivier took *King Lear*, on a specific request from the Foreign Office, to Paris to appear for a week at the Théâtre des Champs-Elyées. The Old Vic was already functioning as a National Theatre in all but name.

"I should have been the fucking knight!" a piqued Olivier was heard to exclaim just before making his imperious entrance as Lear in January 1947. It was Richardson who, as the first choice to lead the company, and as the older leading player, was first granted the accolade. The announcement was made the day of a Cyrano matinée. The stage staff hurriedly fixed a brass plate inscribed SIR RALPH RICHARDSON to his dressing-room door. Olivier's dresser echoed the turbulence, "My guv'nor would never take a knighthood, he'd only take something bigger!"

Sir Ralph, now called by the staff "Sir-Rano", gave his best-ever performance that evening, watched from the wings by everyone who wasn't on stage and given, at the end, a tremendous ovation. The poet Patric Dickinson, then working in the BBC, wrote an encomium:

What gentleman so clearly clubbable?
What actor so discreetly dubbable?
See, how he pledges every part
From the gold tankard of his heart.

But the back-biting in the press grew. The microcosm of backstage dressers was magnified a hundred times. It was asked "If Richardson, why not Olivier?" Only the day before the knighthood was announced, American film critics had picked Olivier as actor of the year. "Does it mean", enquired one with refreshing frankness, "Olivier will feel mighty hurt and quit England, and come to act here?" Grub Street tongues clicked on: Olivier's being passed over was attributed to his divorce, as a clergyman's son, from his first wife Jill Esmond. A further rumour had Richardson and Olivier tossing for the knighthood, and Richardson winning.

No one grudged Richardson his honour: he had been a favourite with the royal family since the Queen had taken the two young Princesses to see him play Bottom. His film appearance as Major Hammond in *Q Planes* had also been much liked by the Queen. But the truth was that Richardson regretted his friend's exclusion. When, six months later, parity was restored, he lent Olivier his black waistcoat for the investiture.

The new knight did not know, however, that Cyrano was to be his second to last role with the Old Vic company, nor that his next part, as Face in *The Alchemist*, would be his last major role with them. The success of this production, directed by Burrell, with George Relph as Subtle, Joyce Redman as Dull Common, Alec Guinness as Abel Drugger, Nicholas Hannen as Mammon and Peter Copley as Ananias, surprised everyone.

It was a time of power cuts, coal and fuel shortages. *The Alchemist* cast was forced to rehearse in the circle bar of the theatre. Every day Richardson came in and asked exactly the same question, "Why do we have to rehearse in the bar?" One Friday the *Daily Express* made a devastating front-page attack on Emanuel Shinwell, the Minister responsible for power. When Richardson came in that morning and asked the inevitable question the paper was handed to him in silence. He read it carefully, his eyes slowly moving down the columns. He stopped. He looked perplexed. Could it be that he had not understood? After some time he pronounced, accenting the second syllable of the name, "Shinwéll, Shinwéll. Bad notices."

On the morning of the first night Burrell called the company together to run through words. George Relph retorted, "That's the very thing we can't do. We don't know them!" They rehearsed until forty minutes before opening, when they heard the house coming. Relph declared: "If I don't have a cup of tea, I won't be able to play it." Richardson dried on his first line. But the performance took off, notices were good, and *The Alchemist* drew full houses during the hard weather of the spring of 1947. Tynan wrote of George Relph—"His eyes pop with avidity. Mr Relph plays gallantly down to allow Ralph Richardson, as Face, to climb on to his back and then hoist the play squarely on to his own shoulders." Richardson, he went on, "is opportunism itself, shuffling and grimacing most impertinently, pushing in his lines swiftly and selfishly, as if each were a last straw at which the play might catch."

But conditions backstage grew dire; washbasins froze, and the cast were reduced to making up in overcoats. Rehearsals for *Richard II* had to be abandoned until the thaw.

Friendship thrives on restraint; in the Old Vic a kind of healthy family obligation flourished; in such a theatre company people were obliged to live together and to tolerate each other. The pattern for this, without which these seasons would not have been possible, was Richardson and Olivier's friendship, based on disinterestedness, or at least a pooling of ambition, and on mutual admiration. Neither was easily offended by the other; neither gave away the other's confidences: neither could be forced into insincerity. One cannot talk to Richardson about Olivier without feeling this fundamental respect: the deep friendship is maintained with the strictness of a vow.

The charming little double act when, at the end of performances in which they appeared together, each in turn held the curtain for the other, carried out more or less as a joke, typified those first three seasons at the New. Simplicity, understanding, and consideration, were, until the spring of 1947, the hallmark of this company's excellence stemming from Richardson and Olivier's behaviour towards each other.

But in January 1947, Olivier departed to make his film of *Hamlet*, while at the end of the season, in May, Richardson too began filming in earnest, one of his finest film roles: Karenin in *Anna Karenina*. He had worked three years for a pittance, by his standards, though he had managed time to appear in 1946 in Peter Ustinov's film *School for Secrets*. Ustinov in *Dear Me* (1977) impishly described the third day of shooting of that film. Richardson appeared "half Falstaff and half himself, bellowing his delight at being alive, but whistling like a kettle on certain sibilants"—having, according to Ustinov, left his bridgework at home. Ustinov, sent his assistant to telephone Richardson's home and in the meantime tried to delay shooting with various technical excuses, all of which Richardson at once tried to rectify. At last Richardson was called to the telephone reacting, on his return to the set, by being "suddenly overcome" by migraine, "the whole incident made more menacing by its understatement." A small packet was delivered by chauffeured car twenty minutes later, and ten minutes after that "Ralph appeared, once again in high spirits."* After *School for Secrets* the time had come for the long arranged break.

Richard II, the next Old Vic production, was intended to set up Alec Guinness as a substitute for the departing giants, but this failed. First of all Guinness, only just turned thirty, did not have the towering temperament of the other pair, nor was he yet at his peak, nor did he have the authority to be a figurehead. Moreover the production marked Richardson's début as a director, a necessary experiment, but one which, with hindsight, should prob-

*Richardson comments: "R. R. has never had false teeth."

ably not have been tried at such a critical moment in the
fortunes of the Old Vic.

John Gielgud's *Richard II* of 1938 overshadowed Guinness even before he had begun. Guinness asked Richardson what kind of Richard he had in mind. "I'll tell you, old
fellow," he said, and catching up an ordinary pencil, crack-
ed and grubby, waved it in the air. "Like that. Sharp and
slim. That's what we want." Capping even this, there was
more than a hint of self-caricature in the vagueness of his
instructions to Michael Warre, who had moved from playing juvenile leads to designing:

RICHARDSON:	I'm not sure how you're going to do this, but I have a strong feeling that the set should all be wood. All made of wood—perhaps moveable about the stage. You should be able to go in and out of it.
WARRE:	Permanent for the whole play.
RICHARDSON:	Yes. Perhaps we could change it from time to time; move it back for the lists, close it for Gaunt, use a raised bit for Flint Castle, enclose it again for the deposition and bring it right downstage for the prison.
WARRE:	We must have an upstairs for Flint Castle and probably for the lists too . . . this is leading us towards a formal structure, with an inner room, an outer stage and an upper stage. In fact Elizabethan.
RICHARDSON:	Why not?
WARRE:	Costumes?
RICHARDSON:	Why not Elizabethan structure . . .
WARRE:	With fourteenth-century costumes?
RICHARDSON:	Don't worry about that. The most important thing is that the actors should be at home on the set, which should be a prop they know and love. They must use

	it—handle it lovingly . . . so it should be made of beautiful wood.
WARRE:	What sort of colour?
RICHARDSON	(*pause*): Wood colour. The colour of beautiful wood . . . like . . . like this (*picks up a pencil*).
WARRE:	Cedar.
RICHARDSON:	Make the whole set of wood.
WARRE:	Homogenous.
RICHARDSON:	That's a five-dollar word.
WARRE:	It won't be a five-dollar set.
RICHARDSON:	Now go away dear chap and think about it. Do some sketches and we'll talk about it again. Remember . . . wood.

Warre claimed he was inspired by this boyish other-worldliness. For Tynan the set was easy game: "Possibly the most impractical that man ever devised. One cannot but stare when Northumberland, swarming with difficulty through a maze of pillars and posts, complains of these wild hills and rough uneven ways; and it is even odder when Bolingbroke . . . extracts a splinter from his arm and refers to the set as the grassy carpet on this plain. It was about as carpet-like as a porcupine." But the main difficulty remained with Guinness whose instinct was to play the role like Gielgud, but whose determination to be different made him play it against himself.

30   *Great holes in the skin*

He said he could discover great holes in my skin; that the
stumps of my beard were ten times stronger than the bristles of
a boar; and my complexion made up of several colours
altogether disagreeable. . .

Gulliver's Travels, Book I

Before leaving for Australasia with Olivier, Vivien Leigh
made the film of *Anna Karenina* (1948), with Richardson as
Karenin. Only the scenes with Richardson in them come
alive; Vivien's failure to respond to such a cardboard
stereotype as Kieron Moore's Vronsky is only too evident
in every sequence. George Moore had observed: "*Anna
Karenina* was written to prove that if a woman lives un-
happily with one husband and leaves him for the man she
loves, her moral character will deteriorate." According to
Anne Edwards, Vivien fell into a state of depression during
the filming because she identified with Anna, the pattern of
whose life, she saw, exactly followed that of her own.

Richardson was so persuasive and convincing as the
wronged husband Karenin—whom Vivien identified with
Leigh Holman, her own first husband—that for Vivien the
whole development of the story was reversed: in her scenes
with Karenin she was alive, responsive, doing her best to be
good; in her scenes with Vronsky she was remote and
implausible. Richardson with his long, round moustache
and spindly beard, his cherubic glow of vitality, not only
eclipsed everyone else but remained remarkably close to
the original. His enjoyment was evident in the detail of
Karenin's appearance—the large ears, for instance, or of
manner—the way he would crack his knuckles—which he
took directly from Tolstoy. Fortunately he ignored the
advice of the director, Julien Duvivier, who had a striking
sense of visual authenticity, but who told Richardson he
preferred not to hear every word he spoke.

Still repaying his debt to Korda, Richardson followed
Karenin with what many believe is his finest piece of screen
acting: the butler Baines in *The Fallen Idol* (1948), Graham

Greene's adaptation of his own short story, directed by
Carol Reed. Like *Anna Karenina*, *The Fallen Idol* was shot
at Shepperton Studios. Unlike Karenin, Baines is a weak
man, and Richardson was able to show with great subtlety
his fear and his aspiration towards goodness: in both parts
he captured a sensitive paternal tenderness, which had
become more of a reality to him since the birth of Charles.
These two intricate character studies, together with the
masterly portrait he was to draw in Hollywood in 1948, of
Dr Sloper in *The Heiress*, adapted from Henry James's
Washington Square, were an immediate reflection of the
run of luck he had had at the New. They were copies from
the matrices of the demanding stage roles which had
brought his career to its peak, copies which he could now
realize with almost infinite, subtle variations of tone.*

His only stage role of 1948 was as Marcus Ivanirex in
Romilly Cavan's *Royal Circle*, which he directed himself,
and which opened at Wyndham's Theatre in April. This
venture into management, his first, lasted only a short
while, for he was due to sail for America on the *Queen
Mary* in late May with Smallie, now three years old, and
Mu. *Royal Circle*, which was booed by the audience and
derided by the press, did not stretch to fill the time to his
departure.

In the meantime Olivier and Vivien Leigh had set sail on
the *Corinthic* for Australia, stopping on the way briefly at
Las Palmas and at Cape Town, where Gwen Ffrangcon-
Davies gave a broadcast, before finally docking at Freman-
tle in March. They rehearsed with their company on board
ship, opening at the Capitol Theatre in Perth. Olivier wrote
to Burrell, addressing him "Dear Johnnie boy":

> Strange birds jabber and laugh and squawk at us in
> various hitherto unknown ways. We have managed to
> see quite a lot of the place, and I think the Co. have had a

---

*Richardson had said, while in New York, "I find I cannot increase my
talent by working in pictures any more than a painter can do so by
increasing the size of his brush."

very gay time, being entertained by all and sundry, though our job, of course, has made it necessary for more serious matters to be allowed for. . . . Last night, Vivien and I gave a very jolly party on the beach after the show. Everybody swam and drank wine and ate delicious oyster patties, and I think a good time was had by all.

After telling him of the myriad social engagements thrust upon them by their hosts Olivier goes on to fill Burrell in on the fortunes of the shows:

It was quite a task as you may imagine to bash over Sheridan's gossamer trifles (*School for Scandal*) in a way that would be appreciated by 2,280 people. Many complaints of not hearing after the first night—although the entire company was roaring and spurting out consonants like machine-gun fire, giving all they had with every word. . . . It is the first live show that has played in this theatre for ten years, and I think a great deal of the inaudibility that was complained of, is on account of their having forgotten how to listen. This I have told them at every function in no uncertain terms, and sold them the idea of building their own theatre.

Olivier sounded very cheerful, but the tour was gruelling. The heat was intense and at night they were torn to pieces by mosquitos. Everywhere they went he and Vivien were treated like royalty, with all the attendant stresses and strains. By the middle of April, when they were settling down in Melbourne for a two-month period, the company was becoming very tired. But Olivier, now Sir Laurence, having gained confidence at the head of his own company, was still making brilliant speeches everywhere he went. His film of *Hamlet* had just been released in London and in May Burrell cabled him enthusiastic reactions.

Richardson had arrived on the other side of the world, in Hollywood. Burrell meanwhile had fallen ill, showing the strain now placed on the pivotal pin of the directors-in-triplicate, and went off to Ireland for a fortnight to recover. Richardson, Mu and Smallie sent him a food parcel full of delicacies to aid his recovery. Richardson told him he had instituted the innovation of driving on the left-hand side of the road in California.

Burrell was enthusiastic about Richardson's Old Vic replacement, Cedric Hardwicke. He is "most enchanting", he wrote to Richardson; further, "I have become greatly attached to him." Hardwicke had been engaged to play Gaev to Edith Evans's Madame Ranevsky in *The Cherry Orchard* and, in the autumn of 1948, Sir Toby Belch in *Twelfth Night* and the title role in *Doctor Faustus*.

There was no disguising the fact that the company had passed through something of a winter of discontent without the glorious suns of Richardson and Olivier to warm it. Burrell did not command the authority to hold together a conglomerate swelled with newcomers but from which the wartime spirit of unity had departed. Divisive factions sprang up, self-interest was rife, in particular among members of the Old Vic Board, who sought to exploit any weakening of the situation for their own ends. All might have yet been rectified by some foresight, some generosity. Such generosity was not forthcoming in such key figures as Lord Esher and Tyrone Guthrie. What was to happen became comparable, in the words of Charles Landstone, in his book *Offstage* (1949), to a Greek tragedy, overhung by the primal curse of a National Theatre.

At first a whispering campaign began, the detractors of the company exaggerating its decline, deceiving those who would listen—though apparently not one member of the Board, an elderly canon who would arrive at meetings and without removing the hat of his office, fall asleep—over the absence of its two leading players, and over the extent to which the company had become a two-star (some went so far as to say one-star) vehicle. These same detractors would gloat over items which lauded "Sir Laurence Olivier's Old Vic company" on the Australian tour; "Whose Old Vic?" they would ask in superior fashion. They raised their eyebrows over Richardson's much-publicized film roles, even though the fulfilment of his obligations to Korda had been agreed between Richardson and the Board. The prestige and the box office earnings that would accrue from his exposure to the film public would more than offset his temporary absence, it had been argued at the time—justifiably, as it was to turn out. While as for Olivier, what could be more directly in the line of duty of a National Theatre after a World War than to be leading a tour of the Dominions?

But Richardson and Olivier had miscalculated as to the quality of the company they left behind. They can hardly be blamed for this, for they chose the best actors available. With hindsight, those they picked increased their reputations many times over, with the exception of the already established Cedric Hardwicke. If Alec Guinness had not quite the weight to plant himself in the giant footsteps of his predecessors, he was still the outstanding actor of a generation ten years junior to Richardson and Olivier. Guinness appeared not only in *Richard II* but in *Saint Joan*, with Celia Johnson acclaimed in the title role, in Gogol's *The Government Inspector*, as Menenius in *Coriolanus* in which John Clements and Harry Andrews also took part, and he directed *Twelfth Night*, which featured Robert Eddison as an unusual Feste, as well as Hardwicke as Sir Toby. And the company also included Trevor Howard, Patricia Burke, Edith Evans and Faith Brook; while both Hugh Hunt and George Devine were to direct, as well as Burrell; hardly, one might think, a roll call of insignificant talent.*

In the spring of 1948 the behind-the-scenes machinations of the Board grew more intense and tortuous. Lord Esher, who had been in charge of the planning committee, now succeeded Lord Hambledon, who died in March. Amid the plotting and counter-plotting one crucial faction against the triumvirate stood out: the committee set up the previous year to amalgamate at some future time the Old Vic with a

*In the Governors' minutes for December 1947, it was reported that the Old Vic company at the New Theatre was doing good business, especially with *Saint Joan*; the provincial tour of *Coriolanus* and *The Government Inspector* made a surplus. So did the New (of nearly £2,000).

National Theatre, a scheme over which Lord Lytton had presided till his death. Olivier recalled a meeting at the time the committee had been formed: "Ralph said to me, 'You know, old fellow, this will be the end of us. These boys are not going to stand for two actors having all this power.' But under Lord Lytton we'd had our wicked way with the Board. It was lovely, everybody did whatever we said. Then Lord Esher came on the scene."

Oliver Lyttelton, another key member of the Board, was enthusiastic over this new committee of Esher's, calling it "a contract of marriage pending the consummation of the marriage", and Esher now managed to persuade Sir Stafford Cripps to earmark £1 million of Treasury funds towards building a theatre. Lord Keynes, however, as spokesman for the newly formed Arts Council, which had superseded CEMA as the body by which Government money was to be channelled into the scheme, displayed a more prophetic cynicism: "All betrothals do not end in marriage," he said.

In June 1948 the Board, with Esher, Violet Bonham Carter and Tyrone Guthrie as its more militant members, made final its plans to remove the directors-in-triplicate. They were helped at this stage by the fact that the 1947–8 season had made a small loss, the first of its kind, necessitating an increase in the subsidy. On the whole it is a rule of committees that they refuse to vote money unless they can control its spending: the new era was one of burgeoning committees seeking room to expand, pioneers of the great bureaucratic dawn ahead. As Richardson put it: "We never borrowed from the Arts Council or British Council although our budgets were underwritten. So up to then we didn't need them. We'd go along to meetings and sit there rather bored. They'd say, what are you doing next, and we'd say, well, you know, we haven't quite made up our mind and when we have we'll let you know. Why should we doff our caps, when we hadn't got a penny of subsidy?"

But now the case was being carefully prepared against him and his partners, and many arguments were put forward. One claim made was that without Olivier the company could do no good work: they had clearly forgotten *Cyrano*, *The Alchemist*, *An Inspector Calls*. Tony Guthrie described Olivier and Richardson as trying to "have the cake and eat it". Both he and others saw their opportunity while both men were away from England and unable, at short notice, to return. Their very lack of response would be interpreted as showing their want of commitment. Someone quoted from Ibsen's *The Pretenders*: "Norway has been a kingdom. It must become a people."

CHESTER TERRACE, *16 October 1979:*

Richardson is talking, I am taking notes, trying to pretend I am not: since the previous occasion I have become conscious that he possibly does not like having his words recorded.

"MGM asked me to go to Hollywood to make *The Heiress* with Olivia de Havilland," he is saying. "Laurence and Vivien had stopped off on a tour; suddenly we got this letter from Lord Esher: 'We don't want to renew your contracts' . . . they fired us. . . Yes, we thought we'd left a reasonable company behind . . . but it was all wrong, it had gone to pot; and then I think the whole thing fizzled out after that . . . later Esher died and they asked Laurence to start a National Theatre—I was in America. But the parts he offered were very dull; odd dukes and the like. Still I'd rather not talk about Laurence: I was always happy with him on an equal basis but I wasn't very happy with him as the boss . . . he was schoolmasterly; you know, 'Come to my office,' he'd say . . ."

I begin to notice a further change in Richardson since our first attempt at collaboration the week before. On that occasion he talked more about his experiences in the Fleet Air Arm than about the theatre. This week I have been asking him specifically about the parts he played in the New Theatre seasons and about other actors: on both subjects he is increasingly difficult to draw out. Of other actors he gives only brief descriptions, such as "Warre did the soft parts", Joyce Redman, "she was very pretty, very nice, perhaps a shade too much so for Doll Tearsheet." Of the conditions of work: "very little by way of sets; we were allowed good costumes."

This time I can hear the grandfather clock ticking and I am aware of the space around us. I sense Richardson is not interested in talking about himself; while he might, for form's sake, have prepared something in advance, it is not something he warms to instinctively. I try to get him to outline how he approaches a part, but his resistance is such that I find myself beginning to feed him with statements he has made elsewhere, as if recycling old propositions just to convince myself I am receiving them at first hand. They never work the second time.

I experience a flashback of some six years to an earlier meeting of a similar kind: with Samuel Beckett in the Café Flore in Montparnasse. There was in Beckett the same resistance to being drawn out. He, I remember, called it "the sore subjects of myself and of my work". He and Richardson share a deep need for privacy. They also share this curiosity about others, which I fear is about to break out in Richardson. If he begins to question me, the game is up.

I was asking Beckett about Jean Genet: "What do you think of Jean Genet?" "Genet?" he replied. "Yes, Genet," I repeated. "Genet?" he said a second time, as if I was trying obscurely to confuse him. "Jean Genet," I repeated so there should be no doubt. "Oh, *Jean* Genet," he said at last with a flicker of recognition.

Some examples of the same kind of thing with Richardson, slightly better on the whole.

G.O'C.:   What did you play at Belsen?

R.R.:   I don't remember playing Belsen.

G.O'C.:   Who were the actors whose performances
           made you conscious of certain elements about
           a part?

R.R.:   There weren't any.

G.O'C.:   How, for example, did you set about forming
           your idea of Peer Gynt?

R.R.   (*displaying great reluctance*): It comes from
           many different ways . . . something you see in
           someone's eyes; you find a character bit by bit;
           but it's all got to come out of yourself; it's a
           combination—it all comes from oneself, you
           might notice a bit, a memory; a statue out of a
           gallery, a foot . . .

Then it happens; the incident, small though it is, is
indicative, to me at least, that we have reached the limit of
Richardson's power to tolerate questions and of his willingness to go back over the past. Later I hear that Olivier who
has begun at this time to write his autobiography, with a
collaborator, has taped fifty hours of recollections.*
Richardson, I surmise, would be capable of perhaps half an
hour. But what a half hour it would be: all original, all to the
point even were there to be no point in particular. For as I
proceed I see that he is in possession of an extraordinary
power, by now highly cultivated, of never repeating himself.

Now we are sitting in his room: I am waiting for a reply:
"How do you view your approach to playing a new part, Sir
Ralph?" or something in this vein. Suddenly his left arm
shoots forward, as if unable to contain some inner demon.
It strikes with devasting accuracy his coffee cup and upsets
coffee all over the lid of his desk, and over the carpet. He

*It is because of this that Olivier, to whom I had written to ask if I could
talk to him about Richardson, replied in April 1980: "I selfishly, very
much lean towards trying to keep my own history, anecdotes and feelings
regarding this wonderful person for my own book in which, of course, you
may be sure, Sir Ralph will figure very prominently, as so much of my life
has been in companionship to his."

jumps to his feet, grabs blotting paper from the desk and starts mopping it up, saying, "How stupid and clumsy! Oh dear," and other expressions of regret. It is then I realize the deep nervousness which has been underlying his mood. The session is over.

But as we proceed to the ground floor, crammed together in the confining lift, he seems at once to relax. The ordeal is past, and in contrast to the constraint and refusal of the previous forty minutes, which he attributes to being nervous about his forthcoming appearances—as Old Ekdal in *The Wild Duck* at the National Theatre, in the other, longer-term project of *Early Days*, in a television play by Roald Dahl ("He's Scandinavian or something—not a name that it's easy to get one's teeth round")—Richardson is positively forthcoming about the present. Of a current production of *Richard III* with John Wood he remarks: "Hate it . . . no respect for Kingship—unless you take being a king seriously the play doesn't begin to exist—he kills in order to become king—unless you sympathize with these objectives . . . but if you turn him into a clown in motley the whole thing means nothing." On the subject of *The Wild Duck* and its director Christopher Morahan he supplies a vignette: "*The Wild Duck* is a fairy story . . . 'Oh,' said Morahan, 'I've got a Wild Duck who's fine.' 'What does she look like?' I asked. 'She's very plain.' 'Oh,' I said, 'well you can't have that, is it too late; can't you start the contract again?' 'Oh no,' said Morahan, 'I see her as plain. . . .' 'But,' I said, 'it's a fairy story . . . and there's a sacrifice: she sacrifices herself, and what's the point if she's not pretty?' But he's got this modern view. . ."

Richardson's behaviour at this second interview has created a mystery whose meaning I totally fail at first to unravel. When I try to work out its implications I am led more and more to the conclusion that it is the key to understanding him both in human terms and as an actor. I shall call it, for the present, his secrecy. I have become, in this last meeting with him, almost afraid of it—afraid of disturbing it, perhaps is more accurate: but I have, too, to admit that it is this secrecy which makes Richardson so fascinating a subject. One image, at this point, remains strongly in my mind. At the previous interview, he had offered me his pocket diaries covering a period of the war. They remained on my lap a few minutes only, and while he was talking I had the opportunity of leafing quickly through. Entries were virtually non-existent; odd sums of money (£38) on certain days; a dentist's appointment; a squash fixture or two. But suddenly the diaries were gone: he had gathered them up and whisked them away into the next room. Yet he cannot have failed to notice the gleam in my eye. His passion to conceal is what excites the curiosity he is so keen to discourage.

31   *The assassination of the giants*

ENOBARBUS:	There's a strong fellow, Menas. (*Points to the Servant who carries off Lepidus.*)
MENAS:	Why?
ENOBARBUS:	A' bears the third part of the world, man.

Antony and Cleopatra, II. vii

On 9 July 1948, a cumbrous document entitled *Private and Confidential Memorandum on Future Administration* was sent by Lord Esher to Richardson, Olivier and Burrell. In what seemed to Burrell like a calculated insult to Richardson, Esher omitted to tell Burrell he had sent Ralph a copy, with painful results for both. "Time, in its tiresome way, has marched on since you have been away. . . . I am sorry to bother you with these things," wrote Esher languidly in his covering letter to Olivier. The four closely typed pages of memorandum he enclosed specified first of all that an institution such as the Old Vic was about to become —including as it now did the Young Vic, the Theatre School, the experimental theatre as well as its other ramifications like the Bristol Old Vic—must have a permanent staff, and "cannot be administered by men, however able, who have other calls upon their time and talent".

It was therefore proposed, instead of the directors-in-triplicate, to have in the future a full-time administrator, who during his term of office would be debarred from acting and producing; an Artistic Director (just one) would be appointed annually. (The idea of downgrading the Artistic Director's post, and making him subject to a civil servant, had been the suggestion of Llewellyn Rees, Drama Director of the Arts Council and its nominee on the Board of Governors, who had given up acting in 1940 to become General Secretary of Equity. It was Rees's desire himself to become first administrator of the Old Vic and, despite some experience as a producer before the war, he was quite prepared to be debarred from acting or producing.) By these means it was hoped to give the future National Theatre a "corporate entity".

Esher ended his stab in the back to Richardson and Olivier with some fulsome appreciation of their work. To Olivier he wrote: "We fully realize the sacrifice you have made and the unceasing and exhausting work that the great position you have made for yourself entails."

In Hollywood Richardson received his copy of the Memorandum four days later. He wrote immediately, on the same day, to both Burrell and Esher. To Esher he replied in a tone, almost, but not quite, of sad regret; "The only expression I would make about that now is a personal one, which may have little bearing." He went on to say that he still wished to have a permanent association with the Old Vic, and "by that I do not mean a permanent cluttering of its stage with one's acting", but that he did not see how his desire could be granted, as the position of the director was defined as "not to act save in very exceptional circumstances". He concluded: "The actor seems to have vanished out of the picture! I believe there are actors capable of exercizing helpful influence in the theatre and it is my ambition to become one. We are busy here with a story by Henry James. The climate is most beautiful."

Richardson it seems had at first supposed that Burrell was conniving with the Governors behind his back, for he could not conceive of the Memorandum having been prepared without Burrell's knowledge. In his letter to him he adopted a concealing, joky tone. "How are you old bird? . . . I am working pretty hard at the studios—the director of the film [William Wyler] and the actors [including Olivia de Havilland] are very good—I cannot act for nuts—*and* nuts are cheap and plentiful in this country!"

He then continued, in his wily way, "Received a very charming letter from Esher," next telling Burrell he was enclosing his own reply to Esher. That was the only reference he made to his dismissal. He asked Burrell to give his love to Margaret, Burrell's wife, and said he was suggesting to David Niven that Niven's children, who were coming to England, should visit the Burrell family: "about the weight of your team, would recommend a tea fight—they are charming little beasts." For all its jocularity the underlying tone was a hurt one, with a faint trace of acid.

Two days later, on 15 July, Burrell cabled Richardson at Holmby Avenue, Westwood, Los Angeles:

DEAR RALPH ESHER HAS SENT ME GOVERNORS MEMORANDUM ON REORGANIZATION AND COPY HIS LETTER TO YOU stop WISH TO STRESS THIS PREPARED IN CAMERA WITHOUT MY KNOWLEDGE stop HAVE REPLIED ESHER PROTESTING AT ONE OUR NOT BEING CONFIDED IN TWO PREPARATIONS AND CIRCULATION OF MEMORANDUM DURING YOUR AND LARRY'S ABSENCE AND THREE REQUESTING NO FURTHER STEPS TILL YOU BOTH RETURN WHEN ALL SEVEN DIRECTORS AVAILABLE FOR DISCUSSIONS stop MICHAEL GEORGE GLEN HUGH ALL VERY ANNOYED AND MAKING DIGNIFIED PROTESTS stop PLEASE DO NOT REPLY ESHER UNTIL YOU GET MY LETTER AND COPY MY LETTER TO HIM AIRMAILED TODAY SINCE IMPORTANT WE REACT IN UNITED WAY AND AVOID ATTEMPTS DRIVE

WEDGES BETWEEN US WHILE SEPARATED stop MIGHT BE PREFERABLE SEND YOUR REACTIONS TO ME FOR TRANSMISSION ESHER stop AM SENDING IDENTICAL CABLE LARRY stop HOPE YOU ARE WELL LOVE BOTH=JOHN

Thus, Richardson's suspicions of Burrell were only too soon allayed. He was, of course, mortified at having held them and at once replied in the warmest possible way:

DEAR JOHN DID NOT REALIZE MEMORANDUM COULD HAVE BEEN PREPARED WITHOUT YOUR KNOWLEDGE SO REPLIED TO ESHER COPY TO YOU AND LAURENCE SAME POST stop WILL OF COURSE TAKE NO FURTHER ACTION stop UNITED WE STAND stop LOVE = RALPH

In Australia, first in Melbourne, then in Sydney, before this blow fell on him, Olivier had been finding the tour an increasing strain. The Melbournese, he noted with irritation, were "piss-elegant" and "nervously smug", and there was a tense humourless fear one was getting at them all the time. In Victoria the same round of shaking the hands of the members of Parliament, lunching with the top boys, and coughing up the identical speeches of gratitude, and being carted round the sights, made it all seem "a bit harder than I thought it could be". Attendances remained good, though the applause was restrained, especially compared to the response the Old Vic had received in Paris or New York. Of the company he had nothing to say but good.

On Saturday, 3 July, during the matinée of *Richard*, in the middle of the fight scene, he slipped and injured his knee. This brought considerable pain and while an X-ray at Sydney hospital revealed no bone damage, the knee continued to give trouble. Vivien too had fallen ill with a bad chest cold.

The Governors' Memorandum and covering letter took much longer to reach Olivier than they did Richardson, and before they arrived he had had Burrell's cable of 15 July. He at once cabled Burrell that the missives had been received, ending "OH ME I SEE THE DOWNFALL OF OUR HOUSE = LARRY".

All Burrell could do was to ask Esher to delay taking any further action until Richardson and Olivier were back in England. "It was indeed unfortunate", replied Esher, "that two out of the three directors of the Old Vic Theatre Co., should have been out of the country at the time when these important matters came up for consideration, but I think I have made it clear that we shall await their return in November." Unfortunate, but highly convenient, he might have added.

It was clear they had already lost. In spite of what they might think or feel over the next three to four months, there was nothing any of them could do without bringing the row out into the open and giving the Board, in their absence, the opportunity to say they were not behaving with the dignity their office required.

Burrell, in particular, deeply resented not having been taken into the Governors' confidence: he interpreted this as meaning that no one placed any trust in him any more. Apart from running the company—and here he obviously lacked the morale-boosting power of Olivier and the paternalistic soothing presence of Richardson—he had been devoting long and arduous hours to planning future seasons. These had been put aside for no apparent reason, and he now saw why. Having an administrator to take the place of the Board of Governors would remove, as he wrote in one angry draft of a letter he never sent to Esher, "the tedium and frustration of fortnightly meetings with fumbling and amateurish Governors, to whom even good manners come grudgingly." But till then, he pursued in his rage, he wanted the Governing Body renewed every five years so as to avoid "Government of the Young and Eager by the Old and Ineffectual". In any case, he concluded, he was off to America where they "know the mysteries of keeping the old men out of the way and giving the younger men a chance to get on with it".

Richardson, who had been trying to fit in enough film work to give himself two years running at the Vic from 1949, was equally dispirited. He had worked hard on a script of Ibsen's *Brand* with James Forsyth, who was adapt-

ing it, ironing out certain difficulties. He was hoping to
broadcast this in late 1948, and, with Burrell directing, to
stage it in 1949. He got his agent to ask Margaret Leighton
to play either Gerd or Agnes, if she were available.

As for Olivier, he felt, as he phrased it in his subsequent
letter to Esher, "more than a little woeful", and "apt to
picture oneself as a pioneer disowned by his country in the
middle of a very distant campaign". He had thought in
terms of continuity and had, he considered, put a great deal
of energy into training a good company for the future. In
fact he had the nucleus of the New Theatre company still
with him.

In that distant campaign they left Brisbane for New
Zealand. After playing 14 performances in Auckland they
flew on to Christchurch nearly 500 miles away, where in the
middle of the dance in *The School for Scandal*, Olivier's
knee played up again. Before setting sail again on the
Corinthic for England, he had it operated on in a nursing
home, and the cartilage removed. His final exit from the
antipodes was achieved by means of an iron crane which
hoisted his convalescent form over the dock on to the
Corinthic.

Richardson was the first to arrive back, cracking jokes
about Hollywood. Not at all as bad, he said, as everyone
made out: William Wyler was "sympathetic, imaginative,
co-operative". Moreover, Richardson was full of enthusiasm for garbage disposal units, and machines that automatically electrocuted flies. Someone had asked him,
he said, "What do you do with your chopped bones in
England?" He had made reply: "In England, sir, we eat
our chopped bones for supper." To Burrell's secretary
he delightedly showed off a new ball-point pen. "Look
—this wonderful new thing—it won't smudge." But it
did.

His exhilaration was much dampened by seeing Cedric
Hardwicke in *Doctor Faustus*, which opened on 7 October
1948. Hardwicke had spent far too long in Hollywood and

grown lazy and accustomed to underplaying.* As he told Gielgud: "My agent reads the scripts for me. I would never agree to do them if I had to choose them for myself." Marlowe's text emerged in some very odd forms. Those on stage couldn't believe their ears at "Was this the face that launched the fish and chips?" while at "Ah, hear me with patience and tremble not at my . . ." Hardwicke would pause, apparently not quite knowing what came next. Words? Ideas? Thoughts? It changed nightly.

The house was only a third full. When the lights came up Richardson looked like death. On him fell, he thought, the main onus of Hardwicke's failure, for it was he who should have played Faustus, and Hardwicke, the old friend and mentor of his early career, had been brought in at his suggestion. And now he had the additional unpleasantness of having to be brutal to him: *Faustus* was withdrawn on 9 November. Strangely enough though, in the one great error of his own career which he was to make later on, he failed to take warning from Hardwicke's example.

Twelfth Night, which had opened late in August in Manchester, was much better. In a cast that included Harry Andrews (Orsino), Robert Eddison (Feste), Faith Brook (Olivia), Mark Dignam (Malvolio), Peter Copley (Aguecheek), Sir Cedric did, in Tynan's words, "for Sir Toby exactly what Sir Ralph did for Sir John Falstaff . . . restored him to the knighthood."

Richardson worked hard on rebuilding morale in the company, with some lighthearted results which belied the gravity of the situation. After one performance of *Twelfth Night*, calling round backstage, he entered a dressing-room where, as Donald Sinden who was playing Sebastian recalled, eight of the cast dressed: "Our dresser, who was notably camp, pranced up to him and lisped, 'Oh, Mr Coward, we haven't met since we were together in *Bitter Sweet*.' Ralph stood his ground, looked him straight in the

---

*In some ways his plight was similar to Peter O'Toole's, coming back to play Macbeth at the Vic in 1980. "Have you seen it?" Donald Sinden asked Richardson at his club. "No . . . No . . . It's not what you expect," was his reply; "it's like having a duff operation at the Middlesex."

eye, and after a pause answered—voice lifting in that strange, grave way—'Ah! Yes—I remember.'"

It was to take more than rock-like imperturbability of manner to shake the Governors. In late November Burrell prepared an appreciation of the situation for himself and his co-directors. In the meantime Esher indicated to Olivier that he would like both Richardson and Olivier to rally round the Old Vic during the Festival of Britain year of 1951. In other words he wanted, as Olivier tersely informed his colleagues, to sack them and have them back when it suited him, to ensure that the Old Vic had some strength when it needed it. He too wanted, in Guthrie's old words, to have the cake and eat it.

When it came to the fateful meeting in early December at which Esher's Memorandum was properly implemented, and while their contracts still had six months to run, they put up little resistance. One by one—and joined now by Saint-Denis, Byam Shaw and Devine—they were summoned before the Governors. One by one they emerged tight-lipped, angry and pale. But silent. Only Saint-Denis, on his emergence, not being English, commented angrily: "They treated us like schoolboys—telling us we spent a lot of money and had not quite got all of it back!"

Predictably there was considerable reaction to the public announcement of the directorate's "resignation": "Old Vic Rumpus" ran the *Evening Standard*'s headline: "The company's future now becomes a matter for conjecture." Cyril Ray put the Governors' case in the *Spectator* on 17 December. Their action was, he wrote, "in recognition of the change for Britain's most distinguished repertory theatre to the National Theatre Company-to-be," and continued, "most people will view it in the light of the failure of the Old Vic's current season which has exposed the present weaknesses." Among these he continually names the influence of Ralph Richardson and Laurence Olivier, quoting, out of context, Harold Hobson, that a film-fan following "replaces knowledge and judgement with sexual hysteria". Even Basil Dean, one of the contenders for the new Artistic Directorship, went so far as to say later in the *New States-*

man: "And the emergence of two supremely good actors, both with screen reputations, and their ability to pack the New Theatre at all performances during the feverish conditions following the grand climacteric of the war only helped to confuse the picture and to delay the day of reckoning." Only in two letters to the *Daily Telegraph*, both written by Stephen Mitchell, the impressario, did the opposing case begin to be put forward. Mitchell cast doubt on the competence of the Board to run the Old Vic, continuing that he might have supposed that the "ardent co-operation and continuance of those two gentlemen [Richardson and Olivier] should have been a *sine qua non* of the Governors' policy". To this Esher replied on 21 January 1948: "Mr Mitchell's general thesis shows that he shares with Sir Thomas Beecham a lamentable ignorance of how things are run in this country."

Llewellyn Rees was appointed Administrator of the new company, while Hugh Hunt became the first Artistic Director, at £30 per week. It is questionable if their achievements in any way approached those of the triumvirate.* Two years later the trio of inspired practitioners appointed by the directors-in-triplicate to run the Old Vic Centre, known affectionately as the "Three Boys"—Devine, Saint-Denis and Byam Shaw—quarrelled with Rees; so many resignations followed in succeeding years that it became a stock joke in theatre clubs to have an approved form to hand round among members to be filled out by "applicants wanting to resign from the Old Vic".

No company has quite achieved such popularity and prestige either at home or abroad since. In January 1946 *The Times* had written that Olivier, Richardson and their company had once more brought the English theatre into

---

*In the new brooms' zeal to obliterate the traces of the old, apparently even the files from the triumvirate's period at the Old Vic were destroyed. According to Kate Ashbury (now Mrs Griffin), "They packed five seasons' letters into huge skips and stored them away in damp cellars where in time the files started to disintegrate. Some years later I went down to the store: all the letters had been sent off to be pulped. But they kept the petty cash vouchers."

an era of great acting. Later Harcourt Williams summarized their achievement:

> Three men of cultural integrity and unquestioned ability in the art of the theatre gathered up the threads of the original organization which the black hurricane of war had blown hither and thither, and wove them into a pattern. . . It was an undertaking that required great courage, foresight and patience. I sometimes think it could never have been done but for the old friendship that existed between Richardson and Olivier.

Burrell, Richardson and Olivier made no public attempts either to defend themselves, argue their case, or even to correct the more flagrant errors spread by the opposition whose stature has with time notably diminished. And while at the end of 1948 the company had a bank overdraft of £8,000, in January 1949 there was over £10,000 of advance booking. For the last six months they played to capacity houses. Sir Laurence's Old Vic company on its Australasian tour had also earned the British Council £42,000 after tax. (The Governors decided not to approach the Australian Government to have the tax repaid.)

Olivier, Burrell and Richardson were, comparatively speaking, all innocents. They were careerists without being politicians, they put quality and the public they served first. Possibly the taste for grandeur shared by the two knights was something in the nature of an Achilles' heel. In the very long run neither of them was to suffer. The only true victim was Burrell whose position, owed as it was to the other pair, had been resented by Guthrie.*

From the Governors' point of view, committed as they were to the idea of a National Theatre, Richardson's

---

*To Margaret Burrell, there was definitely a villain: Guthrie was the "rogue elephant who kicked the whole thing down". In June 1949, when his contract expired, Burrell did go to America as he threatened, to take up an appointment in drama at the Krannert Center, in Illinois. There he remained, with occasional incursions into the limelight as a director, notably for CBS, and once or twice on Broadway, until his death in 1972 from a heart attack.

dismissal was an act of blindness, for it was impossible to imagine anyone more suited by temperament to working in and leading a National Theatre company. His unassuming attitude of mind made him particularly suitable for such an ambitious and difficult undertaking, for it generated support. He had the capacity for equalizing extremes, both in himself and in others. He was a natural figurehead, the outward embodiment of modesty, such as other actors felt affection for and looked up to: it was to "be a daddy", as he said, that Guthrie first asked him to lead the Old Vic, and wisely his first act had been to share, to ask Olivier to join him in running the venture.

Of the sacking he did admit later to feeling "rather badly treated", adding, with his usual self-containment, "but a fired butler doesn't complain of his master."

THREE

Close to the Heart

1949–1982

History adds that before or after dying he found himself in the presence of God and told Him: "I who have been so many men in vain want to become one and myself." The voice of the Lord answered from a whirlwind: "Neither am I anyone; I have dreamt the world as you dreamt your work, my Shakespeare, and among the forms in my dreams are you, who like myself are many and no one."

Jorge Luis Borges

CHESTER TERRACE, *November 1979–February 1980:*

Over the next few weeks I interviewed survivors from the New Theatre seasons, consult newspapers, read through the enormous documentation on Richardson's years as an Old Vic director, preparatory to writing the sample chapter. At his invitation, I spend a morning at Chester Terrace going through his leather-bound volumes of press cuttings which have been carefully stacked for me on a side table in the dining room. (The exercise almost comes to grief, for Richardson at noon generously provides, through the medium of his daily, a decanter of sherry and biscuits. I start on the sherry, but efficiency decreases quickly and I ask for coffee instead.) The earlier volumes have been beautifully arranged and edited by Richardson himself, the reviews impeccably titled with discreet calligraphic flourishes. They present another facet: his strange influence in them is always near. I feel eerily alone in the house and yet I can sense some presence upstairs, as tangible and yet as intangible as the footprint Crusoe found on the seashore. Possible it is José, Richardson's parrot.

On 26 November I telephone Richardson:

R.R.:   Oh my dear chap, how are you? . . .

G.O'C.:   Very well, thank you. I've nearly finished all the research for the sample. When can I come and see you again?

R.R.:   (*very fast and jerky in manner: is he practising Old Ekdal at my expense?*):   I don't think I can . . . just now . . . I'm in such a state . . . I can't tell you . . . I can't find my way . . . can't see how to do it . . . confused as anything . . . it's like a prison . . . a garret (*This confirms it:*

*Richardson has become an old Ekdal and sees
everything including me from the viewpoint of
the old man hidden away in his attic; the jerky
manner he talks in is how he plays the part, with
the extraordinary and sudden effusiveness, too*).
Still, my dear fellow, how are you? . . . let's
leave it at that till the play's opened.

G.O'C.: Could I, in the meantime, come and talk to
Lady Richardson?

R.R.: Oh yes (*Pause: cogitative break lasting some
moments*). Lady Richardson—as you kindly
call her . . . she's watching television . . . yes,
I'm sure she'll see you dear boy.

Even longer break now as he goes to fetch Meriel Forbes.
Although this is the first time I have spoken to her her voice
is warm, friendly. "Yes," she says, she will be "delighted"
to see me, and she will have "lots and lots" to tell me about
Ralph. But she thinks it better if she waits until *after* I have
done the chapter.

I finish the research as best I can, write the sample chapter
—leaving gaps which I hope to fill in later from Richardson's first-hand account—and send it to the publisher. In
February 1980 he rings to say that the reaction is one of
approval. Richardson found it "very interesting", I am
told—but "would you like to wait until the David Storey
play opens", which is in April. "Anyway," says the publisher, his old friend, "why don't you give him a ring?
Ten-thirty in the morning is the best time."

It happens just then to be 10.30 a.m.: with a certain
trepidation, I dial the number. Richardson is in bed. Later I
discover he has always been a late riser. (Robert Speaight
in 1931: "I remember once when at the cottage we told
Ralph that he would have to breakfast at seven in order to
reach the theatre in time for rehearsal. With amazement in
his eyes he asked: 'Is there such a time? I've never heard of
it.'") I am told to telephone again at 11.30. I do. Totally
inconclusive result:

R.R.: I feel terribly guilty, dear boy, for not having replied to you about the chapter. I'll phone you very soon.

Nothing happens for a fortnight, but in the meantime I have decided that with the material I am still quarrying, and which begins to come in from all quarters, I may as well have a shot at the book whatever happens. This small contact with Richardson over the speculative idea of collaboration has revealed sides of him that I might never have hoped to see had I begun entirely from the outside and remained there.

For the present, I leave it that I am dealing with two Ralph Richardsons: First, the man of many secrets and many desires who, it may be, has organized his secrets as all cunning men try to do, to guard one another. The man who is impenetrable, who reveals one thing to one person, only to profess total ignorance of it to another. The man who is clever enough to act at times with a seemingly total transparency that leaves you aghast with wonder; the man who keeps his deep opinions and intentions to himself. Above all the man who, as the record shows, will never consent to be interviewed by the same person more than twice (again, I note, the principle of the game, the home and away match). The Duke of Dark Corners who has a filing system of secrets to which he alone keeps the key. But who, suddenly and unpredictably, will cast all this elaborate indirection to the winds and show he has nothing to hide at all: it is all just a trick, he says, or like Peer Gynt, a peeling of the onion. "Nature is witty."

And there is a second Ralph Richardson, whose interplay with that first is now less and less predictable: less public, more watchful, who has genuine affection for people. The shy man who gives when it is least expected of him. Both sides, which over the years have undergone subtle transformations, are traceable back to his childhood: on the one hand the "character", the role-playing individual whose role has merely attained a super-sophistication of amazed simplicity to match the media technology of the

1980s. But still, on the other hand, the poet who is everything and nothing. People change but remain in essence what they always were.

Ralph No. 1 is most in evidence on our next meeting at 12.30 on 18 February 1980. "How are you dear chap? Book doing well in the States?" (He means my book on Maggie Teyte, just published in America, which he has read.) He goes on at some length. "A minor masterpiece," he calls it. Genuine appreciation or a well-aimed arrow? What *have* I come about??? . . . the mere matter of a book about Ralph Richardson. Oh yes, I've almost forgotten. Then, says Ralph sharply, "Well, you asked to see me, what's it about?"

I notice his sharp eye on mine. "Well—" I swallow, coming slowly to the point. "I have decided," I say, "having gone so far . . . in my research . . . I should like to proceed with a book. After all, with the effort . . ." Gaining courage, I proceed passionately for some minutes. I stop, heart in mouth, to see how he will react.

The intensity has made an effect: he seems quite quizzical. His answer is very calm: "Well I've committed no crimes so far as I know . . . done nothing bad in my life, so you can't libel me. I have never killed anyone—I have sometimes speeded round the Park at seventy miles an hour when no one was looking, but that was a different matter. But yes. Go ahead . . . I won't stop you . . . as long as you don't libel me. If you think you want to write it—and God knows there's not much to write about, then publish and be damned."

That over, thank goodness, we talk pleasantly of lighter matters; I ask him if he has read Jung. "Read some essays by him: very funny stuff, found it on the set, you know they buy books by the load for the set—found a wonderful book about the law—I'll lend it to you. *First Steps in Law.*"

By now he is worried about the time: he has to be somewhere for lunch and is very late. "Shall I give you a lift?" I offer. "Where are you going?" "To the Royal

Academy—the Post-Impressionists . . ." "I'm not going that way—I'll take the bike."

We go down. "Bye bye dear," he whispers through an open door to the Unseen Presence. Turning to me, "Bye bye dear fellow, see you soon."

I might add that I know he is having lunch with his friend the publisher: he does not know I know. For once, I console myself, I am one secret up.

32 *Old vinegar in a new bottle*

> You've been sufficiently assassinated, sufficiently suicided, to be able to stand on your feet, like a big boy.
>
> SAMUEL BECKETT, *The Unnameable*

For a period of nearly three years, from April 1947, when he was still at the Old Vic acting John of Gaunt, until March 1950, when he scored a hit in *Home at Seven*, by R. C. Sherriff, Richardson originated no important roles in the theatre. His only stage success was as Dr Sloper in the play *The Heiress*, in which he appeared with Peggy Ashcroft in early 1949. As the play was the basis of the script of the film in which he had already appeared (later he was to bring off the hat-trick by recording a radio version of it for the BBC), he was not suffering the nervous crisis he usually passed through at the creation of each new role while enduring the disheartening confrontations and meetings that accompanied the break-up of the Old Vic triumvirate in December 1948. But when rehearsals for *The Heiress* began at the

Haymarket, it became progressively clear that John Burrell, whom Richardson had asked to direct, had neither the confidence nor the energy, after the tensions of the past year, to make the best of the script. Dangerously near the end of the rehearsal time, Richardson had to dismiss him. With only five days to go to the opening Gielgud was called in to take his place; Ralph told him gloomily, "We have today assisted at the murder of Caesar."

Richardson gave no explanation to the cast of the change of director. "I don't know what I'm going to do," Gielgud said. "I don't want to change anything, I just want to tighten it all up." But when they had played a run-through for his benefit, and he had witnessed the appalling blocking —they were "strung out from side to side like a football team", he observed—he gutted the production, changed every move, changed the set, had it repainted and even substituted furniture from another time to make the period flavour more exact; and all this within five days. So tactfully and deftly did he achieve this that everyone, including Peggy Ashcroft who had feared Gielgud might want to change too many things, relaxed. The outcome could not have been more successful. "I can see Richardson now standing up against the heavy mantelpiece of his ornate drawing room in Washington Square," wrote Harold Hobson ten years after the event:

> a cruel, relentless figure whose cruelty and relentlessness were due to a great grief within; and I can hear his voice ring out, "That is no consolation," every word spoken as if it were a note in music, resonant, reverberating, echoing down the corridors of interminable years of sorrow. The emphasis on the word "that" was terrible; at one stroke it destroyed all the healing properties of time; and the "consolation" lingered on the air like the distant and dying tolling of a bell.

Sloper's "great grief" was over his wife's death. It is little wonder that Richardson, with his experience seven years before of a similar event, and now his chagrin over the demise of the New Theatre venture, could give the line the energy which communicated itself to Hobson, arousing compassion while it might, in the hands of some equally gifted actor, have awakened disdain and hatred for ruthless self-interest.

While Richardson was now universally accepted as one of England's great actors, his career over the next few years was at its lowest ebb. In some respects these years were for him disastrously similar to the 1930s and while his fortunes underwent redemption and salvation by fits and starts, there was a danger of professional extinction which formerly had not existed.

With Alexander Korda's death, in 1956, he lost the assurance of continuing in substantial film roles in the Karenin–Baines mould. His last work with Korda was as the millionaire inventor (another widower), John Richfield (or "J.R." as he is known by his staff, as he ruthlessly pursues his goal), in *The Sound Barrier* (1952), directed by David Lean,* for which Richardson won the New York Film Critics' Award, and as the Reverend Lambeth in *Smiley* (1956), directed by Anthony Kimmins, which Richardson travelled to Australia to make. *Smiley* was Korda's very last film. Richardson also appeared in Olivier's film of *Richard III*, filmed largely in Spain in 1954, in which he played a much reduced (in terms of text) Duke of Buckingham. The size and impact of what little he did in this film, and in particular the potent and dignified way he turns on Richard when the latter sends him to his death, remain memorable.

He also lost, and was to continue for the next 25 years to be without, the environment which suited him: that of a repertory company. Having been with the Birmingham Rep in its prime, and with the Old Vic in three of its finest periods, he was now to be homeless in this respect until well past the age of seventy, for him as important a turning-point as his performances as Peer Gynt and as Falstaff.

Nothing more was heard of Esher's proposal that

*Richfield was, like Dr Sloper, a widower. Lean, as had Wyler in *The Heiress*, made a point of filming Richardson largely in long shot, making the close-ups, when they came, all the more effective.

Richardson and Olivier rejoin the Old Vic at some future date. Indeed, the very reverse happened. In a calculated insult to the pair Guthrie asked Donald Wolfit to lead the company during the showcase Festival of Britain year of 1951. After initial glory and success—Wolfit, as might be imagined, was superb as Tamburlaine—the arrangement began to go sour. Wolfit resorted, in the words of his biographer Ronald Harwood, to "the petty-cavortings of the actor-manager: up-staging, fidgeting while others spoke, prowling, jumping in on speeches before the other actor had finished, giving endless notes on their perform-ance to his colleagues, and generally making himself dis-agreeable." Guthrie, having accused Olivier and Richard-son of behaving like old-fashioned stars, had now replaced them, in a key season, with the real thing. Wolfit's be-haviour led to an angry reprimand from Guthrie which in turn led to Wolfit's resignation from the Old Vic.*

Following his performance as David Preston in *Home at Seven*, at Wyndham's in 1950, Richardson had another respectable West End run, as Vershinin in *Three Sisters* at the Aldwych, before joining Anthony Quayle's Shakespeare Memorial Company at Stratford-upon-Avon in 1952. There he intended to prove that the Old Vic Governors had been badly mistaken in dismissing him two and a half years before. He was offered Prospero and Macbeth, neither of which he had yet attempted but be-lieved were within his grasp. The latter he had performed before the war on the wireless, to much critical commen-dation, while Prospero should have appealed to his poetic faculty—though the role, while deceptively that of a magi-cian, lacks the fantasy of Bottom or Falstaff. And as he had pulled off Face in *The Alchemist* against the odds, in Burrell's production in 1947, it was a natural progression to

---

*In May 1952 Wolfit, like a ghost from the previous dispute, rose up at a public luncheon of a right-wing organization, to deliver a tirade against the Old Vic: "And so the sorry tale goes on—public money—your money and mine is poured out to keep alive this monstrous pretence of a National Theatre. . ."

play Volpone, his third big role in this season.

The Tempest was a revival of a Stratford production of the year before: with expensive designs by the Australian Loudon Sainthill, and with Michael Redgrave as Prospero, Richard Burton as Caliban, and Alan Badel as Ariel, it had been so successful with the public that it seemed wrong to consign it to oblivion. Richardson, therefore, had been persuaded to take over Prospero ("You could never see me as Prospero," he said later with the advantage of hindsight). Alan Badel was replaced by the tall and statuesque Margaret Leighton, which caused a few raised eyebrows from those who didn't know that for a long period of theatre history Ariel was traditionally played by a woman (Leslie French in 1922 had been the first male Ariel this century). Leighton and Richardson were to resume their New Theatre partnership not only in *The Tempest*, but as the Macbeths. But whatever the relationship between the pair, both off-stage and on, it went awry, for soon after joining the company Margaret Leighton met Laurence Harvey, and their affair became the *cause célèbre* of the season.

Richardson's and Leighton's professional connection had been a rich one: they had played together in *Peer Gynt*, *Arms and the Man*, *Cyrano de Bergerac*, and, most recently, in a radio version of Ibsen's *Brand* which they had hoped to perform at the New Theatre in 1949. (The outstanding sections of the broadcast were those played between Richardson and Leighton, the latter as Brand's wife; Richardson's Brand was noble and regretful, rather than following the more generally accepted view of the character as passionate, even perverse, in his defiance of conventional values.) But at Stratford, unfortunately, this fortunate relationship had clearly come to an end. While Margaret and her lover met in secret, Richardson appeared to be undergoing a humiliation which, in his roundabout fashion, he was to purge and make public through his performance as Macbeth.

33 *Meeting with the goddess of drama*

The ill-fated *Macbeth*, its protagonist too early translated for Richardson into a nightmare character, opened in June 1952. Richardson wore a red wig, having sent down his wig-maker into the stalls during one matinée of *The Tempest* to snip a lock of schoolgirl's hair he decided was just the right shade. Kenneth Tynan in the *Evening Standard* began, as Agate had done in the Thirties and with some of Agate's magisterial tone, to consign performance after performance of Richardson's to the tumbril with a swift downward flash of the pen. He first took to task the director of *Macbeth*: "It was John Gielgud, never let us forget, who did this cryptic thing, Gielgud, as director, who seems to have imagined Richardson, with his comic, Robeyesque-like cheese-face, was equipped to play Macbeth. . . The production assumed, or so I took it, that the audience was either moronic or asleep." As for Richardson, the outward appearance pellucidly revealing the inner condition, he appeared to Tynan as a "robot player, a man long past feeling, who had been stumping across the broad stage as if in need of a compass to find the text". After a momentary flicker of life, his "numbness, his apparent mental deafness, returned to chill me; Macbeth became once more a sad facsimile of the Cowardly Lion in *The Wizard of Oz*." The formal crystal ball, as Richardson liked to describe the actor, had become "the glass eye in the forehead of English acting".

Richardson, without in any way blaming the depressing black velvet Gielgud had chosen in his desire for the non-realistic—the kind of extended-metaphor approach Peter Brook was to adopt more successfully later with *A Midsummer Night's Dream*—took this all very badly, as might be expected. He externalized his sense of failure in a self-deprecating style which was embarrassing to others, for Anthony Quayle too often behaving like "a great big whale—a whale standing on end—makes a lot of wet —everyone gets upset." "Has anyone seen a talent," Richardson remarked, waiting for notes in the Green

Room the day the reviews appeared. "Not a very big one, but I seem to have mislaid it." One night after delivering the great dagger speech he came over to two members of the cast standing by the curtain and said: "I've lost the knack; if I was a member of the audience, I'd ask for my money back." At another time later in the season, during a performance of *Volpone*, he took aside another actor: "Give me five pounds." "What?" said the puzzled colleague. "Give me five pounds." The actor began to wonder if Richardson was still sane. Richardson: "If you don't give me five pounds I'll have it put about that you were in my *Macbeth*."

The damage was done; 1952 became known as Richardson's disaster season, despite his Volpone having some merit. Afterwards he could find fault with himself for not being able to apply his more circumspect methods to Shakespeare's most monolithic, most straightforwardly tragic figure—he hadn't, he said, Olivier's splendid fury, he couldn't blaze because he was not "in the first division"; and this in some sense may have been the trouble, for Macbeth is above all a character who needs frontal assault. Yet there was a more serious impediment of which he himself was only dimly aware, and which made him inhibited with Macbeth, as he had been inhibited with Othello: his inability to portray a character who is the helpless victim of some blind, driving passion within him. In Othello's case it is jealousy, in Macbeth's, ambition: both are too extreme, too inhuman, too near the old basic morality figures for Richardson to feel at ease with them. It had been the same with Caliban at the Old Vic in 1931: Harcourt Williams and Gielgud had difficulty, then, in bludgeoning him into evil. He never could enjoy sheer basic devilry, for in whatever he did the goodness shone through. Because he could not identify with either Othello or Macbeth, he argued that he would never be any good as Hamlet or Lear: but those are both much more mixed characters, more accessible to his kind of compassion and confirmation of contraries, his calculated unevenness.

"Sir Ralph and Shakespeare's 35 children," ran an unusual headline in the Stratford-upon-Avon *Herald* of 25 April 1952. Perpetrating one lapse from his best while preparing a second—in Stratford an unmitigated failure in a production hangs, like an albatross, round an actor's neck all season—Richardson was responding to the toast of "The Drama" at a luncheon in celebration of the 388th anniversary of Shakespeare's birth. Part of his speech ran:

> To speak for all drama there should be tears and pity and horror. There should be grace and wit and laughter. There should be tension, too, perhaps the air torn with a shriek. And all this after lunch! And last, the most important of all, something of moment should be said, some response from on high delivered. I assure you this worried me a lot. I practised a bit. I put on a very deep voice. I did not like it. I tried another voice. It was bad. My shriek was not a success. I wore myself out with worry. I went to sleep. And then I had a dream.

In his dream he conversed with the great goddess of the drama herself. He hoped she would give him some message to pass on, but she was more concerned with telling him how originally she was a Greek lady, how she had gone to Rome, and of the theatres they had built for her. But she did say Shakespeare had been her greatest love—"We had the most wonderful affair; I think we had thirty-five children. I think it was thirty-five—there were one or two about whom no one is certain."

The subject of love, of mistresses, of affairs, if our diagnosis has been correct, perhaps at a more personal level, was not far from his mind: but turning it all, transforming the weight and sense of disaster inside, into lightness, in some curiously resourceful and paradoxical way, his innocence managed to rise above.

Which comes first, great critic or great actor? Or, one might add, bad critic or equally bad actor? They are as essential and as consequent one to the other as night to day; as Pope pronounced in his *Essay on Criticism*, there is as much danger in judging ill as in writing ill.

Richardson's distinctness on stage has always appealed to the outstanding critic. In a strange shift of perspective, Tynan, assuming in the Fifties Agate's mantle of influence (though Harold Hobson of the *Sunday Times*, less wizardly descriptive, remained on balance possibly more influential), was projecting in *The Observer* and elsewhere as fixed a view of Richardson's acting as had Agate in the Thirties. The terms and conditions of theatre reviewing were much altered since Agate's day, but in some essential qualities the two critics were alike. Both were hedonists, both well-read intellectuals who despised ordinariness, who loved the outlandish, the récherché, and, when they could make literary capital out of it, the vulgar; Agate's love of the grand became transmuted, in Tynan, into an inflation of the television cult personality (Johnny Carson, for example). The difference was that Agate preserved some integrity and authority, as a disseminator of opinion, to the end; it is hard not to feel that Tynan became lost in, and seduced by, various pipe-dreams beginning with bull-fighting, turning to Marxism, then *Playboy* sex of the most juvenile kind—though towards the end of his life, notably in his *New Yorker* profile of Tom Stoppard, residual traces of a certain Agate-like steel suggested the reformed sinner once again seeking quality.

Both Agate and Tynan despised the common man; neither could find virtue in ordinariness, in the rapport Richardson could establish with the man in the street who in Richardson saw himself in larger-than-life form. While for Agate Ralph could never be moving because he was so blunt and straightforward, by Tynan, who had to go Agate one better, he was pilloried for transforming that bluntness into what Tynan saw as vacancy or lunacy. Vacuity, for the newly formed *Zeitgeist* of the Fifties and Sixties was an early stage of madness, deadness signified not just itself but burnt-out life, insoluble tension, spiritual bankruptcy or social deprivation. While the man of action had, in Ibsen's time, been supplanted as protagonist by the artist-hero, the artist-hero was soon in turn to be supplanted by the actual lunatic—the first of the three figures Shakespeare lumps together as being akin in imagination, the lover and the poet being the other two. So Richardson's Macbeth was not only dull, it was "sleep-walking", while Gielgud's production left Tynan "unmoved to the point of catalepsy". What Tynan had not noticed was the prophetic element in Richardson's interpretation.

On his next appearance, in *The White Carnation* by R. C. Sherriff, opening at the Globe Theatre in March 1953, Richardson's transformation into this persona of Tynan's imagination was complete; dullness, bluffness had become total unreality:

> Over the past few years the resemblance between Sir Ralph's demeanour on stage and that of a human being in life has been getting progressively more tenuous. He has taken to ambling across our stages in a spectral, shell-shocked manner, choosing odd moments to jump and frisk, like a man through whom an electric current was being intermittently passed.

Skilfully, as the review proceeds—but only after his main point has been ineluctably driven home—Tynan does actually reveal that Richardson is meant to be playing a ghost—a "perplexed phantom" returning to the bomb site where his terrestrial existence ceased in 1944. Tynan did not see that Richardson, in his instinctive way, was beginning to progress towards a new style of acting, which meant a new way of being himself, to suit the changed circumstances of his time. Dimly, he must have glimpsed all those lunatics lining up to take over our stages, beginning in 1966 with Brook's Theatre of Cruelty season and then with his *Marat-Sade*. But as that time, the early 1950s, had little or no identity, or none which found an outlet in the theatre and with which he himself could identify (anger and kitchen-sink realism when they came were both beyond, or beneath, the scope of his art), Richardson would remain at sea. Just as he could not find it in himself to exemplify Agate's vision of the classic actor, he could not identify with Tynan's long-term destructive power as the apostle of Frantic Stimulus, beginning as it did with Osborne's anger.

Richardson belonged to some quieter, but more substantial, ebb and flow of fashion.

In 1953, during the run of *A Day by the Sea*, Samuel Beckett, whose *Waiting for Godot* was under a six-months option to Donald Albery, called on Richardson in his dressing room in the Haymarket Theatre. It is almost impossible to imagine two men looking less alike: Beckett so spare, so ascetic, the long Irish features, the wiry and electric hair, the deeply cerebral expression into which, nevertheless, a strong element of Celtic dreaminess has been woven; Richardson, genial, ruddy-faced, flat-headed and now balding, his face betokening the healthy indulgence of appetite, a disdain, at least on the surface, for anything too intellectual; his tremendous sang-froid beside which Beckett, for all his coolness in danger as a French Resistance courier, must have appeared an anonymous acolyte.

Richardson had been asked to play Vladimir in *Godot*, and Alec Guinness had been approached for Estragon. Gielgud had read the play and pronounced it a "load of old rubbish", though Richardson had not altogether agreed:

> Albery got I and Beckett together; he arrived with a knapsack over his shoulder like this [showing how]. I said to him, "Let me have your knapsack." He said, "No, I'll keep it." Oh, I thought; well I said, can you explain one or two little things . . . I had a little laundry list. "On the whole I like it, but there's something I can't work out. Number One, who is Pozzo [*he pronounces this to rhyme with Gozo*]. "I won't explain," said Beckett. "There's nothing to explain. . . ."

Richardson admitted he sadly misjudged the play out of literal-mindedness, not being able to bear obscurity, distinguishing it strongly from mystery: "For me, the child in *Waiting for Godot* was mysterious, but Pozzo was baffling and obscure. Like a fool I didn't do the play. Very great mistake—one of the greatest mistakes of my life." He did not yet appreciate Beckett's capacity to give obscurity, as opposed to mystery, concrete expression; that, moreover, "the solitude, the despair, the commonplaces of non-communication", in Sartre's phrase, were "profoundly and essentially bourgeois". When he did so, with his slow, measured, but profoundly sure sense of craft, he was able to place himself firmly in the Beckett tradition, not in any works by Beckett himself but in tailor-made, less obscure and more ephemeral works by Harold Pinter and David Storey which drew heavily on the Beckettian mode, and which were at the same time fashioned in the manner of the 1920s and 1930s as star vehicles for Richardson and Gielgud.

34 *Notes of nervous tension*

N. C. Hunter's *A Day by the Sea*, which opened at the Haymarket in November 1953 with Richardson, Sybil Thorndike, Lewis Casson, Gielgud and Irene Worth and directed by Gielgud, although it "figured among the best writing the stage had to offer" at the time, and confirmed the now much closer friendship of Ralph and John, who had ridden out *Macbeth*'s failure with impunity, was hardly the play to revive Richardson's fortunes and reputation. But with this glitteringly cast production, and others like it from the H. M. Tennent stable under Hugh ("Binkie") Beaumont, the Haymarket became for some years a *de facto* National Theatre, at least until Olivier started the Chichester Festival in 1962. Beaumont brought together the best of established talent, and added promising newcomers from time to time—notably, over the next few years, Anna Massey and Alan Howard. Richardson had a main role as adviser in these productions.

With the part of Dr Farley in the Hunter play, Richardson returned solidly to a portrayal of human weakness expressed by means of strong drink—a "brilliant study in aggressive failure", Milton Shulman called it in the *Evening Standard*. Having been involved in a much-publicized court case a month before the opening, Gielgud was worried at the effect this might have on an audience and upon his own reputation. Richardson insisted on changing their first-night entrance so they could come on stage together, thus giving his friend visible support. Even so Gielgud found the first night an ordeal, and his performance was, as Shulman noted in his review, "on a note of nervous tension that almost shrieked."

Gielgud's fears proved groundless. The public, far from being alienated, rallied to his support; in subsequent years his acting benefited enormously from having cleared this hurdle of secrecy over an element in his private life. *A Day by the Sea* ran for almost eighteen months, but closed prematurely, in May 1955, when Gielgud was forced to retire to bed for some weeks with double vision.

Richardson and Mu managed to escape for the rest of 1955 to Australia, acting on tour together (as they had two years before in *The White Carnation*, in which Mu had played the librarian with whom Richardson's other-worldly visitation falls in love). In Australia they joined Sybil Thorndike and Lewis Casson, the quartet appearing together in Terence Rattigan's *The Sleeping Prince* and *Separate Tables* (Rattigan attended the Australian premi-ère in Perth).

They played to packed houses, the takings often exceeding £1,000 a night. According to Sybil Thorndike, "Mu gave an exquisite performance [as Elaine Dagenham in *Separate Tables*], almost too subtle for all but the most perceptive audiences. But our audiences were very percep-tive. Ralph was, as usual to me, perfect in both plays."

What struck Richardson initially about being in Austra-

lia, as he wrote later, was something of which the atlas gave
no hint, namely that the Australians and New Zealanders
"thought a great deal about us in Great Britain, a great deal
more, I should say, than we think about them". It proved
difficult for him to redress the balance, as he hoped to, at
least socially:

> One is asked . . . in the morning before lunch when tea is
> served; one is invited to lunch and after lunch tea is, of
> course, served. The most unusual cup of tea I can
> remember was one night at the trotting races. At about
> nine o'clock I was invited to the Stewards' Room, and a
> whisky and soda leapt to my mind; but, inexorably, there
> was some splendid tea and hundreds of scones and cakes!
> I am afraid I sadly shirked my duty . . . perhaps . . . I
> could have shown a little more how grateful I felt that the
> people of Australia had the kind thoughts of us in Great
> Britain. But, to tell the truth, I put in so poor an
> appearance and was so ill at ease when tightly packed
> among a great many people, however kind, that I felt
> that I was the worst possible advertisement both for my
> theatre and for my country.

Dame Sybil also commented on how little keenness the
Richardsons showed in exploring places and people:
"Actually, I think Ralph is rather shy. He considers an
actor should display his feelings in his art, and off the stage
be as private as he wishes. Mu understood this and backed
him up in his unwillingness to meet people. And of course
we respected his point of view, although we didn't share it."

In Sydney they opened the new National Theatre, and
one night Richardson was going to the theatre in a taxi
when the driver said to him, "How do you like it out there
at this New Elizabethan?" (the name of the theatre). As
Richardson recorded:

> "I like it very much," I said, "it's a very nice theatre."
> "You don't say?" said the driver.
> "Oh yes", for some reason I went on, "very nice
> theatre to play in, very nice to speak in."

"You don't say," said the driver. I said no more.

"I drove two old ladies home from the Elizabethan last night, mister," the driver turned round to inform me, "and they were saying, in this cab, that they couldn't hear a word you said!"

But, apart from the astonishment of finding infants in arms among matinée audiences—the company played, as Richardson said, to "gurgling wails" and a "powerful and sustained infantile trumpeting"—he found the whole experience bracing and enriching.

Over the next eighteen months Richardson did not appear in the West End, though he did surface briefly, and inconclusively, in a further season at the Old Vic in the autumn of 1956, in his sole assumption of Shakespeare's most self-flagellating role, Timon in *Timon of Athens*. Timon, and, eleven years later, Shylock, were his only new Shakespeare parts after 1952, (though he did play Bottom a third time in 1964 and, on radio, John of Gaunt, again, in *Richard II* in 1960 and Hamlet in several scenes from *Hamlet* in 1961). It is a crucial question: why should he have omitted all the wonderful older characters within his range—Polonius, Caesar, Leontes, a dozen others, even Lear—and turned only to two of the most wayward and eccentric of Shakespeare's creations, whose only apparent trait in common is paranoia in advanced form? There would seem to be a personal answer to this as well as an artistic reason. The reduced circumstances of Timon's power and, later, of Shylock's, in some distorted mirror or glass reflected his own narrowed sphere of influence; but neither is a minor role, both represent a still-ongoing creative force. Paranoia is by its very nature unfinished, and by wrestling with the problems of these two characters, and, true to form, trying to emphasize the sympathetic sides of their natures, he was trying to find his way out of an impasse; that way, ultimately, would lead also towards a widening of his own imaginative resources.

Now came two great roles in which his underlying soundness revealed itself, above all his sense of size. The first of these was General St Pé in Anouilh's *The Waltz of the Toreadors*, which ran for four months at the Coronet Theater in New York in Harold Clurman's production (it won the New York Drama Critics' Award for Best Foreign Play). Again compassion was the keynote of his performance—a touching, poignant quality underneath the crusty exterior of the old soldier. The critical reception given him in New York far exceeded that given to his Falstaff— Anouilh's popularity in America has always been greater than in England—and the play could have run much longer than it did, but for the rare intervention of illness.

He thought he had cancer. He awoke one day near the beginning of the run and found a hard lump had formed in his throat. It may, he says, have been something to do with being out of England for longer than his system could tolerate—he needed his old haunts, the Coffee Room of the Athenaeum, his steady hobbies, the bit of speed on the bike, his contact with nature through his pets, originally the white mice, now the ferret, or a white rat which may or may not have originally featured from time to time. He struggled on but his voice was reduced to a whisper, and before finally withdrawing from the run he had been absent for 34 performances over the 12 weeks. No one could diagnose what was wrong, except to say it was a "pachydermous condition of the larynx"—causing a hardening of the membrane coating the vocal chords. He returned to England very lowered in spirit, expecting he might have to have a throat operation. But after some weeks away from New York his larynx mysteriously returned to normal.

His early return to London did enable him to play in an untried playwright's first major work which Hugh Beaumont wanted to put in straight away to fill the Haymarket, a theatre which had become Richardson's second home, and in which his runs would ultimately total seven years. The play was Robert Bolt's *Flowering Cherry*. Bolt's talent was greater than the play: later, in his preface to the published text, he confessed he had tried "with fatal timidity, to handle contemporaries in a style which would make them larger than life"—but the casting of Richardson did ensure it achieved just that dimension. *Flowering Cherry* ran for over 400 performances* and subsequently toured, enabling Bolt to give up his teaching post.

Bolt acknowledged his debt to Richardson:

On the first night, no one knew what kind of play it would be; Binkie, Frith Banbury [who directed] both hard men. . .

Binkie observed "Well I suppose you know we don't hold out any great hope." Then it opened. Ralph transformed the play, lifted it to a level it didn't deserve. It was a triumph. After I went round to thank him. "Well old boy," he said, "just a printing edition!" He is a genuine eccentric. He had a white rat which followed him everywhere. He played a naughty trick on Celia Johnson [who played Isobel Cherry]. He got the rat out and made it crawl up his leg. You should have seen Celia's face. Conversation became very restricted. Eventually Mu threw a mackintosh in his face to stop him. "What's the matter?" he said. "You know what the matter is," said Mu.†

Flowering Cherry was also Richardson's first solid stroke of luck for some years, for in spite of Bolt's comment and in spite of its conventionality, the play is meticulously sound. It was craftsmanship of a kind which the West End sorely needed. Richardson's own style benefited from the conven-

*The actor Clive Swift recalled as a student visiting Richardson after one performance. Knocking timidly on the dressing room door, he was called in. Richardson stood in one corner, wearing a dressing gown, and never once looked at him. Swift declared how much he'd enjoyed the performance, adding that, as a student of theatre, he had come up to London from Liverpool. "Oh, yes," said Richardson. "What are you seeing next?" Swift, suddenly flustered, couldn't think of any other shows on in London. Taking his time, Richardson came to the rescue. "Why not try Sir John Gielgud?" he said. "He's appearing in *Ages of Man*. Jolly good—once he gets going!"

†"What white rat?" comments Richardson. More probably it was a white mouse—the same one that accompanied him in Oxford where he was once seen with a police escort—to shine a torch in its path to make sure it did not vanish down a drain.

tionality and he began to channel those frisky, odd mannerisms into a form of language or symbolism. To take one
instance, in Cherry's scene with his son's girl friend, when
he has drunk rather a lot—a scene which unfolds with a
certain repressed sexuality in its gentle parody of courtship
—Cherry says: "To you I must seem as repulsively old as
you are young—", Richardson could be seen, apparently
inconsequentially, tapping with his foot on the floor. But
this could be taken to signify restrained desire, and far from
departing into the unknown, waywardly representing the
supernatural, Richardson was cleaving to his old preoccu-
pation with basic gesture, with the exaggeration which is
an individual's distinctive quality—Benson's scraping of
his sword on the floor in *Hamlet*, Mrs Patrick Campbell
practising her pistol shots in *Hedda Gabler*. In accordance
with his poetic temperament he was further, and with
subtlety, to develop this symbolism, redirect this repressed
aggression into curious baroque structures of art from
which a sense of inner conviction and truth were rarely
absent. He was to learn, in the very end, to balance the
outer eccentric with the inner man. But not before some
pretty odd tilts at windmills.

CHESTER TERRACE, *June 1980:*

I telephone Richardson one evening. Mu answers: "I'll see
if I can find him." Long pause. I imagine the message
travelling several levels through Chester Terrace but producing no response. He may well have forgotten who I am:
always a chance of this with him.

At last he comes to the telephone. The voice is very high—into its other-worldly register:

R.R.: What a terrible day. Has there been a storm where you are?

G.O'C.: Yes there has: a terrible one.

R.R.: Oh awful—got trouble with the roof: water pouring in.

He has identified for me my uncertain sense of his location: he actually sounds as if he is speaking from under the roof—there is joist-hanging tone to his voice.

Sometime after April 1980, the notion somehow revives among all concerned that Richardson and I might collaborate. Although I have said I will go ahead on my own, Richardson has never actually given a final answer as to whether or not he will be involved, always pleading greater involvement in *Early Days*. On the back of the brown envelope in which my sample is returned are notes he has written in pencil:

The Family
27
my father
60 companies
on tour
Stop the trains
and talk
to each other
leave each other
notes at the
digs

So every now and then I send him a suggestion as to how we might combine without resorting again to the direct question-and-answer technique which proved so unsatisfactory to him on the second occasion. These suggestions include asking him to talk on various themes, such as friendship, or meeting in various locations connected with his life which might act as a spur to memory, such as the Haymarket

Theatre, the real tennis court at Lords, where he says he still plays—and indeed does, every Friday at 3 p.m..

But now, like many actors and actresses, he has rocketed off into the obsessional orbit of his work: spinning fast he no longer approaches normality from the same angle. Only he knows the law of the unique craft at whose control he sits. But if contacted he indicates, invariably, friendliness and willingness to be helpful, to meet, to talk it over further on some future unspecified occasion when circumstances will be much easier.

It is hard not to believe, for the next few months at least, that our relationship is other than that of hunter and prey. However hard I may try to conceal it from myself, or however decent and honourable I profess my intentions are, or whatever the self-imposed conditions I make over the use of such material as I might find—even to the extent of not using it at all—none the less my purpose is to find out all I can about one Ralph Richardson. The contact I have already had with him, the meetings with those close to him that I have yet to have, and the personal contacts still to come, are crucial to my task. My behaviour becomes characterized by a peculiar blend of patience and impatience: to be too patient is to become passive, but to be too impatient means that the hunter's cover is broken too soon and all will have been in vain.

At this point perhaps one ought to ask: Surely actors like publicity? Surely, 99 out of 100 "show people", as Tynan dubbed them in his last book, would be only too flattered and excited to be the subject of a biography or object of an autobiography? Not Richardson. He remains undazzled by, even indifferent to, the idea of self-revelation. I recall him, in somewhat melancholy voice, relating that he had just met Ingrid Bergman at a party and she was telling her life story into a tape-recorder, including the intimacies of her sexual behaviour. Clearly he didn't think this was his line. Perhaps the revelations would be too dreadful. "We all have original sin," he has said. "I would much rather be able to terrify than to charm." Was he serious? At another time: "When I'm asleep, I'm earning my living if I have a nightmare. I get murdered a good deal. I get stabbed quite a bit."

More to the point, Richardson knows, of this I am only too sure, as de Gaulle knew in the world of politics ("one has scant reverence for what one knows well"), and as Henry James knew in practising the art of the novel, that secrecy lies at the core of power. Here is yet another variation of the old paradox: is it really a desire for power, using secrecy, or is it a fundamental modesty and reticence? Perhaps both, again. And if I, as biographer, am lying in wait to record, is not Richardson, to an even greater degree, doing the same? His own sensitivity, his own identity, is not his concern. "Great poets, great actors, and, I may add, all great copyists of Nature, are the least sensitive of all creatures," wrote Diderot in 1778. "They are too apt for too many things, too busy with observing, considering and reproducing, to have their inmost hearts affected with any liveliness. To me such a one always has his portfolio spread before him and his pencil in his fingers." To see Richardson sitting at his sloping desk, with Regent's Park before his eyes, is to know just what Diderot meant.

Thus I realize that Richardson, too, is lying in wait for those vulnerable secrets and possibilities of himself which he will be able to use in his next play—which, it so happens, is in itself a veritable act of self-revelation. Indeed it may be that his withholding of himself from me has given him a sense of the biographical process, which, as it turns out, is at the heart of David Storey's play *Early Days*. One of the most important elements of his acting in this play—apart from the fact that he is living, to some degree or other (one cannot be too definite) the character he portrays— becomes his creation, out of his own biography, a structure to make the character he is playing appear at times factually (as well as imaginatively) real. The logical conclusion of this, as I am to appreciate soon after, is that Richardson and I, for different ends, are deeply in competition. I want from him what he needs for his part.

But with Richardson everything is also a game. He and I, exchanging roles, are engaging in a form of play. With him a game is a privilege as well as a stimulus, for one knows he will play generously and with humour. Even when, as in the old swashbuckling movies, he has flicked the sword out of your hand, he will pick it up and throw it back to you to resume the bout. Like Cyrano he holds that the greatest thing in life is good craftsmanship, be it in love, in arms or with a pen.

35 *Famous tales of eccentricity*

As Richardson grew into late middle age, change became slower and outwardly dramatic events dwindled: the volume of work remained huge, and his energies were equal to it. As a craftsman gradually and steadily creating better and better conditions for himself to work in, he had eliminated the distractions of an extreme life-style so that he could find freedom to perfect his talent, refine it and remould it into different forms as occasion demanded. As he expressed it at this time in a BBC interview:

> After a hundred performances quite a finished little job, as a jeweller or goldsmith might fashion a jewel or a cup or indeed a little crown; it's perfect and it fits nice. And you might say you've got those, to comfort you, surely they give you assurance; they don't somehow; I don't know why: we've got a certain amount of talent but it's of no use until it's refashioned . . . We have to pull it out and melt it down and fashion it out again . . . Every part is a new beginning.

His son Charles progressed satisfactorily through preparatory school in Oxford to Stowe—father and mother used to arrive in a grey Rolls, providing an unforgettable image on the sports field or in the quadrangle. Later Charles went up to Christ Church, Oxford, to read English, acting with distinction in the University Dramatic Society, sometimes uncannily resembling his father.

Richardson had built himself up an establishment figure, distinctly cosseted, one might say; he would find a garage in the West End in which to park his Rolls; if not travelling under his own steam he knew a car was ready to pick him up and drop him off; in every town he knew exactly the hotel in which he wanted to stay. (Asked once about the difference between first and economy class in an aeroplane he replied, "Don't know, old chap. I've always travelled first.")

The actor Nicky Henson recalled being invited to Bedegars Lea for a birthday party when he and Charles Richardson were small, and spotting on his way across Hampstead Heath a huddled figure in an overcoat—it being January —sitting by Whitestone Pond. "The house is full of children," said Richardson mournfully. "—I can't stand it." (He was not as extreme as Olivier, who once dressed as Father Christmas for a children's party and so terrified the children they burst into tears, his own son Richard among them.) If Richardson sometimes expressed bizarre or contradictory feelings about children, it was perhaps because, in the eternal boy he remained—or became more of in time, as if to make up for his own loss of a real boyhood —there was an element of refusing to abdicate his own childhood in favour of his son. Actors have to be children. They have to be able to make-believe on such a scale. Much of childhood is being in a spellbound state in which events are not grouped in time, a state of innocence before a choice has to be made. In order to spellbind others the actor has at all costs to preserve this. He has to experiment; as Kean says in Sartre's play, "Every morning I put on the me that matches my coat."

Possibly Richardson never became sufficiently realistic as a father, at least judging by what he said much later, in

America in 1976, in a newspaper interview: "My son Charles is . . . thirty? Yes, I think he is. I always forget. I always think he's about three. He's working for English television as a stage manager."

Nothing was denied Richardson—no honours either (these had begun two years before his knighthood of 1947 with the Star of Olav conferred by King Haakon of Norway for his *Peer Gynt*). He had become the English actor *par excellence*,* symbolizing in his own person those qualities with which the ordinary Englishman identified, even loved, because ordinariness in him carried such weight and importance. His sensitive and moving portrayal of the cuckolded dentist, Victor Rhodes, in Graham Greene's resounding stage success, *The Complaisant Lover*, at the Globe in 1959, deepened and refreshed this image of ordinariness. Yet Richardson still carried his hat at a rakish angle. He still behaved in that other great English—the Johnsonian—tradition of eccentricity.

Some nights he might be seen, this imposing figure, striding down the Haymarket tapping affectionately with his cane the bonnets of cars parked alongside the curb. "Lovely little Austin," he'd say. "Perfect grand old Rolls —sound old Sunbeam," and other endearing invocations. He believed machines had souls. The unwary and unsuspecting newcomer at one of his clubs might find himself subjected to a ritual exhibition of the awesome size and quality of his personality. Michael Meyer, the biographer and translator of Ibsen, related how very insignificant he felt when he first joined the Savile and found himself sitting at the long communal table with other members. Who should arrive but Richardson: great eyes, noble expression, the embodiment of the famous English actor. A waiter

*He remained a staunch royalist. In June 1974 he telephoned to *The Times* complaining that the flag in Portland Place was not flying at half-mast during court mourning for the Duke of Gloucester. "Even Austin Reed's have got theirs at half-mast," he said. "And so have London Weekend Television." Once, on a Caribbean cruise with Mu, he was taught how to play Bingo by Princess Alice of Athlone. (On the same cruise he accused the captain of turning round the ship, thereby blinding Richardson's team with the sun, in order to win a game of deck cricket.)

Peer Gynt, the dreamer: above with the Green Woman (Margaret Leighton). *(John Vickers Archive, London)*

and below with Aase (Sybil Thorndike). *(John Vickers Archive, London)*

Falstaff: Rembrandtesque study, by John Vickers. *(John Vickers Archive, London)*

As Falstaff, with
Doll Tearsheet
(Joyce Redman).
*(John Vickers
Archive, London)*

As Face in *The
Alchemist. (John
Vickers Archive,
London)*

In defence of tobacco.
*(John Vickers
Archive, London)*

On a jeep-borne razzle with Olivier in Hamburg, 1945.
(Imperial War Museum)

Some Korda film roles: Karenin in his library in *Anna Karenina*, 1948). *(London Films)*

Some Korda film roles: with ace pilot Olivier in *Q Planes*, 1939. *(London Films)*

With Mu, at a glittering Korda Première. *(Associated Press)*

The landscape artist at work. *(The Mander and Mitchenson Theatre Collection)*

Rehearsing for *No Man's Land* with Peter Hall's shadow in foreground. *(Anthony Crickmay)*

Spooner and Hirst in action. *(Anthony Crickmay)*

As Kitchen in *Early Days*, attended by Gloria (Mary Cruickshank). *(John Haynes)*

A new motor bike, 1975. *(Times Newspapers)*

came up and asked, "Will you take beer or wine, sir?" Richardson thought for a moment and then voiced his quandary, in declamatory tones with appropriate pauses.

"Shall it be beer? Or shall it be wine? It shall be neither, it shall be milk—a pint of milk, bring me a pint of milk."

The waiter, flustered, withdrew to fetch the order, came back and set it down. Richardson, with a grandee gesture, picked up the tall glass and quaffed it in one long draught (Meyer was trying to finish his soup); he then turned, showing Meyer the great white mark round his lips:

"Nectar!" he said.

Thought Meyer, I'm not coming here again in a hurry.

A formidable encounter during lunch at the Beefsteak between Richardson and the literary critic and novelist Cyril Connolly was once witnessed by J. W. Lambert of the *Sunday Times*. Connolly was wearing a wide-striped suit, 1920s style, rather flashy:

RICHARDSON	(*after eating in silence for some time*): That's a very nice suit.
CONOLLY	(*unimpressed*): . . . Oh.
RICHARDSON	(*getting intrigued*): How many suits have you got?
CONNOLLY	(*puzzled*): Eh? . . . Nine.
RICHARDSON:	I've got forty-two, but of course it's different for me.

He fished in his pocket and produced his visiting card which had his honorary degrees and clubs listed, handing it to Connolly to peruse.

RICHARDSON:	Some of my friends have said you don't need all the letters—*
CONNOLLY:	Oh yes. You just ought to put your name—unless you're a Jesuit.

Richardson abuptly turned to the neighbour on his right. A pause. He then returned to the attack:

*Richardson comments: "R.R. was asking for advice for which he was grateful."

RICHARDSON: Do you know the edition of
Shakespeare's work, the Nonesuch
edition? I've been collecting them.

CONNOLLY   (*muttering*):   Oh yes . . . beautifully
bound, I believe.

RICHARDSON: I don't know if you know, but the
leather comes from one single breed of
sheep raised in the Sahara for that
particular edition and when they die
there will be none of that leather left.

CONNOLLY: Oh no . . .

Later Connolly stomped along the street outside. "Do you believe that about those sheep?" Connolly asked Lambert. "I think it was just to pay me out for the visiting card."

Some years later in the Savile, Michael Meyer had got to know Richardson much better. One lunch hour he found him by the cashier's desk where members pay before leaving the club; suddenly Richardson said aloud, as if his own private train of thought was utterly self-evident and everyone had been following it, "There's nothing particularly odd about a jam omelette, is there?"

Meyer asked what the matter was. Richardson replied, "I ordered a jam omelette from the waitress, and she told me, 'Sir we have all kinds of omelettes, ham, tomato, cheese, but I don't know if there's a jam omelette.' So I said to her, 'Well, you know, a jam omelette's not all that difficult, once you have the general idea of an omelette,' and so in the end she said 'I'll go and ask the cook.' So off she went and came back and asked, 'Cook wanted to know who it was for—what name am I to give?' I gave my name and off she went; a second time she returned: 'I'm very sorry, sir, cook says they can't do it for you.'" At this point Richardson turned to Meyer and said, "What I want to know is, who do you have to be in order to get a jam omelette?"

Perhaps the crowning glory of this eccentricity was to come a few years later, when Richardson acquired a parrot.

He learned in time to combine its company with his other hobby, that of motor-cycling. Parrot perched on shoulder he would set off, more slowly now, for a spin—sometimes with pipe clenched between his teeth.

Eccentricity appeared to have overflowed into art, at least in Enid Bagnold's *The Last Joke*, Richardson's next West End play after *The Complaisant Lover*. The title must have tempted the worst in Richardson, or so the authoress put it about. *The Chalk Garden*, produced successfully some years earlier, had given everyone high hopes. But even before rehearsals began John Gielgud, who had refused the part of the Tycoon and wanted to play the Romanian prince "who lived in Chiswick Mall and fell half in love with easeful death", telephoned Hugh Beaumont, from New York. Bagnold's intention had been that he take poison, but, she reported in her autobiography: "John Gielgud wanted to shoot himself. And amid fireworks . . . For so great, so beautiful, so perfect an actor he was being silly. Stars are sometimes silly, but very seldom he."

Bagnold against her better judgement agreed. But then: "Suddenly there was a new development. Unasked and uninvited, Sir Ralph Richardson wanted to be in the play. He wanted the part of the Levantine Millionaire Art-Collector who, moreover, had to change his trousers on stage." "But he isn't . . . he hasn't . . . I just don't see him," she told Byam Shaw, the play's director. Box-office, replied Byam Shaw. "It'll be madness to refuse." "'But you can manage *both* of them?' (The two knights, I meant.) Glen considered. He smiled (at the situation, at himself). 'No.'"

They rehearsed a week without Richardson who meantime was in Cyprus, filming in the role of General Sutherland in *Exodus*: during this week they appeared, still according to Bagnold, to be getting on brilliantly.

At the end of the first week Richardson arrived, tough as oak and looking like wood. While in Cyprus he had decided his movements and at what place on the stage he would say certain lines. He began about some long gloves [in the second act] counting out his steps as he spoke. He walked, driven by his own pre-imagining, about the stage. He walked all over Glen's planning. Glen looked aghast. Silence.

"Aren't you going to . . . *say* something . . .?" I whispered, also aghast—for him. He walked up to Ralph. Ralph turned his empty pipe upside down and began to look like Priestley. Glen said his polite say. Ralph smiled across his pipe-bowl and said nothing. Nothing was achieved. That was the beginning of the end. That, and the fact that he had "heard" himself beforehand delivering a certain speech so that the flesh crept. It didn't creep because of the situation; it crept because of him.

Richardson has declared that he sometimes—with no disrespect meant—likes to think of playwrights as dead, thereby giving himself the same freedom with their plays that he has with those of Shakespeare or Congreve. At one point, Bagnold reported, he put his arm round her shoulder, smiled at Gielgud and said, "We must save her from herself!" In fact, as Gielgud said later, both he and Richardson were very unhappy about the play. But Bagnold remained unsoothed: on the eight-week pre-London tour when all the cast, as another of them, Anna Massey, said, were "at sea", "the two knights galloped in different directions" in the third act, "tearing the body apart as in the Middle Ages." Some feverish rewriting was going on. Bagnold further commented, this time sourly, "The knights turned author on their way to London. They were my words, but sorted out and rejammed together." When the play opened at the Phoenix the reviews were terrible. *The Last Joke* succeeded only in living up to its title.

During its short run Richardson received a visitor from the past. Before one matinée Charles Doran, now over eighty years of age, sent up a message. "Does he remember me?" Richardson asked. "Oh indeed he does," said Doran's emissary. Richardson, who was fixing his Levantine toupée, asked Doran up but was told the old actor was quite frail and had lost a leg. So Richardson went down to see his "old guv'nor" who was by the stage door and who gaped with wonder at seeing him again after almost forty years. "Oh Ralphie," was all he could say, "what a beautiful wig-join."

36 *Illusion, ladies and gentlemen . . .*

For the next eight years Richardson avoided new plays and new authors. In April 1962, at the Haymarket, he played Sir Peter Teazle in *The School for Scandal*. This was another sumptuous revival, the cast of which included, at various stages in its lucrative progress, Daniel Massey, Anna Massey, Richard Easton, Meriel Forbes, Margaret Rutherford, John Neville, and, from when he took over right to the end of the run, John Gielgud as Joseph Surface. The first week's takings set up a box-office record of £5,500.

Anna Massey recalled Richardson's Haymarket dressing room with its log fire; the coffee served on a silver tray with biscuits; his first night notes—"how wonderfully witty they were, sometimes with a little drawing." In November 1963 she was having dinner with the Richardsons at Bedegars Lea, together with William Wyler and his wife Talli, when news came through of Kennedy's assassination: straightaway the party broke up and everyone went home.

At the end of 1962 *The School for Scandal* toured America, opening in Philadelphia where the pace of spoken English proved too fast, then transferring to New

York's Majestic Theater for a seven-week season: here, according to Ronald Hayman in his biography of Gielgud, the screen scene, "with John and Richardson collaborating in a succession of expertly timed comic points, was now a superb climax."

In 1963 Richardson passed up an opportunity to play again opposite Margaret Leighton in Ibsen's *The Lady from the Sea*: he didn't like the role of Dr Wangel, he said. It was surprising he didn't do more Ibsen now when he was the ideal age for roles such as Solness, Pastor Manders, Rubek in *When We Dead Awaken*, and even Dr Stockmann in *An Enemy of the People*. He did express a desire to tackle the title role in *John Gabriel Borkman*, and discussed this possibility with the producer David Merrick, without resolving the problem of whom they should cast as the two women; nothing came of it at that time (he was to play it in 1975).

He opened the Mayfair Theatre in April 1963 as the Father in *Six Characters in Search of an Author*: while on tour with the Sheridan Richardson had seen an off-Broadway production by William Ball of Pirandello's masterpiece, and had persuaded Ball to come to London to direct it. The translation was a relatively free one, and a long rehearsal period was arranged, enabling Richardson to do again a more searching kind of prepration than he had been used to under the Tennent management. At the early sessions they sat around informally, read and discussed the play—they were rehearsing in a ballroom near Piccadilly —and Richardson's method of working became more exploratory. But he wouldn't go quite as far, by means of improvisation at least, as the director would have liked. One day Ball said "Let's kick it around—I'd like you all to change characters." At this point Richardson got up from where he was seated and without a word left the ballroom.

Even so, in this outstanding production, Richardson brought a spontaneity and naturalness to the role while preserving the flavour of unearthliness—Pirandello's characters, paradoxically, are real people who also are not real because they are characters: reversible coating, it may be

claimed, for Richardson's own remarkably consistent imaginative kernel—in particular in the directly emotional
scenes with the family. Barbara Jefford, who played the
Stepdaughter, testified to his "delicate suggestiveness" in
the hat-shop scene when the Father re-enacts his own
seduction of her: "so unpredictable . . . so unpredictable,
so naughty; this is the mystery—what is so entertaining
about him is that you never know. But he is meticulous,
every syllable in the text is rehearsed—he underlines different words in different colours—it's planned down to the
millicord."

As the roué seeking his chance, "he never touched me,"
she averred and yet the scene conveyed the essence of
sexual attraction and remorse: it was the kind of indirect
sexiness Richardson was acquiring more with age. The
Father was the first 'poetic' character he had acted for some
years, and if he had again triumphantly returned to the core
of what was best in his acting, and escaped from some of the
dead ends of previous years, it remained for the time being
a turn in a direction in which there was precious little for
him to do.

Then came a majestic Shylock. This, together with the only
reprise of a pre-war part, the Bottom he last performed in
1938, might well seem like a regression to the actor-
manager style, and in a way it was, though on a grander
scale: "Sir Ralph" at the head of a British Council tour,
organized by Tennents and with ambassadorial receptions
scattered along its path, to commemorate the 400th
anniversary of Shakespeare's birth. With Mu as Titania,
they played Mexico City, Caracas, Bogota, Montevideo,
Quito, Lima, Rio, Santiago, Buenos Aires and São Paulo;
then later, Lisbon, Madrid, Paris, Athens and Rome.

The scene changes were slow, the dress rehearsals inadequate, and there was also that grand and yet semi-
improvised way of conducting oneself which conjured up
the time when as a young man with the Doran company he
had bellowed and ranted trying to make himself heard.
Alan Howard, who played Bassanio, recalled the exquisite

playhouse in Quito which had been built as a miniature La Scala and where Bernhardt had once acted, finishing one performance under the patronage of a different President from the one who had been in office when she began it. But grand associations apart, the lighting was little more than naked bulbs hanging down from the ceiling. Howard was standing next to Richardson, who was a traditional, Irving-esque Shylock, at least to look at, with longish hair, bearded chin and nomadic robes made of yards of gabar-dine material—an imposing, powerful presence, with a frightening-looking face. He was resting on the long staff he carried. Suddenly he swivelled round on the staff towards Howard.

"I think we've time," he said cryptically. "Follow me."

He swirled off the stage, down the steps, shouting for his dresser, "John, get out the brilliantine." On arrival in his dressing room he pulled up his sleeves and into his cupped hands had the dresser pour lashings of the waiting brillian-tine, which he began to apply liberally to Howard's hair. "It catches the light," he said.

For Richardson and Howard it was the continuation of a relationship which had begun in a television play by Ter-ence Rattigan called *Heart to Heart*, about a Labour minis-ter who bares his heart in a television encounter as Gilbert Harding had once done with John Freeman in his inquisit-orial *Face to Face*. In *Heart to Heart* Howard had played the politician's Parliamentary private secretary (PPS), and having occasion to call on his superior at his home the two had been obliged to improvise together a few lines of dialogue. Howard had just been acting at Chichester. The first improvisation, purporting to be a conversation of the Labour minister with his PPS, ran:

RICHARDSON: Ah, have you just come up from Chiches-ter?

HOWARD: Yes, as a matter of fact I have.

RICHARDSON: And how is Laurence?—awfully nice man.

HOWARD: He was well.

RICHARDSON:　Did you come by steam-roller?

The second improvisation, several days later:

RICHARDSON:　Have you been for a fitting?
HOWARD:　　　Yes.
RICHARDSON:　Have you got your striped trousers?
HOWARD:　　　Yes.

It was two years later before Howard and Richardson met again. Called to audition for Bassanio, Howard was setting out on to the darkened stage to deliver his piece when he heard a familiar voice call out from the back of the stalls, "Hello, Stripey, how are you?" From that day on Richardson always called him "Stripey."

At the end of the tour the company took leave of one another at London airport—by this time all were exhausted and the goodbyes were emotional. "Ah Stripey," Richardson said, coming up to Howard. "You've got great potential, your performances have grown and grown, but"—he paused here with considerable import—"keep your thumbs down!" It was advice Howard never forgot.

Richardson's Shylock was, for others as well as Howard, more than old actor-manager's hamming. When *The Merchant* was revived for home consumption in 1967 (while it served to excite affectionate mockery in some quarters) it became for the poet and teacher Nigel Frith a model performance:

> The best bit of Shakespearian acting I have ever seen, in the sense that it might most profitably stand as a model to others . . . I had read in those learned, arty, critics' books that Richardson was not really a Shakespearian actor at all, so I did not expect much. It was not a spectacular evening, and I don't think the old boy was trying very hard. In fact he had a temperance that may give it smoothness to a T. But the point about it was it was so deliciously easy to watch. You didn't have to feel embarrassed. You weren't watching a realistic portrayal of what it is like to be victimized by wicked bourgeois society . . . or any other of those pseudo-artistic experi-

ences which fashion finds so precious. You just sat back and enjoyed it. Richardson walked through the part nobly and eloquently. He struck the most expressive and striking attitudes. His speeches seemed to make a kind of music. . . . When he tossed down his knife at the end of the trial, he did it with such a wealth of contempt. It was as if he were saying: you crew of raw, half-finished, trivial trendies, I despise your cliquishness. . . .

With Graham Greene's next play, *Carving a Statue*, it was hoped to recreate the fortunate partnership of playwright and leading actor that had succeeded in *The Complaisant Lover*. To Greene both plays were a similar game played with the same extremes of mood. But Greene's new personage, based on the painter, B. R. Haydon, who had a passion for Biblical subjects, was in no way so good a character as the dentist Victor Rhodes; above all he lacked the rich seam of ordinariness. While Richardson tried, to no avail, to make him human, Greene, it appeared, wanted Richardson to "send him up", to show the character to be worthy of ridicule: "surely a farcical character though he came to a tragic end."

Richardson had never been a *farceur*, he was incapable of the mechanical exactitude required in farce: too late he saw it was a thin piece and wanted to add something of his own, falling back on his known strengths. As J. W. Lambert succinctly defined it: "Richardson made him a Michelangelo; Greene made him a great ass." The upshot was that in a very restrained and gentlemanly manner, playwright and leading actor fell out. Greene complained to Hugh Beaumont who said he would raise the matter with Richardson. Beaumont conveyed Greene's feelings to Richardson through Mu, but Ralph kept unwaveringly to playing the role as he saw fit. Greene, as had Enid Bagnold previously, blamed the whole failure of the play on Richardson. In his 1965 preface to the published text, which he entitled "Epitaph for a Play", he wrote, "Never before have I known a play like this one so tormenting to write or so fatiguing in production. I am glad to see the end of it, and to that extent I am grateful to the reviewers [who had savagely demolished it] . . ." Later, Greene added to the preface, when it was reprinted almost in full in 1980, a blunt reference to Richardson without naming him: "Alas! The principal actor saw the play quite differently from me. He believed he was playing Ibsen."

Greene wrote Richardson an angry letter voicing his continuing grudge. Richardson took it and pasted it inside the front cover of an illustrated book on Henry Moore's sculptures; "Well . . . sculptor . . . carving a statue," he answered when asked by a friend why he had chosen this particular book.

37 *Sidelight on José the parrot*

SCENE: *The Savile Club during one lunch hour. Richardson comes over to a group of members.*

RICHARDSON: Does any of you fellows know the best place to buy a parrot?

All look non-plussed.

STEPHEN WATTS: Have you tried Winsor and Newton?

RICHARDSON: Isn't that where they sell painting tackle? No, I meant parrot, not palette.

Several months later Richardson is being filmed in the role of Alexander Gromeko in *Dr Zhivago*. His agent —now Olive Harding, since Cecil Tennant, who had acted since the 1940s for both him and Olivier, died in a motor crash—receives a telephone call asking if she would arrange an import licence for a parrot. "When are you going to bring it into the country?" she asks. "I'm bringing it with me," he says. Meanwhile Richardson in Spain has to fix an export licence. "What's its name?" asks the Spanish official who is filling in the request. "It doesn't have a name," replies Richardson. Official scratches his head. "Name of animal, it say on the form." "Ah well," says Richardson, clicking, "his name is José Parrot."

José, his presence in England duly licensed by Richardson's agent, becomes a new presence in Ralph's and Mu's life. Some weeks later at the Savile:

> RICHARDSON: I was walking in the market place in Madrid—what do you think I saw—the finest parrot I ever clapped my eyes on—tricky thing to bring it in, but Her Majesty the Queen issued a passport just for my parrot.
>
> CLUB MEMBER: Does it talk?
>
> RICHARDSON: No, there's the snag. Only Spanish—but I'm having lessons!
>
> CLUB MEMBER (*commenting out of earshot on Richardson's well-known lack of linguistic ability*): It'd be cheaper to send the parrot to Berlitz than Ralph!

In spite of the language barrier Richardson and José become good companions. In 1971: "I get great happiness with [him]. Parrots seem to settle. When we get very cross with each other, I call him a bastard or a brute, and he answers me in fluent, swearing Spanish. I wish I could understand it."

An elegant dinner in 1968. Richardson in black tie; Sir John Gielgud in green corduroy jacket; Ivor Brown in ordinary crumpled suit, accompanied by his wife Irene Hentschel. Michael Meyer also present.

> RICHARDSON (*to Meyer*): I forgot to say what to dress in so I thought, what if you turn up in a black tie—so I put one on, just in case you did!

After dinner the ladies retire. Richardson goes to find cigars. After a little while emerges with a bottle of brandy in one hand, a box of cigars in the other—and José on his shoulder. "Johnnie," he says, "dear fellow, have a cigar," leaning over to offer him the box. The parrot spreads it wings and goes *Squawk*!! Gielgud recoils, hand to brow. "Oh my God, Ralph, what a fright!"

José gets even more out of hand. He bites Mu on the ankle. Even worse, in terms of disturbing domestic efficiency, he continually claws the chauffeur on the wrists. "I had to have his wings clipped," Richardson tells Meyer mournfully one day. "That chauffeur said he'd leave unless I stopped him having his little game. It means he can get no exercise—so I'm going to take him round the Heath on my bike!"

38   *The case of the missing phallus*

A feathered biped leaving scars on the wrists may seem a far cry from *What the Butler Saw*, but the two may have more in common than is immediately discernible. Both stimulated a sense of danger—this is what Richardson saw in the play by the new *enfant terrible* Joe Orton. But was Richardson, as he had with other *enfants terribles* who had come his way, going to try and tame Orton, remove his wings and claws in his desire to make him accessible to a large West End audience?

When he read the play he had been having a thinner time than in any other five-year period of his career. There had been a few distinguished parts, though at ominously wider intervals, in Tennent revivals at the Haymarket—the Waiter in *You Never Can Tell* (January 1966), Sir Anthony

Absolute in *The Rivals* in September, followed by Shylock again in the following year. But in the late 1960s Hugh Beaumont fell ill and with his withdrawal from Tennents (he died in 1973) an era was closing. "Corrupting power has never made him vain," Richardson said, paying tribute to him. "I have never once seen him 'show-off'."

In this lean time of good parts, films still steadily supplied Richardson with the means to maintain his comfortable life-style: for his part in *Dr Zhivago*, released in 1965, he was paid £15,000. This was followed by a more extended role in *The Wrong Box*, for which he requested, and received, permission from Bryan Forbes, the producer, to wear the same coat he had worn as the Tsarist officer in *Zhivago*. The year 1966 also found him in *Khartoum*, opposing a blimpish Gladstone to Charlton Heston in some strong scenes: echoes here of *The Four Feathers*.

Olivier too appeared in *Khartoum*, as the deadly Mahdi, eyes rolling and his Othello accent virtually unmodified —but the two old friends played no scene together. Kenneth Tynan had upbraided Olivier at the start of that year's Chichester Festival. In an "Open letter an an open stager" he wrote: "Within a fortnight you will have directed three plays and appeared in two leading roles. It is too much. Do you recall the triumvirate, made up of John Burrell, Ralph Richardson and yourself, that ruled the Old Vic in those miraculous seasons between 1944 and 1947? Why not recruit a similar team to run the National Theatre?" Tynan was sounding like a ghost of Lord Esher, though stood on his head. Olivier's blistering fury at this attack duly transformed itself into Machiavellian sweetness—he would place the upstart critic where he could do least harm; on his staff at the National.

After *The Wrong Box* Richardson had roles in no less than six films released in 1969—*Oh What a Lovely War*, *The Midas Run*, *The Bedsitting Room* (in which he played the lunatic Lord Fortnum of Alamein, giving Oscar Lewenstein, the film's producer, the notion he could succeed in Orton's play, to which Lewenstein owned the rights), *The Battle of Britain*, *The Looking Glass War* (he played the head of the Secret Service) and *David Copperfield* (he was Micawber).

"Four hundred years ago they'd have gone to Bedlam for the afternoon. Now a director and actors recreate a madhouse in a theatre. Let's look at mad people," wrote Joe Orton in his journal on 14 March 1967, presaging his efforts at making psychiatric disruption equivalent to farce. In Orton's last play, posthumously presented in March 1969 at the Queen's Theatre, Richardson was cast as the unfortunately rational doctor, Rance, who tries to find order and form among the delusions and shenanigans unfolding in a clinic for the mad: the role was equivalent to that of Goole in *An Inspector Calls* of twenty years before, but the play gave a more extreme and hysterical vision than Priestley's of a society unbalanced. Deserting the comfortable log fire in his Haymarket dressing room, Richardson was now to confront the yawning abyss of schizophrenia, of homosexual delusion, of riot and pandemonium.

As far back as July 1967, recorded Orton's biographer John Lahr, Oscar Lewenstein had thought of Richardson for the part. Orton wrote: "I'm not sure. Although I admire Richardson I'd say he's a good ten years too old for the part." The play as Lahr describes it—"Torture, nymphomania, transvestism, incest, blackmail, bribery parade across the stage while psychiatric prattle turns the experience into meanings all its own"—hardly looked like an ideal vehicle for Richardson's catching up with new writers.

But he appeared to respond to its spirit: "it piles one thought on another, like mille-fois [sic] pastry." And Rance has a number of sensible and thought-provoking lines which tempted Richardson, such as "Lunatics are melodramatic. The subtleties of drama are wasted on them." This line in particular might have served as an epitaph for the play, were it not that, even beyond Orton's own spectacularly violent and sordid end in 1967, it was just that challenge of making lunacy subtle that playwrights were turning to. *What the Butler Saw*, for all its confusion and crudity, was a prophetic piece.

Richardson had been reluctant at first and did several times turn down the part; but in the end he put some of his own money into the production. Lahr in his book is politely censorious of his effect on the production, again on the principle that the playwright knew best. He quotes evidence that Richardson changed entrances, he couldn't pronounce "nymphomaniac" correctly, and took refuge in protective mannerisms. To Orton's agent, Margaret Ramsay, whom Lahr also quotes and who saw the pre-London run in Brighton, it appeared that Richardson was neither enjoying the play nor feeling any zest. Stanley Baxter, also in the cast, summed up the effect of the angry old ladies who had come along to see Sir Ralph in some more palatable vehicle for his talent: "Ralph got terribly depressed . . . he thought he'd made a terrible mistake in taking part in what he came to regard as a dirty play." Richardson answered by hand every complaint served on him by his public.

Another change Richardson made in the script was to substitute a cigar for the phallus of Sir Winston Churchill which is uncovered in the final moments of the play. Lahr calls this moment, as originally intended by Orton, "Perhaps the purest expression of the antic spirit in modern theatre"; and Orton himself is quoted earlier in the book as saying, "Greek pederasty was a noble ideal. I hope one day to see it practised in this country alongside the Christian virtues. . ."

Even with the deletions made by Richardson, much of the West End opening night audience was vociferously hostile. "Give back your knighthood", was distinctly heard from the gallery, alongside more predictable comment. Orton's rising posthumous fame was given a boost by headlines such as the *Sun*'s "Dead Playwright Booed by Gallery".

Richardson throughout betrayed his classic symptoms of non-identification with the role, with the purpose of the play and with Orton's stated intention, to shock and be obscene. His main stricture on Orton's work, in spite of a conscious effort to overcome it, came from deep within him: it was, as Orton's agent said, that he could not relax and enjoy himself. He was unable to find anything of himself in the role which would enable him to relax; he was unable to play himself. While his instinct had been in the right direction, he needed a vision or view of madness less obscene than Orton's with which he could identify and, through himself, lead the ordinary public to a new source of poetic fantasy. Madness might be fashionable in the hands of Peter Brook, who could select its visual or emotive moments of brilliance, it might feed the antichrist aspirations of Orton's followers, but if Richardson was to add his weight and authority to it, it had to be more ordinary, normal and human. More comfortable and reassuring.

THE MICHAEL PARKINSON SHOW (BBC TV),
13 December 1980:

My impression that two interviews with Richardson—home and away, as it were—are the maximum is reinforced by his second appearance on the Parkinson Show. The return engagement is a less happy affair than the one in 1978, when Barry Sheene was the other guest, for now he is ill-matched with the sombre presence of the Rt. Hon. Enoch Powell, M.P.. Powell's sustained bout of monomania at the start of the show is fascinating, but saps interest in what might follow. Powell has overrun his time; even Parkinson's introduction of Richardson this time sounds hollow—"one of the most beloved institutions of the English theatre." Richardson enters, wearing bright yellow socks, clearly daunted at the prospect, suffering from deep ego withdrawal. He compliments Powell: "fine speech with a wonderful plot—your own life." Ostensibly he feels no inclination to compete.

Laboriously Richardson and Parkinson try to pick up the thread of their last successful encounter and talk about Barry Sheene, as if mirroring their inner uncertainty. The show seems really over, this should have been in next week's programme. They raise the question of relaxation in public. Powell, who needs no audience, answers Richardson's observation that "You can't do anything great unless you relax", rather as if he hadn't even heard it: "You need to be tense when you speak—the times when I'm most frightened are when I'm not frightened." The master of uncertainty, namely Ralph, has met his match, the master of certainty.

Parkinson, whose instinct is always sure, bravely turns to concentrate wholly on Richardson. But no repeat is possible of the easy interchange between Sheene and Richardson. Under considerable pressure Parkinson produces, like a conjurer out of a hat, some impressive statistics: "Your play, *Early Days*," he says to him, "is your ninety-first part on the London stage." Richardson, as in our second interview when I questioned him about Falstaff, has lost confidence: the delightful contradictory spirit has vanished, and he straightforwardly tells a story he has clearly worked on beforehand, about how acting is a trick, of a stoat he had seen when

my wife and I were sitting on a bank in a field. A stoat—a very beautiful stoat . . . and not far away from the stoat there was a baby rabbit and the stoat was after the rabbit: it moved very carefully very slowly, watching the rabbit and then it came to a blade of grass. One tiny little blade of grass . . . the stoat stood behind the blade of grass, convinced himself that the blade of grass was hiding him and to the rabbit the blade of grass did hide the stoat because he then jumped forward, surprised the rabbit and the rabbit was dead. I'm not always able to do that to every member of the audience . . . it's a silly story, isn't it . . .

(One week earlier, at a rehearsal of *Early Days*, according to David Storey, he has told the same story, acting out the stoat and the blade of grass.)

But now with Parkinson, while he has lost confidence, he has not given up hope; he fights back hard, changing subjects, trying to escape the trap, avoid the awkwardness. There is no coffee cup conveniently to hand to upset this time. He has to face it out. Parkinson offers him one avenue of flight: Charlie Chaplin. The next week Richardson is due to unveil a plaque in Leicester Square to this great comedian. He launches into hyperbole about Chaplin which at first is largely dismissable, but then gradually becomes peculiarly self-revealing. At one level it is oddly fictitious, as when he refers to how he got the notion of becoming an actor—not, as he has carefully detailed twenty years before from watching Benson as Hamlet, but this time from seeing Chaplin in a film shown at his school around 1916. Here, as vividly as ever, we see how much he is someone he himself has invented.

But then, while championing Chaplin and also out of his desperate need to dominate Powell's presence—he cannot flee, he cannot rearrange the encounter on his own terms—he comes the closest he has ever come in public to expressing his deep-rooted egotism. His audience always knows unconsciously that the egotism is there, for ultimately it is what gives him his authority and his weight, although all he lets us see is the lightness, the flight of the comet, the trajectory of the arrow—but the greater the flight, inevitably the heavier the weight or thrust needed to carry the object into space. He talks about himself through Chaplin and what he says is the most directly revealing and impressive statement he has ever made about himself. It shows also the extraordinary and instinctively generalizing turn of mind of which he is capable.

To begin with he has called Chaplin "the greatest actor who has ever been in our time—Olivier, Gielgud . . .

illustrated and illuminated great poets and playwrights. But
Charlie Chaplin invented a character part for himself,
pretending he was terrified of the world . . . love was in his
heart all the time." Pursuing this panegyric for all the
mileage he can get out of it, he pushes it to such an extreme
that, finally, he has won over his audience. Parkinson now
ventures to bring in Enoch Powell, asking him about
Chaplin. Powell indicates polite indifference. Attention is
wholly on Richardson. He shows how Chaplin was in-
fluenced by Little Tich.

Then he comes to the climax of his thought, the intuitive
flash which fuses, in a single definition, both his own and
Chaplin's genius:

> RICHARDSON: The audience didn't realize how odd he
> was because he was so near to reality in his madness.

The audience is rapt. The moment is wholly sublime.
Bang—in a puff of green smoke—Enoch Powell has
vanished. I recall Chaplin's own remark: "I remain one and
one thing only, and that is a clown. It places me on a far
higher plane than any politician."

"Near to reality in his madness . . ." Here, as the search
for the real identity of Ralph Richardson enters its final
stage, is perhaps at last a solid clue.

39 *Playing himself*

> We walk through ourselves, meeting robbers, ghosts, giants,
> old men, young men, wives, widows, brothers-in-love. But
> always meeting ourselves.
>
> JAMES JOYCE, *Ulysses*

With *What the Butler Saw* Richardson had reached the
bottom and could only light on easier times: but it was with
extreme scepticism that he and Gielgud approached the
next script which they were offered jointly in 1970 by the
Royal Court Theatre. This was *Home*, by David Storey, set
in the surroundings of a mental hospital which are only very
lightly shaded in. Compared with Orton's it was a vision of
madness and decline softened at the edges, made comfortable, accessible, as if Storey had grasped the essential point
that people wanted to sit back in their increasingly expensive theatre seats and ejoy a certain distance and luxury of
contemplation.

Both Richardson and Gielgud were nearer seventy than
sixty and both had the feeling that they may have been
nearing the end of the road though, as Richardson expressed it, "Actors never retire: they merely get offered fewer
parts until they are offered none." The long friendship of
the two actors which had begun when they played Hal and
Hotspur together had notably misfired on the last occasion
they had appeared together in a new play, *The Last Joke*.
On the other hand, *A Day by the Sea* and *The School for
Scandal*, where the acting objectives were tangible, had
been brilliant successes.

Both approached *Home* in chastened mood, though to
each the script could not, at least superficially, have presented a less auspicious prospect. In it the two inmates they
had agreed to play, Jack (Richardson) and Harry (Gielgud), sit at one point for 25 minutes without moving; the
dialogue was cut back to the minimum, while the part of
Harry was elaborately self-concealing, and met by his
friend with silence, the odd word, three dots. All had to lie
in the suggestiveness of feeling the two old friends could

conjure up between them, the interaction of hidden impulse, for neither of the pair could face the damaging experience which had consigned them to being where they were and what they were, namely borderline cases.

The technical problems apart, how would the world at large view the pair's attempt to catch up, a little late in the day, with the avant-garde? Was theatrical 'royalty' being forced to sup modestly at the Court with the class renegade Lindsay Anderson as director—scion of the British Raj, Anderson had been photographed as a child on an elephant, wearing topi and gaiters, had been at Cheltenham and Wadham, Oxford, but was now a pillar of the anti-establishment (through his film *If*)—and in a play by the Yorkshire ace craftsman David Storey, master of demotic rhythm? Or, to take the opposite view, was the new drama, having exhausted itself in ephemeral social realism and newspaper headline drama, returning to the traditional source of renewal—the great actors of the past? It certainly was, as Storey recalled, a "combination of strange temperaments".

Anderson and Storey were an experienced team, and they could afford to be empirical about the two knights. Storey remembered vividly his and Anderson's first visit to Chester Terrace to discuss *Home*. Richardson opened the door for them and began at once vigorously barking like a dog: "Uncanny," said Storey, "this imaginative transforming of himself into an animal—in everything but the literal sense he was a dog." They followed him down the dark corridor to the dining room, whereupon Richardson threw out a leg and neighed like a horse. His extraordinary, very plastic quality completely caught Storey's imagination.

In rehearsal Gielgud expressed his nervousness about *Home* in a variety of ways; he developed the weird habit of taking from his pocket a pair of scissors and cutting out those sections of the text which did not concern him or his part until his copy was in ribbons. Richardson, more depressed, kept a check on his apprehension, trying to show he was impervious. Once, about three-quarters of the way through rehearsals, and obviously perturbed by the lack of business, he approached Storey to ask, "Could we have a necklace somewhere I could discover in a fireplace?"

Fortunately Storey and Anderson remained firm: Anderson was undeferential but allowed Richardson and Gielgud their head, giving them time to exhaust themselves in all directions, to push at the text, invent what they wanted—"like a couple of race-horses," said Storey, "hoping they would run out of steam before they reached the cliff." Gradually Anderson brought them under control. Richardson had after so long at last found a director who could treat him as an equal, and this became significant in the revival of his fortunes. A bridgehead had been established on the theatre's other bank. (Most younger directors were of Jonathan Miller's opinon—"I don't like great actors . . . you're always deferring to them.")

Home and Lindsay Anderson gradually won Ralph and John's confidence. Ronald Hayman, in his book about Gielgud, describes how at one rehearsal John went out front to watch a scene between Richardson and Dandy Nichols: "He immediately saw that there was an extra dimension to the dialogue." Gradually a rhythm was created to which both actors could give their allegiance, and they wove on it a rich and intricate web of hesitation and odd explicitness. In Hayman's words, "the main passages of dialogue became set with a musical precision . . . the contrast between their voices was exploited with very careful scoring."

When it opened in June 1970, *Home* became a showcase for Richardson's and Gielgud's new-found rapport, and the no less new, informal style of their work—as Gielgud was reported saying later in the *Los Angeles Times*: "now I try not to speak too perfectly." Under Anderson's sensitive direction the play became a living museum preservation of impeccable British acting, moving from the Royal Court into the West End at the Apollo, and later to the Morosco in New York. By this time so sure were the pair of acting together that like an old married couple they virtually ignored one another while unconsciously being perfectly in tune: "One reason I so enjoy working with Ralph Richardson," wrote Gielgud later in *An Actor and his Time* (1979), "is that we are old friends and we laugh a lot and seem to balance each other's style in a very happy way. It is wonderful to play with somebody who is so absolutely opposed to you in temperament: we are a tremendous contrast in personalities." Storey found them so inextricably part of one another's style that it was hard to know sometimes if they were conversing with one another, or saying lines from his play. One night during the run at the Apollo a man in the stalls suffered a heart attack and the commotion was such that the stage curtain was lowered. Uperturbed, almost academic in their interest, the two knights sat on stage discussing the break in performance. "Was it your cue that was missed, or was it mine?" They seemed unaware of the cause. The dream remained unbroken. They continued with the play.

So taken was Storey with what he saw as Richardson's unused possibilities that he subsequently dashed off, "in a couple of days," a draft of a play specifically for him, about an elderly politican who was "sketched just in terms of temperament". He sent it to Chester Terrace. Richardson, Storey said, "didn't like to say no, but was rather noncommittal." This was the beginning of *Early Days*.

After *Home* Richardson went back again to the Royal Court, appearing next as Wyatt Gillman in John Osborne's *West of Suez*, which later transferred. Stories were told of Ralph's wilful, or instinctive, means of getting his own way with a text which, typical of Osborne, was too wordy by far. He would miss out passages, and plough on through questions unnecessarily placed in the mouths of other characters as if they weren't there. Osborne was well known for hating to have his text cut, and when he heard Richardson doing this he went straight round backstage after one performance. Richardson forestalled him, putting his hand on Osborne's shoulder just as he was about to open his mouth: "Dear fellow," he said, "I must be getting senile, I'm afraid I miss out bits here and there, can't help it—the old memory's going, I'm afraid."

From respectable acclaim in *West of Suez* Richardson
returned to long-running triumph in his next part, in which
he was to remain for the next two years. This was more
typical West End fare: *Lloyd George Knew My Father*, by
William Douglas Home. No uncertainties, this time, over
Richardson's reaction to the text: "There's something
underneath the surface," he told Douglas Home. "Don't
ask what it is, because I don't know. Nor will I ask you,
because you won't know either." Richardson had spotted
an extra dimension to the dialogue, some mystery element,
some thread of magic. They discussed who should play the
leading lady. "Who would you like, Sir Ralph?" the im-
presario Ray Cooney asked.

"'Edith couldn't do it now,' [Ralph] said, more to himself than to us. 'Old Edith couldn't do it, could she? I should
doubt it, poor old Edith!' He stared into the middle distance, summoning replacements out of the four corners of
the restaurant for 'poor old Edith'."

"'Peggy,' he said, suddenly. 'I might give Peggy a ring.'"

Peggy Ashcroft was duly persuaded to take the party of
Lady Boothroyd, with Richardson playing General Sir
William Boothroyd. All went well until just before the
opening night in Oxford, when Douglas Home met Laurence Evans, who had been General Manager of the New
Theatre seasons in 1944–6 and was now Richardson's
agent. "Ralph's depressed about the play," Evans told
him. "He just thinks it isn't any good. In fact he wanted to
get out of it this morning, but I told him it was too late.
That's why I came down—to quieten him down." Richardson was not the first great performer, growing older, who
had needed to externalize his nervous symptoms in this
way.

The play is ostensibly about Lady Boothroyd's
announcement that, if a motorway is cut through the
Boothroyd estate, she will take her own life. (It is, and she
doesn't.) But the currents in the Boothroyds' lives run
deep, for Sir William suspects his wife of infidelity, many
years before, with an Army colleague. When it opened at
the Savoy Theatre on 4 July 1972 the *Financial Times* critic

judged it a lighthearted comedy on the eccentricities and
foibles of the upper classes; laughter, he said, automatically
greeted the lines spoken by Sir Ralph and Dame Peggy, "as
if they had been spoken by members of the royal family or
prime ministers at a party conference." But Harold Hobson, writing in the *Christian Science Monitor*, picked up the
"extra dimension" Richardson had discerned, in the scene
in which Lady Boothroyd

> says after dinner the night before the motor way is to be
> cut that she has never looked at another man than Sir
> William. With quite extraordinary bitterness, Sir Wil-
> liam replies, "You looked at Tim Carson all right." And
> then comes the story, brought up out of the stores of
> memory . . . Lady Boothroyd laughs merrily at the
> recollection. She and her husband are old people now.
> They can afford to treat their previous peccadilloes as
> jokes . . . But Sir Ralph sits immovable, his face half
> turned away from her. When the curtain falls there has
> been no forgiveness.

Richardson had perceived that within his limitation of class
and subject matter Douglas Home had the same capacity as
Ibsen for using the present to bring out of the past a series of
closely related incidents.

Richardson's seventieth birthday, on 19 December 1972,
fell on a Monday when he was appropriately enough in
Ibsen's actual company, as Judge Brack in a film of *A
Doll's House* being made at Elstree. *The Times* had sent
along a man to the Savoy the Saturday before, just prior to
the matinée: "Hey, hey, hey, how are you?" Richardson
boomed to him. "I was thinking coming down that when I
was young my birthdays were always red letter days for me.
I always waited for the postman because my aunt every year
sent me a ten shilling note, which was red in those days. But
times have changed. I have no more aunts and they don't
make ten shilling notes any more."

The *Times* man asked him why he had never worked for

the National Theatre but he dodged the question. Olivier himself delivered a birthday tribute on the BBC beginning with an obscure remark which to those paying careful attention could have sounded like a slightly jealous rebuke at the now much closer relationship of Gielgud and Richardson: "Ralphie, Ralphie boy, my dear old cocky. I'm probably your oldest friend. I know I'm not your best friend but I believe I am the one who loves you the best." Olivier continued, having adopted a style owing much to his childhood years as a vicar's son, to finding 'essences' for Ralphie:

Cloth: Rough tweed
Flower: Evening primrose
Redolence: Firm tobacco
Scent: New mown hay
Drink: Drambuie laced with Highland whisky
Animal: A Buckingshire horse
Music: Elgar's *Enigma Variations* (Nimrod)

Richardson become a grand old man—and the sainted eccentricity, always latent in his character, could be given full rein. Peter Lewis of the *Daily Mail* also interviewed him at the Savoy, when he found him waiting for tea "rather as a retired general waits on a country platform for a delayed train to Paddington." After pouring his tea carefully into the saucer—"Excellent tea here, but it wants to be drunk from something of shallow shape"—and exhorting his visitor to do the same, he then, on Lewis's prompting, talked of his ferret, Eddie:

You remember Eddie! He's off. Escaped. I loved Eddie. I believe Eddie loved me. I could wake him up by pulling his tail and he could only look at me as if to say: "What is it, Papa? Do you want a word with me?"

Lewis proceeded, having disposed of the eccentricities: "I had always been intrigued by Sir Ralph's description of acting as 'dreaming to order.'* Those quirkish nods and quivers of the head which occur in his performances are, I believe, a sign that he is dreaming in public again. He wasn't doing them now." But Richardson had the last word:

He turned towards me and I got the full power of his hypnotic stare. "Even in life," he said, "nothing is *really* true. You are never completely in control of what is happening. Even if you say to a girl, 'I love you very much,' it's not *wholly* true. Part of it is what you've decided to say. It's part of a dream.

'Put it this way," he said. "Persons are not what they seem to be. You are not just what you seem to be this afternoon. I am not. A person is a whole pack of cards." He chuckled again to himself. He rose abruptly. Like Eddie, he was off.

"A whole pack of cards," he said in farewell, and shot away across the carpet.

---

*"Acting is to some extent a controlled dream. In one part of your consciousness it really and truly is happening. But, of course, to make it true to the audience all the time, the actor must, at any rate some of the time, believe himself that it is really true. But in my experience this layer of absolute reality is a comparatively small one. The rest of it is technique, as I say, of being very careful that the thing is really accurate, completely clear, completely as laid down beforehand. In every performance you're trying to find a better way to do it, and what you're re-shaping, the little experiments, may be very small indeed, and quite unnoticed by your fellow actors; but they are working all the time. Therefore three or four layers of consciousness are at work during the time one is giving a performance." (Richardson, quoted in *Great Acting*, 1967.)

40 *Looking for the Gabriel*

Lloyd George could have run indefinitely but first Peggy Ashcroft left the cast, and then her replacement Celia Johnson departed, prompting Richardson to declare: "I've had two leading ladies shot from under me and I can't take any more." So they took *Lloyd George* off to Australia, where Mu stepped into the shoes of Lady Boothroyd. "The play," wrote the Australian critic Leon Glickfield, "is a vehicle for Sir Ralph . . . but the real driver is Lady Richardson." The venerable vehicle itself gave an ominous shudder and threatened to overturn on arrival at Sydney airport. Richardson fainted in the airport lounge and a doctor was summoned. But if fate was laying a hand on his shoulder, he was determined to be defiant. Downstairs the press were waiting with a Honda 1000 he had agreed to pose with. He put on his mackintosh and down he went: to everyone's amazement he climbed on the bike and rode off—he was gone for ten minutes and the place was in uproar as they wondered if he would ever return.

But he more than lived out the tour which continued in North America: Christmas 1974 found him safely back in Chester Terrace, writing affectionately and in jocular mood to William Douglas Home with some new ideas for a play they had discussed previously: "I have just woken from a xmas pudding dream—my dream was about you—it was about a thought we have had together of *The Blood-stained Mouse*." As the letter continued he gradually came round to what he had just begun rehearsing:

> I think of you often; I get close clippings of news of you from our mutual friend at Truffits the barber—I know that you had a haircut just a few days ago. I watch you!
> . . . There is not YET in my life at the moment no PRESENT—am working for a rival author of yours—comes even NORTH of you—had a beard—name of IBSEN. Awful fellow.
> But back to my dream.
> The DE[TE]CTIVE perhaps arrives late in the play after the

audience have been fascinated with the characters and the events that have brought the CRIME about. The audience know all, the de[te]ctive nothing! In act ii you see him fumbling about. HE IS WARM HE IS COLD a child's game that we and we all have played so often! Near and near he comes to put the missing piece in position! He fumbles again—what a fool he is *WE* all know! Of course in the last few moments he does it! But, the puzzle picture he makes is not at all the one that was expected! Perhaps the stupid de[te]ctive hardly knows why he has done it!

And he ends his playful suggestions:

I hope you do not get too many xmas dinner letters like this! I am sure you have a large

waste basket to put them in, but I have done two years hard with you and have been happy and I would like another sentence.

Richardson had had three years of unbroken pleasure in modern dress parts, and now, in 1974, he was rehearsing the title role in a classic he had always wanted to do. The supreme stroke of good fortune had come about when, Olivier having retired, Peter Hall had won the fight to succeed him as Director of the National, and Richardson was at long last installed by Hall in his rightful place at the head of a National Theatre company.

He and Hall had never worked together, although, some twelve years before, Hall had gone along to Bedegars Lea to try and persuade him to do Falstaff again. Richardson told him then, "Those little things which I've done in which I've succeeded a little bit, I'd hate to do again." Instead Richardson took Hall for a spin along the North Circular Road on the pillion of his Norton. They stopped in a private road. "You have a go," Richardson told him. Hall took the bike, careered a bit down the road and fell off. Later Hall had been asked to direct Richardson in New York in *The Waltz of the Toreadors*, but in the end this had proved impractical and Harold Clurman had done it.

Now they were working together on *John Gabriel Borkman*. During rehearsals Ralph quipped at one point, "I've got the John, I've got the Borkman, I'm still looking for the Gabriel"—and it was the archangel's name, though Richardson professed not to know this, that Ibsen had intended to symbolize Borkman's 'genius', the poetic side of his character which he shared with Ibsen's earlier, autobiographical creation of Peer Gynt.* Here was the ageing artist-hero figure, his wife and her twin sister rivals for his active part, symbolized by his son Erhart, caught between a desire for freedom and remorse over the past. Ultimately, as the artist-hero, does he run his women, or do they run him? On this score Ibsen's answer is not absolutely clear, though Borkman's final escape is through delusions of power.

Richardson's method of work was appropriate for this Ibsen role so near to himself in many aspects. Hall found that he would "dig deeper and deeper into himself. He is not a great imitator. But he is the most complex and complete actor we have because he reveals so much of himself."

Hall called him, moreover, "the freest, most experimental of the great actors"—meaning Richardson, Olivier and Gielgud. At rehearsals Hall found that Ralph had a low boredom threshold and "does not enjoy the

---

*Ibsen told this to his doctor in later years; the English name John was meant to characterize Borkman as a businessman.

modern institution of note-giving, because he likes to be doing it in work." In sum, Hall said, he "makes you feel a hell of a good director—all great actors make you feel like that."

Outwardly, as Borkman, Richardson was romantically spruced up: with a wig of wavy grey hair, straight nose, moustache brushed elegantly to either side, he looked like a distinguished musician or literary figure. When the production opened in January 1975, the acclaim it received was not unmixed with criticism from those who felt either that his interpretation was too poetic, or that his capacity to link opposites metaphorically was a form of inconsistency. Harold Hobson again stood out as Richardson's most powerful apologist. Writing in the *Sunday Times*, he said:

> Sir Ralph is in my opinion the most extraordinary actor in the world. Other great players have a wide range, but he is the only one who can be at both ends of the range at the same time. He can be simultaneously the totally ordinary embodiment of kindly domestic commonsense and a man whom the chaos of the universe has driven out of his mind. There are moments in this performance when Borkman speaks utterly prosaic words in a manner entirely normal, and yet it is evident that the man is completely and frighteningly mad. There is something both wholly natural, given Borkman's character, and strangely disturbing in the Napoleonic gesture of hand-stuck-into-the-shirt-front when he receives a visitor.

We might condemn Agate, for, all those years before, saying Richardson should never play another Ibsen role, Solness—who, he said, "is as mad as a hatter, whereas Richardson is as sane as all the hatters in London put together"—but we must, in mitigation, remember that Hobson was Agate's deputy. Time had brought about a form of justice.

Hall had remembered Ralph's great roles at the New, which he had been just old enough to see, and had set out to extract the poetic essence from *John Gabriel Borkman.* The cunning of his production, with its central performances not only from Richardson but also from Wendy Hiller and Peggy Ashcroft as Gunhild and Ella respectively, was that it did just this: released the potential poetry, set in motion the trolls and epic scenery of *Peer Gynt*, injected fresh air and provided an almost operatic expansiveness in which Richardson's own size could reach its proper dimensions. Commented Gielgud, "I shall never forget the noise he made when Borkman died. As if a bird had flown out of his heart."

Borkman might strike anyone as the ultimate goal of an actor in his riper years, but it was only the beginning of this actor's richest creative period, which up to this day shows no sign of falling off. Richardson had still two more outstanding achievements at the National: one of them in tandem again with Gielgud in Harold Pinter's *No Man's Land* (directed by Peter Hall), and the other in the central role in Storey's *Early Days*. *No Man's Land* skilfully and impeccably translated the double act of Jack and Harry in *Home* into Hampstead surroundings. The roles were somewhat reversed, and Pinter substituted suspense and mystery for Storey's gentle degree of reality, or lack of it. The play worked no less well than *Home* (many American reviewers commented on the slightness of the writing) and went round on virtually the same refulgent circuit, with the two knights now become, as Gielgud put it, like the "brokers men in *Cinderella*. People even mix us up and greet us by each other's names, particularly in America where titles often confuse the public."

Richardson and Gielgud's near-fifty-year-long relationship was as strong and secure as any in the theatre, and their affection for one another—it wouldn't be going too far to call it a deep though platonic love—was based on mutual tolerance of very opposite qualities. At home, and abroad, when on tour, they kept to their own, now perfected and very separate styles. Richardson would visit the zoo or play the occasional game of tennis, otherwise keeping himself to himself; Sir John would sign copies of his numerous books in the bookshops, and dine out glamorously in the places to be seen in with show people, or repair to the local movie house to glut his appetite for sensation (in Toronto, for example, seeing *Murder by Death*).

They would come together to dispense endless bounty to gossip-hungry journalists, in interviews in which reality danced in perfect harmony with the fictions of themselves which they had, over the years, been no less subtle in forming:

SIR RALPH: Shall we live it up now?
SIR JOHN: Certainly.
SIR RALPH: You're looking very well by the way.
SIR JOHN: Thank you.
SIR RALPH: I haven't seen much of you lately.
SIR JOHN: We meet in costume.
SIR RALPH: We meet as other people.

Then they would depart to their separate waiting cars or Cadillacs—the latter "usually about that size", said Richardson one night in New York surveying a lengthy specimen parked outside. "Or longer."

Richardson also devoted his energies to playing with characteristic precision of detail several minor parts at the National, in Tolstoy, Congreve and Ibsen. In 1978 he had, typically, yet another reverberative, half farcical failure in the West End, in a play called *Alice's Boys* by Felicity Browne and Jonathan Hales; trapped in poor material, he again took refuge in eccentricity. In *The Kingfisher*, originally commissioned for Richardson as a successor to *Borkman* at the National Theatre, William Douglas Home provided a further though shorter sentence for him to serve—Richardson referred to it as "two bits of cobweb stuck together with stamp edging and sticking plaster"—in whose text Richardson, in an exchange of letters with Douglas Home, suggested useful modifications.* He and

---

*One of the delicate points Richardson raises with Douglas Home is that he does not want the part of Cecil, which he is to play, to become too absent-minded. "This quite destroys," he wrote, "what I deem to be your magical conception of Cecil—who is so alert, so swift on the ball, so dexterous in any situation with not a grain of goofiness or bumble about him."

Celia Johnson, who played opposite him, with Lindsay Anderson directing, again created a standard by which the West End might be judged.

41 *In my end is my beginning*

I'm amazed that I'm as old as I am. I always had the idea that when I was old I'd get frightfully clever. I'd get awfully learned, I'd get jolly sage. People around would come to me for advice. But nobody ever comes to me for anything, and I don't know a thing.

RICHARDSON, London Weekend Television, 1975

Early Days, David Storey's play about the elderly politician Kitchen, was put away for six years. During that time Storey occasionally took it out, read it, scored out a passage or two, or added something. Then in late 1978 Peter Hall got hold of a copy; Lindsay Anderson had already seen the copy: both tried to persuade Richardson to play the part, but Richardson, now in his seventy-seventh year, was scared of losing his memory. In the end they prevailed over his fears, but Richardson wanted to include in the contract a proviso that if he had not been able to learn the lines by such-and-such a point in rehearsal, he would have the option to withdraw. This in time was forgotten. Even so, learning remained difficult. He would telephone Storey at weekends: one weekend—"I have learnt up to page 33." "Good," would say Storey. Next weekend: "I have learnt up to page 27." Storey: "But last weekend you had learned it to page 33." Richardson: "Oh yes, but that wasn't very thorough." Next weekend: "I've learnt to page 12—I really know it." Before the first out-of-town night, in Brighton, Storey found Ralph in the stalls looking "so old and tired, his wig all wrong". Imagining himself to be entirely on his own Richardson had sunk down in a stall seat, uttering in a tone of the deepest despair, "Oh, for a cup of hemlock!" He had then, realizing too late that Storey was still there, turned and looked aghast.

But, Storey remembered, at that first night in Brighton, only an hour or two later, being amazed by Richardson's complete transformation. As soon as he had made his first entrance Storey noticed his tremendous appetite for being on the stage; from being terrified out of his wits, pleasure irradiated his countenance. He strode forward into the lights eager for battle. He did not give a damn, and the uncertainy he felt over remembering parts of the text became immaterial: he was in control of the dream. Later, in that try-out week, at a matinée, he had "dried" quite frequently but had walked over to the prompt corner* and taken the lines he had forgotten without dropping the pace of the play, as if forgetting was the easiest and most natural thing in the world. In the passage where he has to insult in son-in-law in his daughter's presence—"The man is like a fetish"—the actual word "fetish" eluded him on more than one occasion. He went into contortions to find substitutes: once, after turning his back to the audience and flexing his shoulders as if lifting a great weight, calling him "a . . . mollusc"; another time he delivered himself of the ultimate epithet—"a . . . croissant!"

June 1980:

RICHARDSON (*on telephone to me*): Yes, old chap, you come along and see *Early Days* again. Let me fix you up a ticket . . . We'll have a drink together. I shall be going away to shoot a film shortly. In Wales. I'm preparing it

*"Jolly useful chap, that," he once remarked to an audience, of the prompter.

now.* *Early Days* closes at the end of the week but
there's a plan to transfer it to the West End in October.
They're thinking of Wyndham's. Don't know whether it
will work. Doesn't need too big a place. Maybe it will
sink without trace . . . Still, it may be worth a try.

A week later, the last Thursday night of the run at the
Cottesloe (the small auditorium of the National Theatre),
at the stage door. I pick up a ticket from Hal, Richardson's
apple-cheeked dresser who walks with a slight limp. Earlier
I have caught a glimpse of Richardson arriving in his Rolls
and being guided by Hal on to a privileged lot by the
dustbins. The audience on this night includes not only the
director, Lindsay Anderson (recognizable instantly in the
description Richardson gave to William Douglas Home
when Home and Anderson were due to meet over *The
Kingfisher*, at Marcelle's in Sloane Street—"You will see a
little Caesar in a leather jacket"), but also a serene figure of
tall classic beauty, Jocelyn Herbert, the designer of *Early
Days*, whose screens of subtle gauze greens evoke a strong
memory image, and Peggy Ashcroft, who is herself soon to
open at the National Theatre in a Lillian Hellman play. The
evening's performance is, I am later told by Storey, the very
best performance Richardson has given.

The play begins with Alan Price's hauntingly cheeky
music: fluting hints of the priapic faun, with old gnarled
features but the sexual urge remaining intact. Richardson
as Kitchen enters on his own in a light suit, bow tie, blue
scarf knotted round his neck. He wears a grey wig with a
balding crown; the effect, intensifying reality, is to make
him look more himself as well as years younger. By now he
is near the front of the stage, open on three sides. His
overwhelming presence fills not so much the stage, because

*This was *Dragonslayer*, shot in Wales, which finds him in the role of an
ancient magician. In one scene he is challenged to a test of his magic. A
dagger is thrust into his breast and for several seconds it is hard to know if
he is alive or not. In *Time Bandits*, another recent film, he plays The
Supreme Being, first appearing as a disembodied dark head, at the end as
himself, in crumpled lounge suit. "Back to creation," he says. "I mustn't
lose any more time."

it has no proscenium, as the whole of the small auditorium.

He suddenly stops as if he's thought of something to say, but as usual that something implies that you have been following his previous line of thought—it comes over as arresting, even quite shocking, because it is *his* thought: acting and reality are one. He raises his right hand in a conventional gesture. I'm glad to see this time he has cut the eyebrow shooting up which he used in the preview I saw and which gave it an artificial air. But the thumb is almost shaking, though well down (his parting words to Alan Howard, "Don't forget, Stripey, keep your thumbs down"). One's gaze is riveted by that thumb: one asks—is it connected to the rest of his body, or have the sinews been severed?

> KITCHEN: At the seaside. Travelling in a coach beneath a bridge. I see the bridge, which is really a footwalk, so high above me—it seems I have passed beneath it ever since. . .

It continues, the audience clearly mesmerized by what Irving Wardle calls, in his later review in *The Times* of *Early Days*, upon its transfer to the West End at the Comedy, "the most pricelessly irreplaceable instrument in [the National Theatre's] collection."

At the end of his solo passage Bristol, appointed by Kitchen's daughter and son-in-law to keep an eye on the old man, enters. He brings on tea, hands it to Richardson who holds the cup and saucer elegantly as if it were a fan, then continues his monologue about the past and about going on voyages—"Michelangelo, Rembrandt, Milton: they are people who made a journey of scarcely any consequence at all and subsequently never travelled further." Again, as in the first speech, the dialogue is full of deft strokes with which Richardson can begin outlining the richness of the character's temperament, which of course is virtually the same as his own. Storey's skill, at once evident, is to have achieved exactly the right distance to enable Richardson to do this: perhaps uniquely, the playwright has become part of the actor's process, not the other way about. At least some of the time they're interchangeable. The tension between text and actor seems exactly right.

Kitchen describes his memory: at this point I find my attention sharpening with a vested curiosity as to whether Richardson's observation of me attempting his biography may be brought into use.

KITCHEN: It's been suggested I should write my memoirs.

It is. Big pause. Wait for it.

KITCHEN: I can't remember anything.

Huge, deserved laugh. Another thread established. We shall see what becomes of it later.

But now, in imitation, or exaggeration of Richardson's own principle of counter-attack, Kitchen goes on to the offensive, asking questions, metamorphosing the answers into his own internal imagery. Two further lines on the "playing myself" principle—but with an extra dimension added: "I'm top dog. I've ruled the roost here for as long as I can remember," and, a little further on—and greeted by another laugh as the audience immediately recognizes the theme: "If they pay me enough my memory might start coming back."

Immediate question to be raised: what about the audience who, unlike me, has not been carefully raking over the live embers and dead ashes of this actor's very combustible presence? How do they manage to respond so patently with affection and recognition to this extraordinarily autobiographical performance? First of all, Richardson is a wonderful communicator and, acting being the medium he has chosen to communicate in, his authority is total. As usual in his best work he is living on several levels at once, and not least of these is his level of audience contact, which is and has always been acute. (The audience for *Home* at the Royal Court he called, "a hand-fed, pet audience. Very nice to play to"; on the Savoy audience for *Lloyd George*, mostly coach trade: "It's like going into a cage of lions. You can frighten them, but you mustn't let them frighten you. Give them half a chance and they'll chase you out through the stage door. . . . You mustn't fool yourself there are five hundred people keen on you. If you're lucky, you've got five." The audience at the Cottesloe, he knows, has all come to see him: it is more like a club, or one person with a hundred or so heads. You try to take them aside separately and give each one a sense you are taking him or her into your confidence. "You're in the end speaking to one person."

That is how, then, without any specialized knowledge, this audience feels in contact. Each member of it feels he or she has met Richardson for the first time, but feels also he has known him all his life: privileged and, in turn, rejected, advanced graciously, and then tripped, so that he falls over flat on his face. The master magician is in control:

> I would say that everything is in some way a trick. The sunset is a trick: if it were not for the screen of the atmosphere there would be no glory, no blaze of majesty, the sun would go down in a penny plain, flake out.

Is this Kitchen speaking, or Ralph Richardson?*

Gestures keep being repeated during the performance, so that after a while the odd shakes of hand or head become the equivalent of what Richardson as a boy found in Mrs Patrick Campbell's delicate, fastidious hand movements, which in turn reminded him of Charlie Chaplin licking the nails of the boots he ate in *The Gold Rush*: tokens of independent life, symptoms of continuity, in Richardson's case visible ripples of thought or energy passing through the character's mind. Somehow they go back, too, to another thread in his life, indivisibly part of him, the symptoms of his first wife's illness; or, later, of his close friend, L. A. Hart, who died of Parkinson's disease. While underlining that Kitchen loves secrecy and has two private notebooks, one which he leaves lying around so his daughter and

---

*Answer: Richardson, in the *Sunday Times* in 1960.

son-in-law can learn of its contents, and a second book which no one reads, Richardson strokes his chin. Then, with the sudden jerky speed with which he changes gear, he shifts from impish levity into the succulent inflections with which he delivers:

KITCHEN: One's childhood is the profoundest period of one's life: after that comes anti-climax.

Hardly much later, there's the vulnerability and tenderness, much more inevitably touching in one who is so patently layered with defences, on his guard against intrusion, of talking about his love for his departed wife:

KITCHEN: I loved her so much I could never tell her. I could never admit I loved her at all. Why did you die, my dear? (*Weeps.*) Why did you leave me all alone? (*Pause.*) How are you getting on with my memoirs, Matt?

Again one particular ghost comes to dominate the stage. Kitchen's evocation of his dead wife is as real as anything Richardson has ever done: the infidelity he forced her into, her peakiness, his own absence and the fact that he could never be left alone with a woman. And again, self-revelation is balanced, held in the exquisite tension of paradox, by the abuse he heaps on his adulterous son-in-law, the admonitions he delivers to his daughter to run off with any man who is available, be it Bristol, or the doctor who later comes to give him a check-up. Yet he stands up for morality, for marriage. Marriage is also, he tells Bristol, like childhood, the most profound experience anyone has, while to his son-in-law he says, "This place has no atmosphere. It is no family. You with your infidelities have seen to that. One girl is followed by another; one deception by another. Disloyalty is a cancer; it eats out the heart of any marriage." One might be tempted to dismiss the character as a silly contradictory old man, were it not for the fact that the authority of the actor who plays him is total, his absolute innocence has ultimately a taming effect, and he unites, as only the great poet who is at the same time both everything and nothing can in his personality unite, apparently disparate and even basically rather unpleasant elements. By this he exalts us and reconciles us to the greatest predicament of all, that of being human.

There are other elements in Richardson as a man and in Kitchen as a character which *Early Days* cunningly and successfully combines: the paranoia, the madness, the escape element, the desire to flee—we don't realize how odd he is, because he is "so near to reality in his madness". Again these are lightly sketched in, for Richardson himself to fill out. Kitchen has exposed his genitals in the village near his daughter's home: as well as wanting to lead his daughter into adultery he wants, as far as an old man is capable, to re-experience the sexual urges of youth which have been curtailed to a token existence. But though hardly referred to, the sexuality, as seen through his acting, is latent and easily accessible. This, as Storey says, is the "key to Richardson's masculinity" which women have, as he has grown older, found more and more compelling.

> Sin is disfavoured
> Virtue is blessed—
> Bring in the ladies
> Let's pick out the best,

he says, tapping with his left foot on the ground, just as, years before, he had done as Cherry in *Flowering Cherry*. Again, there's a taming, reconciling quality in his knowing playfulness: it is like Falstaff, of whom Samuel Johnson wrote, "No man is more dangerous than he that with a will to corrupt hath the power to please." Free, away from his family, he can indulge his fantasy, too: "Look at that window," he says to Bristol; "a man beating his wife. Or is it a carpet." The lines have a Peer Gyntish ring. But the exuberance, the life urge, the libido are no longer expressed in outward virility as they were in the middle part of his career. As Richardson said once, using an analogy from painting, he had a great big tin box full of make-up and covered his face in every conceivable colour that could be found, but as time went by he saw he could reduce his needs until all he had was a tiny little tray with one pencil on it and one pencil sharpener—"you learn that by using fewer and fewer colours you can get a more penetrating observation."

So now, having undergone many subtle changes, he can show exuberance and youthfulness instead of being youthful and exuberant. Life is preserved by continuity, by anticipation and recollection, foresight and hindsight; Richardson has mastered the situation of being old, can hold the mirror up to this process of careful and unending recollection, with all the contradictions and tensions inherent in it. Having learnt to retain the inner exuberance, to serve it instead of it serving him, his power has kept its wholeness and its indivisibility. In old age he underlines the supremacy of his early days: he has kept them fully alive and in watching him, we see he is in contact with that within him which will always live; we are soothed in the perseverance of his essential genius.

Afterwards, in his dressing room backstage, wearing a white gown of towelling with a flap across the chest—very Caesarian—he greets me. The dressing room is a narrow, long affair, with an inner cubicle for the intimacies of changing and an outer chamber. An encapsulating tightness suggests one might be hurtling through space at enormous velocity. As does the close proximity of so many meteoric composites: Jocelyn Herbert, Peggy Ashcroft, Andrew Cruickshank and his wife, Lindsay Anderson make up the party, with one of Richardson's non-theatrical friends, introduced as "from the club". Hal the dresser is in attendance. Holding tooth glasses of whisky or gin, we are pushed up against one another in the narrow corridor, or near a window through which we look down on a concrete pit.

Action centres round the one armchair and its arms: in the chair sits Dame Peggy, recovering from a recent operation on her knee, while Ralph hops on and off an arm. Jocelyn Herbert begins to slide down the wall by the window on to the floor.

RICHARDSON: No! No! You mustn't sit there. Have this
(*he indicates his arm of the chair.*)
HERBERT: I'm used to the floor.
ASHCROFT: I wish I could sit down like that.
RICHARDSON (*still insisting in gentlemanly fashion*):   But
this isn't Borneo.
HERBERT: I haven't been working.
RICHARDSON: But I haven't been sitting down.

He vigorously questions each of the two ladies in turn. In
Thomas Mann's *The Adventures of Felix Krull* the actor's
persona is stripped away when Krull visits backstage to
reveal the insecurity and decaying mortality behind the
great artist; here the magician's mask is ripped off—to
reveal another, equally well formed and potent mask. No
one mentions the play. Richardson keeps the subject well
away from himself until

ANDERSON (*to me*):   Tell him it's good.
SOMEONE ELSE: He knows.
ANDERSON: All actors need praise.

There is no escape. Put on the spot like this, I deliver
myself of some suitable if somewhat forced expressions of
praise. We are all playing a game, with two master magi-
cians—the second being Anderson—who hold all the
trump cards and will cover for one another. Audibility of
certain parts of the performance is discussed: it is mentioned that Olivier, when he visited, could not hear some of
it.

RICHARDSON (*the old diffidence*):   I was tired tonight—it
wasn't at its best.

(Everyone agreed it was the best performance ever).

MAN FROM THE CLUB (*astute, non-theatrical, clear-headed,
a solicitor, wearing a City suit: to Richardson*): Did
David Storey write it specially for you?
RICHARDSON (*masterly playing, totally deadpan*): No . . .
not specially . . . he might have had me . . . in the background.

ANDERSON (*backing up Richardson*):   Aha! That's what great acting is, you see—he makes it seem as if it's been specially written for him!

Conspiracy to the last: the theatre must create mystery or die, defend secrecy or crumble into little segments of actuality. The inner armour against questions is possession of a secret: secrecy goes with danger, for whatever its content, a secret is always dangerous, more dense, capable of causing an unpleasant surprise.

RICHARDSON (*to man from the club*): Been to Lord's recently?

They discuss tennis. Richardson, turning to me, "Are you a cricket man?" At this his friend says goodbye.

RICHARDSON: We must have a game of snooker some-time.

Telephone rings. Hal takes it and informs Richardson that it is Mu to tell him he must not stay up drinking too late. He has been at a late supper party the evening before. Mu the protectress. Everyone quickly takes the hint that he is now tired and must be got home as soon as possible.* A last hilarious occurrence flashes through my mind: Richardson and Olivier dining late at the club and both a bit plastered. Olivier asking Richardson before he leaves for Brighton, if he'd be a good chap and telephone home to let the wife know he'll be late. Richardson on arrival at Chester Terrace, telephoning Olivier's first wife, Jill Esmond. "Laurence says not to worry, he'll be a bit late." "My dear Ralph, I haven't worried for thirty years . . ." Richardson, however, as the others leave, indicates I should stay: he stages a mock collapse on top of the much smaller Lindsay Anderson, who wilts somewhat under the load though supports him with good humour. Wonderful

---

*At home, as he wrote in the *Telegraph Sunday Magazine*, "There will be, perhaps, a bacon sandwich and wine waiting for me and, even after a long talk with the dear one who has sat up for me, I am still not relaxed, and may go to the work room and look for a letter to answer."

sight for the onlooker: wish I had a camera. Anderson takes his leave.

ANDERSON (*to me*):   You're not to tax him.

Richardson changes in his inner cubicle, telling Hal to pour me another drink, muttering, "I must get out of here, I've been here all day," and stripping to light-striped canvas underpants, not bothering to draw the curtain. He changes quickly, asking after my children, and to my reply—I have young children—he answers with a weary sigh, "I find having one difficult enough," as if his own is still at the same age.

By now the tiredness is evident: drooping pouches under his eyes. He finishes dressing and then we depart down the long corridors inside the National towards the stage door. On pushing open one of the many sets of swing doors in front of him, I remark, "I didn't at all notice, in your performance, that you were tired." To which he answers, "It's like making out cheques—doesn't matter what you're doing, you may be pissed, but the signature always comes out right in the end." We drift into the casts of other plays, who are clattering up the stairs, or sweep unexpectedly round a corner. *Hamlet* is playing that night. Seeing one group, Richardson cannot resist attempting to sow confusion. He declaims:

> Light thickens and the crow
> Makes wing to the rooky wood.

Heads turn at this startler. One has the vision that by some act of mad intervention all the wrong cues will slip from their tongues: *Hamlet* will suddenly become *Macbeth*.

At the stage door an autograph seeker stands by the desk waiting for Richardson, a plain-looking woman about forty, wearing glasses.

AUTOGRAPH HUNTER: I don't expect you to remember, but I send you a card every Christmas.

RICHARDSON (*apparently in a total mental blur*):   Who is it?

She gives her name.

Richardson, saying nothing, writes her Christian name on the top of her programme and signs it.

AUTOGRAPH HUNTER: I came to see you at the Old Vic years ago. I queued all day—but you were ill and didn't play.

RICHARDSON (*hand to head, genuinely stricken with remorse, emits a loud cry*): Oah—ah! How awful.

Has she just come to complain about this episode years before, or is it a manifestation of awkwardness?

Hunched over the wheel of his car, and being solemnly flagged out by his dresser, Richardson takes to the road.

CHESTER TERRACE, *2 October 1980:*

A little while later I hear from him by letter. On the long envelope of antique laid paper the thick ink autograph of a hand which carves characters out in separate flourishes, puts him entirely in your mind as if he is in the same room. He has finally abandoned the revived notion that we might collaborate on a book. "Dear Garry", (he writes):

I've had a number of hobbies in my time, these I have found very refreshing. They started with white mice and among the last were drawing and painting.

A time ago I had a letter from you and with it a proof copy of "Miss Tayte"—which was quite splendid. Before this I had suggestions that I might write an autobiography, I was not very keen to do so—but from your letter and from your book—I saw a chance.

Then I thought, No, I am not a star like Miss Tayte; this would be a silly thing to do. . . .

But now I understand how completely he has written his autobiography in *Early Days*, printing out every copy he has printed in his distinctive hand.

By this time *Early Days* is about to open in the West End, at the Comedy Theatre where, having gained even greater authority and decisiveness by virtue of the addition of the proscenium arch, narrowing the audience's aperture, the play makes a sharper, more prosaic and less wistful impact. But attendances fall off swiftly and Richardson becomes irritable and dismayed. Subsequently it starts on a provincial tour, when business again picks up, then goes on to play in Canada and America, where it is a big success.

I see the play four times between April 1980 and April 1981, when the production leaves for America: twice at the Cottesloe, once at the Comedy Theatre to which it transfers in December 1980, and finally, during its English provincial tour, at Richmond, Surrey. On this last occasion, I climb intentionally to the highest seat in the gallery of the tall and elegant Richmond Playhouse: a challenge to Richardson's age as well as his art, my final gauntlet.

It is by far the most enjoyable performance of the four I have seen. His mastery over the part is, though hard to credit, greatly enhanced, the vitality has increased not diminished over the long run, and he is clearly heartened by the wonderful local reception: the ordinary middle-class public which is drawn in by Richardson's name, responds delightedly to the image of ageing and fantastical ordinariness. Flattered by the reaction, he relaxes, and the playfulness increases. Survival, too, in itself fascinates—it is the old man who is "top dog", for his multiple awareness and his experience gives him the edge; crucially he has lasted.

Over all the combinations of opposites the essence of the poet towers. With this essence we began. Perhaps Richardson has no real biography. It is the imagination which has the distinctive features we have attempted to map, the escape from reality as much as the reality itself. Perhaps, as he said of Olivier's white silk canopies hanging motionless from the rafters, he rehearsed it all. "I am a PRINTER that is all," he wrote in his first letter; "there is nothing to say to anyone about such an occupation." This time his missive from Chester Terrace ends, as if framing that earlier reply. "Well, now, here is enough ink."

The Career of Ralph Richardson

PLAYS

d. = director

1920
December

With the St Nicholas Players, St Nicholas Hall, Brighton

Isolated performances (d. F. R. Growcott):

1921
10 January

A Gendarme in *Jean Valjean*, an adaptation of *Les Misérables* by Victor Hugo

18 January

Cuthbert in *The Farmer's Romance* by F. R. Growcott

29 March, 2, 9, 12, 13, 16 April

Banquo and Macduff in *Macbeth*

17, 18, 21 May

The Father in *The Moon-Children* by Constance M. Foot

25, 28, 31 May

2, 4, 7 June

Tranio in *The Taming of the Shrew*

June–August

With the F. R. Growcott Repertory Company, Shakespearean Playhouse, North Garden, Queen's Road, Brighton

Weekly repertory (d. F. R. Growcott):

24 June

Malvolio in *Twelfth Night*

4 July

Revival of *The Farmer's Romance*

11 July

Revival of *Jean Valjean*, with *Waterloo* by Conan Doyle

18 July

Mr Bumble and Bill Sykes in

	Oliver Twist, adaptation from Charles Dickens
25 July	Banquo and Macduff in *Macbeth*
1 August	Defarge, Stryver and the Marquis in *Tale of Two Cities*, adaptation from Charles Dickens
August–September	On tour in the provinces with the Charles Doran Shakespeare Company, opening at the Marina Theatre, Lowestoft (29 August). During the first week's repertoire Richardson played Lorenzo in *The Merchant of Venice*, Guildenstern in *Hamlet* (later in the tour he doubled this part with Bernardo), a Pedant in *The Taming of the Shrew*, a Soothsayer and Strato in *Julius Caesar*, Oliver in *As You Like It*, Scroop and Gower in *Henry V*, Angus (later Macduff) in *Macbeth*. In plays added later to the repertoire his parts were Francisco (later Antonio) in *The Tempest*, Lysander in *A Midsummer Night's Dream*, and Curio (later Valentine) in *Twelfth Night*.

During the tour the Company played five weeks in Ireland, in Belfast, Dublin and Cork.

1922

| January–June | Second tour with Charles Doran. Richardson's parts this year included Banquo (*Macbeth*), Lysander (*A Midsummer Night's Dream*), Horatio (*Hamlet*), Decius Brutus and Octavius Caesar (*Julius Caesar*), Fabian (*Twelfth Night*). |
| 13 February | First London appearance, as Vincentio in *The Taming of the* |

Shrew, with the Doran Company at the Borough Theatre, Stratford, London E.

September–
December

Third tour with Charles Doran. On this tour Richardson played Lucentio in *The Taming of the Shrew* and Sebastian in *Twelfth Night*.

1923

January–June

Fourth tour with Charles Doran. The Company again played a season in Ireland. On this tour Richardson played Cassio in *Othello*, Antonio and later Gratiano in *The Merchant of Venice*, and Mark Antony in *Julius Caesar*.

July–August

Season with the Earle Grey Company at the Abbey Theatre, Dublin. Richardson played Sir Lucius O'Trigger in *The Rivals* by Richard Brinsley Sheridan, and Bobby in *The Romantic Age* by A. A. Milne (both d. W. Earle Grey)

September–
November

Fifth tour with Charles Doran

1924

January–June

Henry in *Outward Bound* by Sutton Vane, Winter Gardens, New Brighton (7 January) and tour

August–October

Fainall in *The Way of the World* by William Congreve (d. Nigel Playfair), Prince's Theatre, Manchester (4 August) and tour

1925

February	With the Birmingham Repertory Company:

Richard Coaker in *The Farmer's Wife* by Eden Phillpotts (d. H. K. Ayliff), New Theatre, Cambridge (16 February), and tour

    The Company played a two-week season at the Royal Court Theatre, London, from 10 August and resumed the tour in September; in December the production went to the Repertory Theatre, Birmingham, for a six-week Christmas season.

December   Dick Whittington in *The Christmas Party* by Barry Jackson (d. Maud Gill), Birmingham Repertory Theatre (matinées from Boxing Day during the run of *The Farmer's Wife*)

1926

January   At the Birmingham Repertory Theatre:

Geoffrey Cassilis in *The Cassilis Engagement* by St. John Hankin (d. H. K. Ayliff)

February   Christopher Pegrum in *The Round Table* by Lennox Robinson (d. H. K. Ayliff)

A Gentleman in *He Who Gets Slapped* by Leonid Andreyev (d. H. K. Ayliff)

March   Lane in *The Importance of Being Earnest* by Oscar Wilde (d. H. K. Ayliff)

	Robert Blanchard in *Devonshire Cream* by Eden Phillpotts (d. H. K. Ayliff)
April	Albert Prosser in *Hobson's Choice* by Harold Brighouse (d. W. G. Fay)
	Mr Dearth in *Dear Brutus* by J. M. Barrie (d. W. G. Fay)
May	Frank Taylor in *The Land of Promise* by W. Somerset Maugham (d. W. G. Fay)
June	Dr Tudor Bevan in *The Barber and the Cow* by D. T. Davies (d. H. K. Ayliff)
10 July	The Stranger in *Oedipus at Colonus* by Sophocles, translated by Robert Whitelaw (d. Robert Atkins), Scala Theatre, for the Greek Play Society (special performance)
August–October	With the Birmingham Repertory Company:
	Robert Blanchard in *Devonshire Cream* by Eden Phillpotts (d. H. K. Ayliff), Prince's Theatre, Manchester (23 August), and tour
November	Arthur Varwell in *Yellow Sands* by Eden and Adelaide Phillpotts (d. H. K. Ayliff), Haymarket Theatre
1927	During the run of *Yellow Sands* Richardson played the following Sunday performances:
24 April	Harold Devril in *Sunday Island* by Harry Wall (d. Fred O'Donovan), Strand Theatre, for the Repertory Players
12 June	John Bold in *The Warden* by

	Michael Sadleir and Gerard Hopkins, from Anthony Trollope's novel (d. Ben Webster), Royalty Theatre, for the Lyceum Club Stage Society
17 July	Sophus Meyer in *Samson and Delilah* by Sven Lange (d. Michael Orme), Arts Theatre, for the International Theatre Guild
11 September	Frank Liddell in *Chance Acquaintance* by John Van Druten (d. Henry Kendall), Strand Theatre, for the Repertory Players
16 October	Albert Titler in *At Number Fifteen* by Alma Brosnan (d. Marion Fawcett), Garrick Theatre, for the Repertory Players

1928

March	Zozim in Part IV and Pygmalion in Part V of *Back to Methuselah* by Bernard Shaw (d. H. K. Ayliff), Royal Court Theatre
April	Gurth in *Harold* by Alfred Lord Tennyson (d. H. K. Ayliff), Royal Court Theatre
April–May	Tranio in *The Taming of the Shrew* (d. H. K. Ayliff), Royal Court Theatre
17 June	Hezekiah Brent in *Prejudice* by Mercedes de Acosta (d. Leslie Banks), Arts Theatre
August	Ben Hawley in *Aren't Women Wonderful?* by Harris Deans (d. H. K. Ayliff), Royal Court Theatre
September	Alexander Magnus in *The First Performance* by Svend Rindom (d. Charles Carson), Strand

	Theatre, for the Repertory Players (Sunday performance)
7 October	David Giles in *Arms and the Maid or Rustic Ribaldry* by Arthur Jagger, Green Room Rag, Queen's Theatre (Sunday performance)
November	James Jago in *The Runaways* by Eden Phillpotts (d. H. K. Ayliff), Garrick Theatre

1929

January	David Llewellyn Davids in *The New Sin* by Macdonald Hastings (d. Nigel Clarke), Epsom Little Theatre
April–August	South African tour with Gerald Lawrence's Company: the Duke of Winterset in *Monsieur Beaucaire* by Booth Tarkington and E. C. Sutherland; Joseph Surface in *The School for Scandal* by Richard Brinsley Sheridan; Squire Chivy in *David Garrick* by T. W. Robertson (all. d. Gerald Lawrence)

1930

February	Gilbert Nash in *Silver Wings* by Dion Titheradge and Douglas Furber, music by Jack Waller and Joseph Tunbridge (d. William Mollison), Dominion Theatre. (Tour before London, opened Empire Theatre, Liverpool, December 1929.)
23 February	Edward in *Cat and Mouse* by Phyllis Morris, Green Room Rag, Queen's Theatre (Sunday performance)

May	Roderigo in *Othello* (d. Ellen Van Volkenburg), Savoy Theatre
	Season with the Old Vic Company at the Old Vic Theatre and Sadler's Wells Theatre, September 1930–May 1931:
September	Henry, Prince of Wales, in *Henry IV, Part I* (d. Harcourt Williams)
October	Caliban in *The Tempest*, Sir Harry Beagle in *The Jealous Wife* by George Colman (both d. Harcourt Williams)
November	Bolingbroke in *Richard II*; Enobarbus in *Antony and Cleopatra* (both d. Harcourt Williams)
7 December	Tom Holt in *Under the Table* by Warrington Jay (d. Cedric Hardwicke), Green Room Rag, Strand Theatre (Sunday performance)

1931

January	Sir Toby Belch in *Twelfth Night* (d. Harcourt Williams). Re-opening of Sadler's Wells Theatre, 6 January
February	Revivals of *Richard II* and *The Tempest*, Sadler's Wells
	Bluntschli in *Arms and the Man* by Bernard Shaw (d. Harcourt Williams)
March	Don Pedro in *Much Ado about Nothing* (d. Harcourt Williams)
April	Earl of Kent in *King Lear* (d. Harcourt Williams)
23 April	Sir Toby Belch and Don Pedro in scenes from Shakespeare in the Birthday celebrations, Old Vic Theatre

3 May	John Morrison in *Revenge*, adapted by J. Wallet Waller from a short story by Lynn Doyle (d. J. Wallet Waller), Green Room Rag, Strand Theatre (Sunday performance)
May	David Reagan in *The Mantle* by Basil Maitland (d. Robert Atkins), Arts Theatre
August	Malvern Festival: Matthew Merrygreek in *Ralph Roister Doister* by Nicholas Udall; Mr Courtall in *She Would If She Could* by Sir George Etheredge; Viscount Pascal in *The Switchback* by James Bridie (all d. H. K. Ayliff)
	Season with the Old Vic Company at the Old Vic Theatre and Sadler's Wells Theatre, September 1931–May 1932:
September	Philip the Bastard in *King John* (d. Harcourt Williams)
20 September	John Morrison in *Revenge* (J. Wallet Waller/Lynn Doyle), Fourth Revel, Arts Theatre (Sunday performance)
October	Petruchio in *The Taming of the Shrew* (d. Harcourt Williams)
November	Bottom in *A Midsummer Night's Dream* (d. Harcourt Williams)
December	Henry V in *Henry V* (d. Harcourt Williams)
1932	
January	Ralph in *The Knight of the Burning Pestle* by Beaumont and Fletcher; Brutus in *Julius Caesar* (both d. Harcourt Williams)

February	General Grant in *Abraham Lincoln* by John Drinkwater (d. John Drinkwater)
March	Iago in *Othello* (d. Harcourt Williams)
April	Sir Toby Belch in *Twelfth Night*; The Ghost and the First Gravedigger in *Hamlet* (in its entirety) (both d. Harcourt Williams)
23 April	In a burlesque *Willy's Choice or An Author in Search of Some Characters* by Farquharson Small (d. Farquharson Small), in the Birthday celebrations, Old Vic Theatre
August	Malvern Festival: Matthew Merrygreek in *Ralph Roister Doister* by Nicholas Udall; Face in *The Alchemist* by Ben Jonson; Oroonoko in *Oroonoko* by Thomas Southerne; Sergeant Fielding in *Too True to be Good* by Bernard Shaw (all d. H. K. Ayliff)
September	Sergeant Fielding in *Too True to be Good* by Bernard Shaw (d. H. K. Ayliff), New Theatre
November	Collie Stratton in *For Services Rendered* by W. Somerset Maugham (d. H. K. Ayliff), Globe Theatre
1933	
February	Dirk Barclay in *Head-on Crash* by Laurence Miller (d. H. K. Ayliff), Queen's Theatre
23 April	Shylock in an extract from *The Merchant of Venice* (in the style of 1999) (d. Harcourt Williams), in the Birthday celebrations Old Vic Theatre

May	Arthur Bell Nicholls in *Wild Decembers* by Clemence Dane (d. Benn W. Levy), Apollo Theatre
September	Sheppey in *Sheppey* by W. Somerset Maugham (d. John Gielgud), Wyndham's Theatre
November	Produced *Beau Nash* by J. C. Woodwiss, Theatre Royal, Bath
December	Captain Hook and Mr Darling in *Peter Pan* by J. M. Barrie (d. Lichfield Owen), London Palladium

1934

February	John MacGregor in *Marriage Is No Joke* by James Bridie (d. H. K. Ayliff), Globe Theatre
September	Charles Appleby in *Eden End* by J. B. Priestley (d. Irene Hentschel), Duchess Theatre
22 November	Spoke a series of verses written by A. A. Milne to accompany cartoons drawn for *Punch* by George du Maurier, in the Gerald du Maurier Memorial Fund matinée in aid of the Actors' Benevolent Fund, His Majesty's Theatre
27 November	Claude Dubois in *French as She Is Learnt* by E. F. Watling, at a matinée in aid of the Heritage Craft Schools and Homes for Crippled Children, Theatre Royal, Brighton

1935

March	Cornelius in *Cornelius* by J. B. Priestley (d. Basil Dean), Duchess Theatre
December	Mercutio and Chorus in *Romeo and Juliet* (d. Guthrie McClintic), Martin

Beck Theatre, New York and on tour both before and after the New York production

1936

February   Emile Delbar in *Promise* by Henry Bernstein (d. Henry Bernstein), Shaftesbury Theatre

May   Sam Gridley in *Bees on the Boat Deck* by J. B. Priestley (d. Ralph Richardson and Laurence Olivier), Lyric Theatre

August   Dr Clitterhouse in *The Amazing Dr Clitterhouse* by Barré Lyndon (d. Claud Gurney), Haymarket Theatre

1937

November   Peter Agardi in *The Silent Knight* by Humbert Wolfe (d. Gilbert Miller), St James's Theatre

December   Bottom in *A Midsummer Night's Dream* (d. Tyrone Guthrie), Old Vic Theatre

1938

February   Othello in *Othello* (d. Tyrone Guthrie), Old Vic Theatre

23 May   Beckett in a scene from Tennyson's *Beckett*, at the Henry Irving Centenary matinée, at the Lyceum Theatre

1939

February   Johnson in *Johnson Over Jordan* by J. B. Priestley (d. Basil Dean), New Theatre, later transferred to the Saville Theatre

1940

12 March	Henry in an extract from *Henry V* (d. Norman Marshall), at a Red Cross matinée, Palace Theatre
23 April	Three extracts from Shakespeare on the theme of Time, in the Birthday celebrations, Old Vic Theatre

1943

24 February	Spokesman in *Salute to the Red Army* (d. Basil Dean), Royal Albert Hall
May	Compèred *The Ship-Shape Show* aboard H.M. Troopship in convoy
12 September	Read *The Little Ships* by J. B. Priestley in *Seascape* (d. Basil Dean), two performances for ENSA, Royal Albert Hall
17 October	In a Navy League concert at the London Coliseum

1944

Season with the Old Vic Company at the New Theatre, August 1944–May 1945:

August	Peer Gynt in *Peer Gynt* by Henrik Ibsen (d. Tyrone Guthrie)
September	Bluntschli in *Arms and the Man* by Bernard Shaw; Earl of Richmond in *Richard III* (both d. John Burrell)

1945

January	Voynitsky in *Uncle Vanya* by Anton Chekhov (d. John Burrell)
May–July	ENSA tour of the Old Vic repertoire in Antwerp, Ghent, Hamburg and Paris (at the Comédie-Française 3–15 July)

Season with the Old Vic Company at the New Theatre, September 1945 –May 1946:

September   Sir John Falstaff in *Henry IV, Part I* (d. John Burrell)

October   Falstaff in *Henry IV, Part II* (d. John Burrell); Tiresias in *Oedipus* by Sophocles, translated by W. B. Yeats (d. Michel St. Denis); Lord Burleigh in *The Critic* by Richard Brinsley Sheridan (d. Miles Malleson)

1946

May–June   New York season with the Old Vic Company at the Century Theatre: *Henry IV, Parts I and II, Uncle Vanya, Oedipus* and *The Critic* Season with the Old Vic Company at the New Theatre, October 1946–May 1947:

October   Inspector Goole in *An Inspector Calls* by J. B. Priestley (d. Basil Dean). Tour before London, opening at the Opera House, Manchester, 9th September

November   Cyrano de Bergerac in *Cyrano de Bergerac* by Edmond Rostand, translated by Brian Hooker (d. Tyrone Guthrie)

14 December   Narrator in *Interlude and Serenade for Voice and Orchestra* by Delius, and Hector's Farewell to Andromache from the Sixth Book of the *Iliad*, for the Brighton Philharmonic Society, The Dome, Brighton

1947

January	Face in *The Alchemist* by Ben Jonson (d. John Burrell)
April	John of Gaunt in *Richard II* (d. Ralph Richardson)

1948

April*	Marcus Ivanirex in *Royal Circle* by Romilly Cavan (d. Ralph Richardson), Wyndham's Theatre

1949

February	Dr Sloper in *The Heiress* by Ruth and Augustus Goetz (d. John Gielgud), Haymarket Theatre
6 November	Narrator in Remembrance Day concert, Royal Albert Hall
20 November	"Three Thoughts on Time" (Shakespeare) ". . . Merely Players", London Coliseum (special performance)

1950

March	David Preston in *Home at Seven* by R. C. Sherriff (d. Murray MacDonald), Wyndham's Theatre
16 April	Orator in Hallé Orchestra concert at King's Hall, Belle Vue, Manchester

1951

May	Vershinin in *Three Sisters* by Anton Chekhov (d. Peter Ashmore), Aldwych Theatre
7 October	Narration in *Salute to Ivor Novello*, London Coliseum (Sunday performance)

*Month of London opening given only; post-war productions have had a pre-London tour, or, as with *Flowering Cherry*, *Lloyd George Knew My Father*, *Home*, etc., a post-London tour.

1952

March–October	Season at the Shakespeare Memorial Theatre, Stratford-upon-Avon: Prospero in *The Tempest* (d. Michael Benthall); Macbeth in *Macbeth* (d. John Gielgud); Volpone in *Volpone* by Ben Jonson (d. George Devine)
November	Opened Kenya National Theatre, Nairobi

1953

March	John Greenwood in *The White Carnation* by R. C. Sherriff (d. Noel Willman), Globe Theatre
November	Dr Farley in *A Day by the Sea* by N. C. Hunter (d. John Gielgud), Haymarket Theatre

1955

Spring–Autumn	Tour of Australia and New Zealand: the Grand Duke in *The Sleeping Prince* by Terence Rattigan; Mr Martin and Major Pollock in *Separate Tables* by Terence Rattigan (both d. Lionel Harris)

1956

September	Timon in *Timon of Athens* (d. Michael Benthall), Old Vic Theatre

1957

January–May	General St Pé in *The Waltz of the Toreadors* by Jean Anouilh, translated by Lucienne Hill (d. Harold Clurman), Coronet Theatre, New York

November	Cherry in *Flowering Cherry* by Robert Bolt (d. Frith Banbury), Haymarket Theatre
1959	
June	Victor Rhodes in *The Complaisant Lover* by Graham Greene (d. John Gielgud), Globe Theatre
1960	
September	Edward Portal in *The Last Joke* by Enid Bagnold (d. Glen Byam Shaw), Phoenix Theatre
1962	
April	Sir Peter Teazle in *The School for Scandal* by Richard Brinsley Sheridan (d. John Gielgud), Haymarket Theatre and (November 1962–January 1963) American tour, Majestic Theater, New York
1963	
June	Father in *Six Characters in Search of an Author* by Luigi Pirandello (d. William Ball), Mayfair Theatre (opening production)
1964	
February–May	British Council Shakespeare 400th Anniversary Tour of South America and Europe (opening at Theatre Royal, Brighton): Shylock in *The Merchant of Venice* (d. Wendy Toye); Bottom in *A Midsummer Night's Dream* (d. David William)

| September | The Father in *Carving a Statue* by Graham Greene (d. Peter Wood), Haymarket Theatre |

1966

| January | The Waiter in *You Never Can Tell* by Bernard Shaw (d. Glen Byam Shaw), Haymarket Theatre |
| September | Sir Anthony Absolute in *The Rivals* by Richard Brinsley Sheridan (d. Glen Byam Shaw), Haymarket Theatre |

1967

| September | Shylock in *The Merchant of Venice* (d. Glen Byam Shaw), Haymarket Theatre |

1969

| March | Dr Rance in *What the Butler Saw* by Joe Orton (d. Robert Chetwyn), Queen's Theatre |

1970

| June | Jack in *Home* by David Storey (d. Lindsay Anderson), Royal Court Theatre; later Apollo Theatre and Morosco Theater, New York |

1971

| August | Wyatt Gilman in *West of Suez* by John Osborne (d. Anthony Page), Royal Court Theatre; later Cambridge Theatre |

1972

July	General Sir William Boothroyd in *Lloyd George Knew My Father* by William Douglas Home (d. Robin Midgeley), Savoy Theatre; later Australian tour (1973), North American tour (1974)
1975	With the National Theatre Company:
January	Borkman in *John Gabriel Borkman* by Henrik Ibsen (d. Peter Hall), Olivier Theatre
April	Hirst in *No Man's Land* by Harold Pinter (d. Peter Hall), Lyttelton Theatre; later Wyndham's Theatre and North American Tour

1977

May	Cecil in *The Kingfisher* by William Douglas Home (d. Lindsay Anderson), Lyric Theatre

1978

February	With the National Theatre Company: Firs in *The Cherry Orchard* by Anton Chekhov (d. Peter Hall), Olivier Theatre
May	Colonel White in *Alice's Boys* by Felicity Browne and Jonathan Hales (d. Lindsay Anderson), Savoy Theatre
1978	With the National Theatre Company:
September	Lord Touchwood in *The Double Dealer* by William Congreve (d. Peter Wood), Olivier Theatre
	Zvezgintzev in *The Fruits of Enlight-*

	enment by Leo Tolstoy (d. Christopher Morahan), Olivier Theatre
1979	
December	Old Ekdal in *The Wild Duck* by Henrik Ibsen (d. Christopher Morahan), Olivier Theatre
1980	
April	Kitchen in *Early Days* by David Storey (d. Lindsay Anderson), Cottesloe Theatre; later Comedy Theatre and North American tour
1982	
	Leonard in *The Understanding* by Angela Huth (d. Roger Smith), Strand Theatre
1983	
June	Alberto in *Inner Voices* by Eduardo de Filippo (d. Mike Ockrent), Lyttelton Theatre.

FILMS

1933	Nigel Hartley in *The Ghoul* (d. T. Hayes Hunter)
1934	The Schoolmaster in *Friday the Thirteenth* (d. Victor Saville)
	William Ammidon in *Java Head* (d. Walter Ruben)
	Hugh Drummond in *The Return of Bulldog Drummond* (d. Walter Summers)
1935	Paul in *The King of Paris* (d. Jack Raymond)
	Morell in *Bulldog Jack* (d. Walter Forde)
1936	The Boss in *Things to Come* (d. Cameron Menzies)

1937   Colonel Winstanley in *The Man Who Worked Miracles* (d. Lothar Mendes)

Manningdale in *Thunder in the City* (d. Marion Gering)

1938   Robert Carne in *South Riding* (d. Victor Saville)

Lord Mere in *Divorce of Lady X* (d. Tim Whelan)

1939   Denny in *The Citadel* (d. King Vidor)

Major Hammond in *Q Planes* (d. Tim Whelan)

Captain John Durrance in *The Four Feathers* (d. Zoltan Korda)

Wing Commander, in *The Lion Has Wings* (d. Michael Powell, Brian Desmond Hurst and Adrian Brunel)

1940   *Health for the Nation* (G.P.O. documentary, commentary by Richardson)

Will Kobling in *On the Night of the Fire* (d. Brian Desmond Hurst)

1942   Lockwood in *The Day Will Dawn* (d. Harold French)

1943   Jaap Van Leyden in *The Silver Fleet* (d. Vernon Sewell and Gordon Wellesley)

1944   As Himself in *The Volunteer*, Ministry of Information film (d. Michael Powell and Emeric Pressburger)

1946   Professor Heatherville in *School for Secrets* (d. Peter Ustinov)

1948　Alexis Karenin in *Anna Karenina* (d. Julien Duvivier)

　　　　Baines in *The Fallen Idol* (d. Carol Reed)

1950　Dr Sloper in *The Heiress* (d. William Wyler)

1952　Captain Lingard in *An Outcast of the Islands* (d. Carol Reed)

　　　　David Preston in *Home at Seven* (d. Ralph Richardson)

　　　　John Richfield in *The Sound Barrier* (d. David Lean)

　　　　The Revd Martin Gregory in *The Holly and the Ivy* (d. George More O'Farrell)

1955　The Duke of Buckingham in *Richard III* (d. Laurence Olivier)

1956　The Revd Lambeth in *Smiley* (d. Antony Kimmins)

　　　　Roger and Clement in *The Passionate Stranger* (d. Muriel Box)

1959　C in *Our Man in Havana* (d. Carol Reed)

1960　Sir Edward Carson in *The Trials of Oscar Wilde* (d. Gregory Ratoff)

1961　General Sutherland in *Exodus* (d. Otto Preminger)

1962　Themistocles in *The 300 Spartans* (d. Rudolph Mate)

　　　　James Tyrone in *Long Day's Journey into Night* (d. Sidney Lumet)

1964　Charles Richmond in *Woman of Straw* (d. Basil Dearden)

1966   Alexander Gromeko in *Dr Zhivago* (d. David Lean)

Joseph Finsbury in *The Wrong Box* (d. Bryan Forbes)

1967   Mr Gladstone in *Khartoum* (d. Basil Dearden, Eliot Elisofon, Yakima Canult)

1969   Sir Edward Grey in *Oh What a Lovely War* (d. Richard Attenborough)

Henshaw in *A Run on Gold* (d. Alf Kjellin)

Lord Fortnum of Alamein in *The Bed-Sitting Room* (d. Richard Lester)

Minister in *The Battle of Britain* (d. Guy Hamilton)

Leclerc in *The Looking-Glass War* (d. Frank R. Pierson)

Micawber in *David Copperfield* (d. Delbert Mann)

1970   Sir Hudson Lowe in *Eagle in a Cage* (d. Fielder Cook)

Mr Benton in *Who Ever Slew Auntie Roo* (d. Curtis Harrington)

Crypt Keeper in *Tales from the Crypt* (d. Freddie Francis)

1972   The King in *Lady Caroline Lamb* (d. Robert Bolt)

The Caterpillar in *Alice's Adventures in Wonderland* (TV; d. Jonathan Miller)

1973   Dr Rank in *A Doll's House* (d. Patrick Garland)

Monty/Sir James Burgess in *O Lucky Man* (d. Lindsay Anderson)

Lacey in *Frankenstein: The True Story* (d. Jack Smight)

1975   Senator in *Rollerball* (d. Norman Jewison)

1977   Cardinal Richelieu in *The Man in the Iron Mask* (d. Mike Newell)

Simeon in *Jesus of Nazareth* (d. Franco Zeffirelli)

1978   Hirst in *No Man's Land* (TV; d. Peter Hall)

1980   The Supreme Being in *Time Bandits* (d. Terry Gilliam)

Ulrich in *Dragonslayer* (d. Matthew Robbins)

1981   Kitchen in *Early Days* (TV; d. Anthony Page)

1982   Pfi in *Wagner* (d. Tony Palmer)

Acknowledgements

While this is not an 'authorized' or 'official' biography of Sir
Ralph Richardson, and has been undertaken on my own
initiative, my first thanks must go to Richardson himself for
providing such a tempting, if elusive, subject to try and do
justice to, and for not wholly discouraging me in my
attempt. I am grateful to him in particular for reading
through the book in typescript, and for his modest and
thoughtful comments, which I have happily incorporated,
sometimes in footnotes.

The book could not have been undertaken and certainly
not finished, were it not for the effort and encouragement
of Deborah Rogers, and the participation and helpful
comments of Alfred Knopf Jr., Ion Trewin and Thomas
A. Stewart. Before and during writing I have had many
valuable talks with Catharine Carver, whom I also thank
for her careful editing. To J. C. Trewin, B. A. Young,
Linda Kelly and John Tydeman must go my thanks for
reading the draft text and for perceiving many errors and
lapses, though I must add that any of either which remain
must be blamed wholly on me.

I must thank the following for consenting to be interviewed, for sending or collecting information, and for help
in one or more of innumerable other ways, as well as—in
many cases—for providing most generous hospitality. For
any names unintentionally omitted I beg to be forgiven:
Harry Andrews, Mark Amory, David Ayliff, Susan Ayliff,
Sally Beauman, Richard Bebb, Eileen Beldon, Diana Boddington, Robert Bolt, Gary Bond, Margaret Burrell, Glen
Byam Shaw, Peter Copley, James Dale, Peter Dews, Frank
Duncan, Laurence Evans, David Fairweather, Leslie
French, Sir John Gielgud, John Goodwin, S. N. Grace,

Kate Griffin, Jonathan Griffin, Sir Peter Hall, Olive Harding, Robert Harris, Nicky Henson, Ian Herbert, Sir Harold Hobson, the Hon. William Douglas Home, George Howe, Alan Howard, Lucy Hughes-Hallett, Angela Huth, Patrick Ide, Jo Inslee, Ruth Jeayes, Barbara Jefford, Linda Kelly, J. W. Lambert, R. B. Marriott, Vivian Marriott, the late Norman Marshall, Anna Massey, Michael Meyer, Tanya Moiseiwitch, J. B. Priestley, Anthony Quayle, Joyce Redman, Max Reinhardt, Mercia Relph, Simon Relph, Mary Richards, George Rylands, Leslie Sarony, Paul Scofield, Maggie Sedwards, the late Norman Shelley, Donald Sinden, Molly Sole, David Storey, Noël Streatfeild, Clive Swift, J. C. Trewin, Wendy Trewin, Michael Warre.

I thank Lord Olivier for his permission to quote on pp 191–191 from unpublished letters to John Burrell. I am grateful to Sir Harold Hobson for allowing me to base my list of Richardson's performances on that published in his monograph, *Ralph Richardson* (Barrie and Rockliff, 1958); to the Hon. William Douglas Home for lending me letters; to Kate Griffin for her collection of Old Vic material, and to Margaret Burrell for letting me consult the late John Burrell's papers. Thanks are also due to Colin Benham and the Old Vic Governors for giving me permission to consult their archives. Without Oliver Sacks's *Awakenings* (Duckworth, 1973), I could not have begun to form any understanding of the symptoms of Kit Richardson's illness.

Much kindness has been shown me by the staff of the following libraries and institutions where I have worked. BBC (Sound and Written) Archives, The Publicity Office, National Theatre, British Film Institute (Elaine Burrows), Imperial War Museum, Colindale Newspaper Library, Bodleian Library, Oxford, Central Library, Westgate, Oxford, John Rylands University Library, Manchester, Cheltenham Ladies' College Library, Denville Hall, Savile Club, Cheltenham Public Library (Roger Beacham), Lewes Public Library, Newcastle Public Library.

Finally I thank Linda Rowley for typing the manuscript, Rita O'Connor for her document searches in central London, Raymond Mander for advice on illustrations, Norma Vickers for showing me her collection of the late John Vickers's photographs, Morag Robinson for picture research, and Victoria O'Connor for help with the index.

G.O'C.

Oxford
April 1982

Sources

Following are the more important contributions by Richardson himself, in the form of published articles and/or broadcast talks or interviews, on which I have drawn:

"The Audience, Broadcasting Shakespeare", *The Old Vic and Sadler's Wells Magazine*, February and April 1931

"What *Peer Gynt* Means to the Actor", *Radio Times*, 8 November 1946

The Mighty Line, BBC Radio, 19 November 1947

Techniques No. 5—Acting, BBC Radio, 9 June 1949

Return Journey to the Old Vic, BBC Radio, 30 October 1949

"Antipodean Report", *Theatre 1955–6*, ed. Ivor Brown (Reinhardt, 1956)

"On Looking Back", *Sunday Times*, 26 June, 3 and 10 July 1960 (broadcast on BBC Radio, November 1960 –February 1961)

Style in Acting, BBC, 30 June 1969

Portrait of Mrs Pat Campbell, BBC Radio, 12 August 1970

The David Frost Show, Metro Media TV (New York), 11 December 1970

Gielgud and Richardson, BBC Radio, 16 November 1971

"Hand Movies", *Theatre 73*, ed. Sheridan Morley (Hutchinson, 1973)

The Michael Parkinson Show, BBC TV, 25 November 1978

"The Age of Innocence", *Vogue Magazine*, February 1979

Desert Island Discs, BBC Radio, 5 August 1979

The Michael Parkinson Show, BBC TV, 13 December 1980

There are few theatrical autobiographies or memoirs, or books on the British theatre or films since the 1920s, that do not contain at least a passing reference to Richardson. The following list includes only those works on which I have drawn most frequently. (The place of publication is London unless otherwise indicated.)

James Agate, *Ego* (9 vols., 1935–48: vol. 1, Hamish Hamilton, 1935; vol. 2, Gollancz, 1936; vols. 3–9, Harrap, 1938–48)

——*Brief Chronicles* (Cape, 1943)

——*Red Letter Nights* (Cape, 1944)

Enid Bagnold, *Enid Bagnold's Autobiography* (Heinemann, 1969)

Deirdre Bair, *Samuel Beckett* (Cape, 1978)

Felix Barker, *The Oliviers* (Hamish Hamilton, 1953)

Denys Blakelock, *Advice to a Player* (Heinemann, 1957)

——*Round the Next Corner* (Gollancz, 1967)

Ivor Brown, *The Way of My World* (Collins, 1954)

——(ed.), *Theatre 1955–6* (Reinhardt, 1956)

Lillian Browse, *William Nicholson* (Hart-Davis, 1956)

Hal Burton (ed.), *Great Acting* (BBC Publications, 1967)

——(ed.), *Acting in the Sixties* (BBC Publications, 1970)

John Casson, *Lewis and Sybil: A Memoir* (Collins, 1972)

Judith Cook, *Director's Theatre* (Harrap, 1974)

John Cottrell, *Laurence Olivier* (Weidenfeld and Nicolson, 1975)

James Dale, *Pulling Faces for a Living* (Gollancz, 1970)

W. A. Darlington, *6001 Nights: Forty Years a Dramatic Critic* (Harrap, 1960)

Peter Daubeny, *My World of Theatre* (Cape, 1971)

Basil Dean, *The Theatre at War* (Harrap, 1956)

——*Seven Ages* (Hutchinson, 1970)

Alan Dent, *Mrs Patrick Campbell* (Museum, 1961)

Fabia Drake, *Blind Fortune* (Kimber, 1978)

Daphne du Maurier, *Gerald: A Portrait* (Gollancz, 1934)

Janet Dunbar, *Flora Robson* (Harrap, 1960)

Anne Edwards, *Vivien Leigh* (W. H. Allen, 1977)

Virginia Fairweather, *Cry God for Larry* (Calder, 1969)

Bryan Forbes, *Notes for a Life* (Collins, 1974)

——*Ned's Girl* (Elm Tree, 1977)

James Forsyth, *Tyrone Guthrie* (Hamish Hamilton, 1976)

John Gielgud, *Early Stages* (Macmillan, 1939)

——*Distinguished Company* (Heinemann Educational, 1972)

——*An Actor and His Time* (Sidgwick and Jackson, 1979)

Val Gielgud, *Years in a Mirror* (Bodley Head, 1965)

Logan Gourlay (ed.), *Olivier* (Weidenfeld and Nicolson, 1973)

Tyrone Guthrie, *A Life in the Theatre* (Hamish Hamilton, 1960)

Cedric Hardwicke, *A Victorian in Orbit* (Methuen, 1961)

Ronald Harwood, *Sir Donald Wolfit* (Secker and Warburg, 1971)

Charles Hawtrey, *The Truth at Last*, ed. W. Somerset Maugham (Butterworth, 1924)

Ronald Hayman, *John Gielgud* (Heinemann Educational, 1971)

Harold Hobson, *Ralph Richardson* (Barrie and Rockliff, 1958)

——*Unfinished Journey* (Weidenfeld and Nicolson, 1978)

William Douglas Home, *Mr Home Pronounced Hume* (Collins, 1971)

John Graven Hughes, *The Greasepaint War* (New English Library, 1976)

Thomas Kiernan, *Olivier* (Sidgwick and Jackson, 1981)

Michael Korda, *Charmed Lives* (Harmondsworth: Penguin Books, 1980)

Karol Kulik, *Alexander Korda* (W. H. Allen, 1975)

John Lahr, *Prick Up Your Ears* (Allen Lane, 1978)

Charles Landstone, *Off-Stage* (Elek, 1949)

Jesse L. Lasky, Jr. (with Pat Silver), *Love Scene* (Brighton: Angus and Robertson, 1978)

C. A. Lejeune, *Thank You for Having Me* (Hutchinson, 1964)

Margaret Morley, *Larger Than Life* (Robson, 1979)

Sheridan Morley, *Review Copies* (Robson, 1974)

——(ed.), *Theatre 72, 73, 74* (Hutchinson, 1972–4)

Nora Nicholson, *Chameleon's Dish* (Elek, 1973)

J. B. Priestley, *Midnight on the Desert* (Heinemann, 1937)

R. C. Sheriff, *No Leading Lady* (Gollancz, 1968)

Robert Speaight, *The Property Basket* (Collins, 1970)

Elizabeth Sprigge, *Sybil Thorndike Casson* (Gollancz, 1971)

Marguerite Steen, *William Nicholson* (Collins, 1943)

Noël Streatfeild, *Away from the Vicarage* (Collins, 1965)

Paul Tabori, *Alexander Korda* (Oldbourne, 1959)

Laurence Thompson, *Behind the Curtain* (Ward, Lock, 1951)

Russell Thorndike, *Sybil Thorndike* (Butterworth, 1929)

J. C. Trewin, *The Theatre Since 1900* (Dakers, 1951)

——*Sybil Thorndike* (Rockliff, 1955)

——*Benson and the Bensonians* (Barrie and Rockliff, 1960)

——*The Birmingham Repertory Theatre, 1913–1963* (Barrie and Rockliff, 1963)

——*Shakespeare on the English Stage 1900–1964* (Barrie and Rockliff, 1964)

——*The Edwardian Theatre* (Oxford: Blackwell, 1976)

Kenneth Tynan, *He That Plays the King* (Longmans, 1950)

——*Curtains* (Longmans, 1961)

——*The Sound of Two Hands Clapping* (Cape, 1975)

——*A View of the English Stage* (Paladin, 1976)

——*Show People* (Weidenfeld and Nicolson, 1981; includes his 1977 *New Yorker* profile of Richardson)

Peter Ustinov, *Dear Me* (Heinemann, 1977)

John Vickers, *The Old Vic in Photographs* (Saturn, 1947)

——*Five Seasons* (Saturn, 1950)

Irving Wardle, *The Theatres of George Devine* (Cape, 1978)

Michael Warre, *Designing and Making Stage Scenery* (Studio Vista, 1966)

Herbert Wilcox, *Twenty-five Thousand Sunsets* (Bodley Head, 1967)

E. G. Harcourt Williams, *Four Years at the Old Vic 1929–1933* (Putnam, 1935)

——*Old Vic Saga* (Winchester, 1949)

Emlyn Williams, *Emlyn* (Bodley Head, 1973)

Audrey Williamson, *Old Vic Drama* (Rockliff, 1951)

Donald Wolfit, *First Interval* (Odhams, 1954)

I am grateful to the editors of and contributors to the following newspapers (London and elsewhere) and magazines in which I have consulted articles, reviews, etc.: *Birmingham Post, Daily Express, Daily Herald, Daily Mail, Evening News, Evening Standard, Financial Times, Irish Times, Los Angeles Times, Manchester Guardian* (and *Guardian*), *New Statesman, New York Post, New York Times, New Yorker, Observer, Observer Magazine, Ryerson Review, Spectator, Sunday Express Magazine, Sunday Times, Sunday Times Magazine, Telegraph Sunday Magazine, Time Magazine, The Times, Vogue.*

Index

RR = Ralph Richardson